THE HORNED OWL

A Sam Chitto Mystery

Lu Clifton

First Edition, First Printing April, 2018
Cover image courtesy of Pixabay

Summary: Mark Twain once said, "Every man is a moon and has a side which he turns toward nobody; you have to slip around behind if you want to see it." ("The Refuge of Derelicts" 1905). This insight into human nature proves to be the driving force behind Sam Chitto's pursuit of justice in The Horned Owl, the third book in the Sam Chitto series. Two Choctaw tribal council members pull Detective Sam Chitto into an unauthorized investigation to prove a teenage boy is innocent of murder and sexual mutilation. Using graphic novels the boy produced, prosecutors enlist the aid of a forensic psychiatrist to prove the boy committed a fantasy murder. Also suspect is the reason the boy gave for being seen near the body after the murder: the Choctaw deity Ishkitini, the Horned Owl, forewarned him in the night that someone would die violently. One case investigation becomes two as Chitto realizes the murder occurred where his father was killed a decade before. Chitto's efforts to discover the moon side of various characters drives the action in both investigations. The juxtaposition of the ancient Caddoan mound civilization with modern forensic methodology adds interest.
1. Fiction—Indian reservation police 2. Murder—Investigation—Fiction 3. Choctaw Indians—Fiction 4. Oklahoma—Fiction Title: Sam Chitto Mystery

ISBN 978-0-9985284-2-7
ISBN 978-0-9985284-3-4 (e-book)

Two Shadows
P.O. Box 154
Davis, Il 61019
Email: info@twoshadows.biz

For my sons, Christopher and Jeffrey

ACKNOWLEDGEMENTS AND DISCLAIMERS

I am indebted to R.D. Hendrix, Director of Law Enforcement for the Choctaw Nation for guiding me through the complexities of the Choctaw Tribal Police organization. Director Hendrix also demonstrated incredible patience as I endeavored to fathom the inner workings of the checkerboard jurisdictional system in Oklahoma.

Setting and places in *The Horned Owl* are factual but, as fiction writers are prone to do, I exercised artistic license in developing characters and plot. Fiction is, after all, invention. If I have portrayed anything incorrectly about the tribal police in so doing, it's through no fault of Director Hendrix.

I'm also indebted to the Choctaw School of Language for help with Choctaw phrases and terms. *Yakoke.*

Last, but certainly not least, thanks to my family and friends for their encouragement and support, for acting as readers and providing feedback, for simply being there.

PREFACE

"Every man is a moon and has a side which he turns toward nobody; you have to slip around behind if you want to see it." — Mark Twain ("The Refuge of the Derelicts" 1905)

CHAPTER ONE

Thunderstorms rumbled across southeastern Oklahoma in the night, leaving waves of rain in their wake. The fall pattern was beginning. More times than not, you could count on rainy weather in April and October. Sam Chitto liked patterns. Patterns were predictable. Now close to midday, he welcomed the thrum of raindrops on his office window. Water had been sluicing down the panes all morning making for empty streets, quiet phones, and a grateful Choctaw Nation police detective needing a quiet Friday to catch up on paperwork.

The loud rasp of Jasmine Birdsong's voice shattered the spell. He looked up to see her trailing behind two women marching his direction, hoods on their raincoats concealing their faces. Without invitation, the cloaked women took chairs in front of his desk and pushed back their hoods. Chitto sighed. Not one council member, but two. And one of them his mother.

"It's all right, Jasmine," he said. The administrative assistant stood behind the intruders, fists on her hips and a scowl on her face.

Jasmine had only been there a few weeks. For years, she had worked as a temp in various offices across the Nation, filling in until a permanent hire was made. After Wanda Gilly, the department's former administrative assistant died,

Jasmine agreed to fill the empty chair temporarily. Then, for reasons understood only to her, she decided to take on the job full time. Chitto didn't know Jasmine well but what he did know about her, he liked. She kept to herself, knew the Choctaw Nation like the back of her hand, and was an ace on the computer. She apparently didn't like to be steamrolled either. Another point in her favor.

Quickly, he introduced Jasmine to his mother, Mattie Chitto, and June Biggers, council members for Districts Eleven and Four respectively.

"Oh, I know *her*," Jasmine said, indicating June Biggers. "I was born and raised in LeFlore County."

"Birdsong . . ." June narrowed her eyes, examining Jasmine more closely. "Yes, I recognize you now. You're descended from that old freedwoman, Violet."

"My grandmother."

Jasmine was neither young nor old, fifty-something Chitto guessed. Today, as always, she had dressed in subdued clothing: brown slacks and tan shirt, leather walking shoes. Earthy colors that complimented her rich skin tone. While Jasmine held her personal life close, her heritage was well known. Her ancestors had been slaves of Choctaws removed to Indian Territory in the 1830s. In the late 1880s, those freed slaves had been admitted to the Choctaw Nation.

Turning her attention from Jasmine to Mattie Chitto, June Biggers said, "Give him the folder, Mattie."

Obligingly, Mattie Chitto dropped a damp manila folder onto Chitto's desk. "This is for your eyes only," she said, locking him in a stare.

Chitto paused, decoding the nonverbal message, then looked at Jasmine. "Make sure no one interrupts me."

"Tried that one already," she snapped.

2

As Jasmine strode away, Chitto turned to his mother. Raindrops glistened on the lapels of her trench coat, shirt collar, high cheekbones. "There's a coat rack up front," he said pointing his chin toward the entrance.

"No need," Mattie said. "We have a meeting and can't stay long." She gave an insistent nod toward the folder.

Sighing again, he opened a folder containing a stack of hand-drawn pictures. Hurriedly, he flipped through crude pictures of fantastic monsters and misshapen people, bloodied weapons and bleeding bodies, all drawn on three-ring notebook paper.

"What am I looking at?" he asked, looking at Mattie.

"What's it look like to you?" she said.

"Are you serious—?" He glanced at the unfinished paperwork on his desk, which he'd hoped to finish before the rain let up and people came out of their hidey-holes.

"Dead serious," she said. "What do you see?"

Giving his head a slight shake, he studied the drawings for a couple of minutes. "Well," he said, looking between June and his mother. "From the similarity in style, I'd say they were done by one kid, probably a teenage boy."

"So," Mattie said. "Pretty normal for a boy to do that kind of thing, huh?"

"Normal . . ." He paused, trying to read the subliminal message in the two sets of dark eyes scrutinizing him. "They're not unlike others I've seen kids do," he said with a shrug.

June gave Mattie a knowing look, saying, "You were right. He *is* the one to fix this."

"Fix what?" Noting the smug looks on their faces, Chitto bristled. "Look," he growled. "I get the feeling I'm being led

3

around by the nose here, which pisses me off." He tapped the folder. "So one of you tell me what I'm looking at here."

"Condemning evidence," June snapped.

"Evidence?" Quickly, he flicked through the stack of drawings again. "Of what?"

"Murder," Mattie responded.

"*Heinous* murder," June added. Her angular face and prominent cheekbones appeared chiseled from stone. "Which he didn't do."

"Okay," Chitto sighed, shoulders slumping. Resigned that he wasn't going to defer this conversation, he leaned back in his chair. "Start at the beginning."

June took charge, telling Chitto about Bobby Taneyhill, a high school boy and member of the Choctaw Nation who had been accused of murdering a young woman at the Spiro Mounds Archaeology Center. The victim had worked at the gift shop on site and lived in Spiro, a few miles away. The boy lived with his grandfather, a maintenance worker at the Center who owned a home nearby.

"I heard something about that," Chitto said, searching his memory for details. "But Spiro Mounds . . . that's state-owned, isn't it?"

"Right," June said. "Which is why the case was filed in the LeFlore County District Court in Poteau. But it doesn't matter. The boy's grandfather said Bobby was home all night and that man would never lie. His name's Charlie Walker and he's a Tribal Elder—an *honorable* man. The boy didn't do it—and you have to prove it."

"*Nuh-uh* . . ." Chitto stiffened, head wagging side to side. "The case is out of my district, not to mention my jurisdiction."

"You've worked in other districts lots of times," Mattie countered.

The Choctaw Nation covered 11,000 square miles and was divided into twelve districts. Chitto was field lieutenant for District Nine; LeFlore County was in District Four. The two districts were on opposite corners of the Choctaw Nation, as the crow flies a hundred fifty miles apart. The distance was not an impossible problem to overcome. Chitto had been assigned to other districts plenty of times to fill in for another field lieutenant either out on sick leave or handling an emergency.

"This is different," he said. "There's no need to send me up there. Besides, you both know how the system works. This country's called the Checkerboard for a reason. My hands are tied."

The problem was an old one, for not only the Choctaw but also the other nations forced to move to Indian Territory. All told, there were thirty-eight federally recognized tribes in Oklahoma and the Removal had been the trigger mechanism for the occupation. For the Choctaws, the Removal began in the 1830s when the people were forced from their lands in Mississippi. Survivors of the march were given the southeast corner of Indian Territory, a section wedged between the Canadian River on the north and the Red River on the south, the Ouachita Mountains on the east and grassland prairies to the west. Sometime later, the federal government redid the treaties, chopping the whole into smaller pieces, in effect making the Choctaw allotment Indians. Sometime later, another government treaty replaced the previous one, opening up land not yet allotted to Choctaws to non-Indians. The mix of tribal and non-tribal lands led to a checkerboard landscape requiring a multi-layered law enforcement system—federal, state, municipal, and Native American. A stranglehold of jurisdictional issues often led to criminals walking free.

5

Mattie's eyes narrowed to slits. "That didn't stop you before."

Before . . .

Chitto fixed his eyes on his mother, knowing full well what she was referring to and wondering where she'd gotten the information. Recently, he'd teamed with Chickasaw and Muskogee police officers looking into murders that spanned their boundaries, a case officially under the auspices of the FBI. He'd made a decision at the end that caused a man to die and him to feel unclean, unfit to do his job. He'd gone to an old mystic named Sonny Boy Monroe for a cleansing ceremony. Had Sonny Boy spilled the beans?

He leaned forward, eyes still locked on hers. "My hands are tied," he repeated more forcefully.

Chitto's mother was missing an important piece of information. The Feds had gotten wind of the undercover operation and made their displeasure known. The bureau didn't like it when other jurisdictions trespassed in their territory, and one FBI agent, by the name of Ramon Rodriguez, had made it his personal vendetta to ID Chitto as the leader of the rebellious act.

"Well untie them." June Biggers crossed her arms, dark eyes glinting. "The boy's being framed. It's all because one of his teachers said something about scary pictures he drew in class—claiming they showed something was wrong with him." She made a circular motion with her forefinger finger and pointed it at her head, the sign for crazy. "The prosecution's bringing in a psychiatrist who specializes in sexual homicides to look at the stories the boy wrote. Comic book stories, not real."

"Graphic novels?" he asked, thinking of the latest rage in books that were especially popular with the younger generation.

"Yeah," she confirmed. "That's what they're calling them. But the state's lawyer is claiming the boy was living out a fantasy, saying the murder was a fantasy killing." Looking at her watch, she rose from her chair. "That teacher's the one who's nuts—that lawyer, too."

"Hold on," Chitto said, looking up at June. "To indict him, there had to be some pretty solid evidence presented."

"Well . . ." She hesitated. "See, a rancher driving down the road saw him walking away from the Archaeology Center where the body was found." She hesitated again. "Bobby went looking for it the next morning."

"Looking for it . . . The body?"

"Yes." Glancing at the rain-streaked window, June pulled up the hood of her raincoat. "He heard *Ishkitini* in the night so he knew someone had been killed."

In Choctaw mythology, *Ishkitini* was the Horned Owl. Hearing its screech in the night was a sign of sudden death, as in a murder.

Chitto suppressed an urge to laugh. "You're saying this kid heard a screech owl and went looking for a dead person the next morning."

"That's exactly what she's saying," Mattie said, pulling up her hood. "We have to go now but you call me later, tell me what you're gonna do. The boy needs an advocate from the Nation."

"June can be his advocate," he replied.

"A *cop* advocate," she said over her shoulder.

"Wait up," Chitto called to the departing women. As they turned, he held up the folder of drawings. "You didn't say how you got hold of the pictures this kid drew. They should be locked up in an evidence locker."

7

"Didn't say they were done by *that* boy," Mattie said. "Look on the back of the pictures. There's a note from another teacher, too."

Chitto opened the folder again. "Well, hell," he muttered, seeing a scrawled *Samuel Chitto* on the back of the pages. The handwritten note tucked behind the drawings was one a seventh-grade algebra teacher had sent to his parents. The teacher described the images as abnormal and postulated that either Chitto was a lazy ne'er-do-well who would never amount to a hill of beans or in need professional help.

"I was bored, not psycho," he mumbled. He hurried toward the front entrance hoping to catch his mother, wanting to ask her why she had hung onto the drawings all these years. Too late, he caught a glimpse of her car leaving the parking lot.

I'll catch up with her tonight, he thought, returning to his desk. She was expecting him to call that evening and he did want to know that she'd made it home all right. It was an hour and a half drive to her home in Krebs, an eighty-mile trip up Highway 69. She was a careful driver but the roads were wet. Hydroplaning could be a problem. Shoving the folder into a bottom drawer, he went back to his reports.

But as Chitto worked, his attention wandered to Bobby Taneyhill's drawings. Graphic novels were stories told primarily through pictures, like the funny pages in newspapers and comic books sold at drugstores and newsstands. An innocuous form of entertainment for children and teenagers. He'd bought his share of comics growing up. In recent years, the art form had developed into something more sophisticated, a novel told primarily in pictures but for a more mature audience. He wondered what the subject of the Taneyhill boy's stories had been and what the psychiatrist had seen in them that indicated he was capable of murder.

Chitto looked up from his work, wondering what a psychiatrist would see in his own drawings. Opening the bottom drawer, he pulled out the folder again. Examining the pictures more closely, he recognized them as subjects of stories his grandmother had told him growing up. Old Choctaw legends and myths, ways to explain how things came to be. Nothing unusual, he told himself. Every culture had its own. Had Bobby Taneyhill's grandfather told him those old stories, too? If not, was there was another logical reason for what the boy drew?

That thought triggered a chain of others and he swiveled his chair, looking toward Jasmine's desk. Being from LeFlore County and having worked in most of the Nation's offices, she possessed a wealth of information. What's more, with her computer experience she would know which rocks to turn over to find what was obscured. Such as why the boy was being raised by his grandfather instead of his parents. If he'd had problems with teachers or schoolmates. If he'd seen counselors, had dealings with the victim.

The next thing he knew, he was wondering if the screech of the owl could have been the scream of a woman. The boy's grandfather lived nearby. Was the place close enough to the murder site for the boy to hear the victim's cries? One thing was certain: honorable men didn't lie. If the boy *had* been home all night, the murderer was still out there. Was this his first murder? Would he kill again?

Chitto selected a stone from the collection on his desk and rubbed it between his fingers. Trained as a geologist, he had put together his collection carefully, selecting various types of rock that spoke to the creation of that part of the country. Spanning eons, the rocks told an ancient story: volcanic eruptions, ancient seas, cracks in the planet's surface that led to earthquakes and faults. The flat, round stone he chose this day, however, was nothing remarkable. He'd picked it up on a fishing trip with his father.

Swiveling his chair, he looked out the window. The rain had let up, causing ground fog to float like ghost vapors in low-lying places. Chitto knew of ghosts. The recent murder was not the first one to happen in LeFlore County. Two Choctaw Nation police officers had lost their lives there a decade ago, his father and Bert Gilly.

Chitto contemplated the misty vapors rising from the ground like restless spirits. From past experience, he knew ghosts had a way of making their presence known. Had he just been handed an invitation to look into a ten-year-old murder case?

His father had been Field Lieutenant for District 11 and Bert Gilly for District 9. But soon after their bodies were discovered, the jurisdictional rigmarole had kicked in and Dan Blackfox, the Director of the Law Enforcement, turned the case over to the FBI, which held jurisdiction. Chitto had not visited the murder site since the case was turned over to the feds.

A decade, he thought now. Ten long years. He had changed his career plan because of the murder, given up a career in geology for a job that would enable him to find the killers. His goal had gone unfulfilled. And though multiple FBI agents had been assigned to work the case, none had made any progress. Would doing a favor for two irate council members be the ammunition he needed to persuade Dan Blackfox to let him off leash?

Returning the stone to his collection, he rose and walked to the front of the office. "Jasmine," he said. "Let me buy you a cup of coffee."

"Um-hmm," she said. "I knew those two were up to no good. Politicians always have an agenda."

Another reason to like Jasmine Birdsong. Her opinion of politicians matched his to a T.

CHAPTER TWO

Until recently, the Law Enforcement Department for the Choctaw Nation was housed in the main building of the Tribal Complex, a multi-storied, red brick building that began life as a college. Now, the department took up part of a single story building behind the main one. Recently refurbished, the back building had been divided into thirds with Law Enforcement on one end, Land Management on the other, and a small cafeteria between. It was a welcome change for the department. Officers no longer had to share desks, being adjacent to the parking lot made for easy access, and the cafeteria eliminated the need for quick runs to a fast food place. Better still, the coffeepot was always on.

Chitto and Jasmine sat at a table in the cafeteria now, steaming Styrofoam cups in front of them. Situated on the far side of the room, the table provided privacy. It also sat next to a window, which allowed a view of the parking lot so they could monitor who was coming and going. He quietly briefed her on the reason for the two council members' visit and the arrest of Bobby Taneyhill.

"I didn't know the family personally," Jasmine said. "But I heard stories 'bout the grandfather." Long, slender fingers rotated a stir stick, blending hazelnut creamer into the coffee. "People have a lot of respect for Charlie Walker. I'm surprised he raised that boy. He's no spring chicken."

"You know nothing about the boy's parents?"

13

Lu Clifton

She raised an eyebrow. "LeFlore's a big county, Sam. And Spiro's way out on the edge, almost in Arkansas."

True, he thought, pulling up a mental image of the area. That part of the Nation was rugged country, full of wrinkles. The Choctaw and the Winding Stair fault lines ran through it. Chert, black shale, and fossilized sponges spoke to an ancient life. The mound builders, pre-Columbian people, had also settled there. LeFlore County proper measured 1500 miles square and was populated by 50,000 people, more or less. The east side of the county shared a border with the state of Arkansas. To the north, with the Cherokee Nation. Meandering like a snake, the Arkansas River served as the boundary line between the two states and two nations. His father and Bert Gilly had gone there to handle a land dispute on that river, from which they hadn't returned alive.

"One of my great grandpa's owners farmed that area way back," Jasmine said. Olive-green eyes, dark hair, and warm-toned skin echoed her multicultural heritage, a mix of African American, Caucasian, and Choctaw. "He was a slave to one of the Choctaws who settled there. He told my mother stories about those mounds, how they plowed around them so they wouldn't disturb the spirits of the old ones. I believe Mr. Walker was descended from those old Choctaws."

Chitto made a low grunting noise. "That would explain the respect the locals have for him. Too bad you didn't know the younger generation."

"I lived in Poteau, not Spiro." She peered at him through tortoise-shell framed glasses. "Something tells me this cup of coffee comes with strings attached. What's that visit from those two politicians have to do with me?"

Noticing increased activity in the cafeteria, Chitto leaned closer. Quickly, he briefed her on his father and Bert Gilly's murder.

14

"I remember that," she murmured. "The woman I replaced was Gilly's wife. Name was Wanda, died of lung cancer."

He nodded. "Wouldn't give up the smokes. Vices come with a price."

She eyed him steadily. "Still doesn't answer what this has to do with me."

"Sounds like this Taneyhill kid needs an advocate, and . . ." He paused, sighing. "Aw hell, if I'm going to be in the area, I thought I'd look into my dad and Bert's murder case, see if I could pick up on something. The case belongs to the FBI so I'd need to hole up somewhere private. Lots of cabins and fishing camps up that way, bet you'd know a good one. And . . ." He made eye contact. "I could use someone here to scout things out for me. Background material on this Spiro Mounds murder for starters. I'm in the dark on it. As for Dad's case, I might need someone to dig into old files, maybe do some computer research."

"Scout things out . . ." A deep frown wrinkled the skin between her eyes. "Like Bloody Knife, you mean?"

"Bloody Knife?"

"Custer's favorite scout. Died at the Battle of the Little Big Horn."

Chitto lifted an eyebrow. "I didn't know you were a student of history, Jasmine."

"Not a student of anything," she replied. "I just like old western movies, 'specially those where the Indians go off the rez."

He laughed quietly. "You would've liked my wife, Mary. She was also a fan of movies involving Indians. Only she was into the newer ones showing their struggle to fit into today's society."

She looked across the table at him. "I hear she died of cancer, too."

"Pancreatic," he murmured.

Jasmine rolled her cup between her hands. "Bloody Knife died at the Battle of the Little Big Horn, the back corner of nowhere."

"That's true," Chitto said as her meaning sunk in. "But if Custer had listened to him, neither one of them would've died."

"You might want to remember that." She eyed him directly. "Am I to assume the boss man hasn't blessed this?"

He leaned back, sighing. "Haven't run it past Dan yet but plan to this afternoon. It would be helpful if he gave me his blessing, but . . ." He let the sentence hang.

She made a sound somewhere between a laugh and a grunt. "Doesn't matter what he says, your mind's made up. Come hell or high water, you're going." She drained her cup, placed the stir stick inside, and stood up. "Want to stay in Spiro or Poteau?"

Sighing with relief, he said, "Somewhere in between. The murders happened in the Spiro area but the courthouse is in Poteau."

∞

"You expect me to buy that cock-'n-bull story?" Dan Black-fox sat with his elbows on his desk, fingers peaked in a steeple. "The *real* reason you want to look into this Spiro Mounds killing is because it would give you an excuse to dig into Will and Bert's murders." His eyes raked Chitto. "No way in hell," he growled. "The Chief got wind of how some of us directors across the nations have been . . ." He paused, eyes indicating he was searching for words. "*Permitting* our people to go renegade." The Chief he referred to was the Chief of the Choctaw Nation whose office was in the main

16

building overlooking the police department. "The order's come down that we're to cooperate with all the other government agencies—and especially the FBI."

"Come on, Dan," Chitto said, fingers splayed. "This kid needs someone in his corner." He quickly retrieved the folder of drawings his mother had given him and spread them across Blackfox's desk. "Something similar happened to me when I was a kid."

Blackfox thumbed through the drawings, read the teacher's note, and looked up at him. "So what you're saying is, 'There but for the grace of God, go I.'"

"Something like that. The difference is I had both parents and a grandmother to fend for me. This boy has an elderly grandfather."

Reading the reproachful note in the folder again, Blackfox chuckled. "I bet Mattie landed in the middle of that teacher with both feet—and Will was probably behind her laughing his head off."

Smiling, Chitto said, "No doubt." Sobering, he said, "The grandfather swears the boy was home all night. He's an Elder, his code of conduct wouldn't condone lying." He paused, exhaling loudly. "And you're right. As long as I'm up there, I'd like to poke around, see if I could find a new lead on Dad and Bert's murderer. All I'm asking is that you clear the road for me."

Chitto had been working on a double master in Geology and Criminal Justice when his father and Bert Gilly were killed. The Criminal Justice degree was to please his father but he'd never intended to follow in his footsteps. He planned to do field geology. The murder altered that plan. He'd visited the murder site only once and that was right after he buried his father. He couldn't explain why he felt it necessary to go there, perhaps because he needed something concrete to prove his father was gone—what psychologists called closure. Seeing the crime scene tape and blood darkened ground had done the trick. Now, however, with a decade of police work under his belt, he would be looking at the site through different eyes.

"*No*—" Blackfox held up a hand, silencing more comments. "I closed the door on that incident a long time back. You learn as you get older you have to do that if you're going to live with yourself."

"It's the Chief, isn't it," Chitto said. "That ultimatum he gave—"

Blackfox raised the hand again, stopping Chitto midsentence. "It's not just because we're under scrutiny. You need to give Rodriguez a chance." Ramon Rodriguez wasn't just the FBI agent trying to pin the illicit intertribal investigation on Chitto, he had also been assigned to handle Chitto's father and Bert Gilly's murder. The last in a long line of agents. "The guy's smarter than you give him credit. Let him do his job. How'd you like to be handed a ten-year-old cold case—especially one dealing with a cop killer? He's got a hard-enough road ahead of him without your interference."

Chitto let out a groan. He didn't cotton to FBI agents in general, who he felt suffered from overinflated egos, but in his opinion, Rodriguez was the worst of the bunch. He not only had a chip on his shoulder but was a clotheshorse to boot. Chinos and a clean shirt were good enough for most feds but Rodriguez decked out in a sports coat and tie every day.

Chitto leaned forward, eyes intense. "Don't look a gift horse in the mouth, Dan. This Spiro murder provides the perfect cover."

"Cover for what?" Blackfox raised his hands, let them drop. "The trail's gone cold. Where would you even start?"

"I'd follow the evidence. Interview the locals, the officials—anyone who might remember something. There would've been a lot of chatter about something that big. Someone up there was involved or can put the finger on who was . . ."

Blackfox waved him off. "More than a decade's gone by. I doubt any of the current people were on the roles when Will and Bert were killed. Turnover's high in this business, especially with elected offices. And you can bet your bottom dollar, no one who knew anything is going to talk. There'd be nothing to gain from it. They know which side of the bread their butter's on."

Chitto leaned back, a stubborn set to his jaw. "Someone knows something, Dan."

"Who? You can rule out our own people. Wayne Drumright's hasn't been field officer up there very long. He replaced Ruth Bledsoe, who went on maternity leave and didn't come back. Pete Brody's been field lieutenant there for years but he'd never do anything lowdown. He's as true-blue as they come, a cop to the core."

Chitto nodded in agreement. He'd had personal dealings with both men. Blinking slowly, he looked away, then back at Blackfox. "Was Pete the one who called Dad and Bert to come up there? You signed off on it, so they didn't go off on their own."

"For a fact, he wasn't." Running a hand through short dark hair showing no gray though he was closer to sixty than fifty, Blackfox turned reflective. "Bert set up that trip based on a phone call he got the night before."

Chitto hesitated, frowning. "And the call went to his house?"

"All I know is it didn't come through here." Blackfox paused a beat. "Not sure if it was to his house phone or cell, but he wanted Will to ride shotgun."

Chitto leaned forward again. "How come I'm just hearing about this now?"

"Because you weren't on the job then, and . . ." Blackfox let out a troubled sigh. "Aw hell, I figured the trip was part personal. Will and Bert went way back. They were always joshing about finding a new fishing hole."

Chitto nodded. He'd gone with his father many times in search of a new place to catch bass.

But he'd never talked about the Arkansas River . . .

"Seems funny Wanda never mentioned that phone call to me," Chitto said. "We were pretty close."

"To me either. But she was pretty much a basket case after it happened. Thought sure she was headed for a breakdown but she pulled herself together."

"Well," Chitto said quietly, "she was a powerhouse there at the end."

"Regrettably." Blackfox sighed again. The former administrative assistant had turned bitter at the end of her life, the result of incurable lung cancer and the need for vengeance. To ease that burden, both Chitto and Blackfox had promised they wouldn't stop looking until they'd found the killers. A deathbed promise.

"We promised Wanda—"

"I remember," Blackfox said, cutting him off. They sat quiet a minute.

"Strange she didn't mention that phone call," Chitto said, frowning. "You think she even knew about it?"

Blackfox let out a snort. "Wanda knew everything about everything."

20

"She did, didn't she," Chitto said, grinning. Wanda had put in decades with the department and prided herself on being a walking file cabinet.

"Anyway," Blackfox went on. "I prefer the men team up when they're investigating something unusual, so I called Will and told him to accompany Bert. Gave Pete Brody a call to let him know they'd be up there, and . . ." He raised a hand, let it drop.

"You couldn't have known what was going to happen, Dan."

"I've told myself that a thousand times. Still . . ." Blackfox ran fingers through his hair again.

A long minute passed. "You think Bert was the target and my dad just collateral damage?" Chitto asked.

"I don't know." Blackfox exhaled slowly. "I ran possible scenarios of what might've happened that day till I was blue in the face. I *do* know Will and Victor Messina had a history. Will had seen so many kids hooked on dope, he took it upon himself to shut down Messina's drug operation."

The Messina family had a long history in LeFlore County with a finger in everything from drugs and prostitution to land swindles. Over time, the family extended its dealings to other counties, including Pittsburg, his father's jurisdiction. Will Chitto had run himself ragged trying to put Vincent Messina, the patriarch of the family, behind bars but thanks to the convoluted legal system, he could never make anything stick.

Blackfox rocked back in his chair, eyes downcast. "And given where they were found, I had no choice but let the feds take over."

Though not sympathetic with the decision, Chitto could understand the logic. His father and Bert Gilly's bodies were found near the boat ramp for the Mayo Lock and Dam, north of Spiro. The U.S. Corps of Engineers administered the Aransas River navigation project, putting the case outside tribal jurisdiction.

"Regrettably, the FBI took the files relevant to the case," Blackfox continued. "No telling where they are now, so many agents have been involved over the years."

"Files be damned," Chitto said, planting his elbows on the edge of the desk. "I know who killed them—or had them killed. Vincent Messina wouldn't have dirtied his hands. He'd have someone else do it."

"You *think* you know. Remember, in our business you're innocent till proven guilty."

"Suppositions keep you chained," Chitto said, leaning back in his chair.

"Besides which," Blackfox said. "I don't think old man Messina's living in LeFlore County anymore. I hear he moved into Fort Smith because there's better medical facilities there. Poor health and age catching up with him, I guess. Or maybe his sins."

"That might be so," Chitto said, "but you can bet he still keeps a finger on things." He paused, recalling something Blackfox mentioned earlier. "You said they were investigating something *unusual*."

"For us it was." Blackfox's gaze drifted. "As a rule, we don't get involved in land disputes, especially those on the Arkansas. That damned old river's a pain in the butt."

Being the boundary line for the states of Oklahoma and Arkansas and subject to erosion and channel changes, the Arkansas River was often the cause of court cases between property owners in the two states, not to mention the state of Arkansas and the Choctaw Nation. The river was designated the line between Choctaw land and state of Arkansas in the

Treaty of Dancing Rabbit Creek in 1830. Since then, the channel had changed many times.

"But it seemed real important to Bert." Blackfox rubbed the back of his neck, eyes askance. "Though he didn't say as much, I got the feeling he knew whoever was involved in the dispute. Maybe a friend or old acquaintance."

Chitto considered this. "Sounds like you think that friend set them up."

Blackfox's fingers began a methodical tapping. "It did occur to me."

Betrayed?

"Of course," Blackfox said, eyes narrowing. "It's possible we could scrounge up some of Bert's old files . . ."

Chitto smiled inwardly. Blackfox's door had just opened a crack.

"Nope—" Glancing toward the main building, Blackfox reasserted his stance. "We're not going down that road. Like I said, it's best to let Rodriguez handle it. He can be more objective. We're both too damned close to this thing."

Chitto paused, thinking in the decade that had passed the FBI had used up their chances. None of the agents he'd encountered ever displayed an ounce of objectivity. They were more interested in what made them look good: high profile cases that got publicity, such as terrorism and drug trafficking along the Rio Grande.

"And what am I supposed to tell my mother and June Biggers?" Chitto asked, taking a new tack. "They're expecting to hear from me later today."

Blackfox shrugged. "Just what I told you."

"*Right*," Chitto said mockingly. "You've known my mother for years. She's a dog worrying a bone when it comes to something she sets her mind on. You think she's going to

23

be satisfied with *that* answer?" He sucked the spit from between his teeth, head shaking. "You leave me no choice. I'll have to sic her on you."

Blackfox's jaws dropped. "You wouldn't . . ."

Chitto raised his palms in a helpless gesture.

"Well, hell." Blackfox let out a long sigh. "Mattie can be a force to be reckoned with when she gets a burr under her blanket. June Biggers, too." He paused, looked away, then made eye contact. "You got any time-off coming? I know you worked some weekends, put in a lot of your own time on that undercover case."

Chitto grinned. "I stopped keeping track, took too much effort."

Blackfox rubbed his neck again, sighing. "Take two, three days off next week. Clean up your desk, give Nate any cases that might need immediate handling, and brief Junior." Nate White was the field officer for District Nine; Junior Wharton, the Evidence and K-9 Officer. "But you're going up there to look into this Spiro Mounds murder, understand? I'll let Pete know you're coming but you will *not* be representing the Nation. So keep a low profile."

"*Low profile,*" Chitto snorted. "No way in hell! I might need to check records at the sheriff's office or the courthouse. How am I going to do that without an official reason?"

"Get creative. You're good at that." Blackfox leaned forward, eyes hard as flint. "And on the offhand chance you run into something on Will and Bert's murder while you're up there, you *will* involve me and Ramon Rodriguez. Don't forget, I watched you program his number into your cell phone—and you sure as hell know mine."

Knowing he'd hit a brick wall, Chitto mumbled "Deal" and reached for the stack of drawings.

"I'll just hang on to these," Blackfox said, picking up the folder.

Chitto stared at him. "What for?"

Blackfox shuffled through the drawings again. "I'm inclined to have a psychiatrist friend take a look at them." He looked across the desk. "I've been trying to figure out what makes you tick for years. These might just shed some light." He paused, grinning. "And if you don't abide by my wishes, I just might be forced to put them into your official personnel folder."

"That's blackmail."

"More like insurance. And one more thing."

More conditions? Chitto's back stiffened. He preferred having a free hand. Conditions put a crimp on things.

"Try not to call at an ungodly hour," Blackfox said. "Makes my wife cantankerous when you call at two in the morning."

Chitto was smiling when he rose from his chair. Funny thing about cell phones, he thought. In this part of the country, they didn't work worth a damn.

"Sam—"

Chitto turned slowly, anticipating Blackfox was about to lay another condition on him.

"You do understand this boy might be guilty. Don't underestimate the psychiatrist's assessment. The kid could have a dark side. Sounds like he was a bit . . . withdrawn."

"Yeah, I know," Chitto said. "We all have a shadow and the more buried it is in the subconscious, the darker it is."

"That more of Rhody's teachings?" Blackfox asked. Rhody Pitchlyn was Chitto's grandmother, who had drilled Choctaw beliefs into him since he was a child.

"Nope," Chitto said. "Guy named Freud."

25

CHAPTER THREE

"Well, blow me down and call me Shorty," Jasmine exclaimed. "Dan is actually sending you up there to investigate the Spiro murder?"

By the time Chitto returned from his meeting with Dan Blackfox, Jasmine had a pulled together a folder of information on the Spiro Mounds murder, including copies of newspaper clippings covering the investigation, a map of the Spiro Archeological Center, and the address and location of the grandfather's place where the boy lived. She had also made a reservation for him at a cabin off the beaten track.

"Not exactly," he sighed. "Dan's going to let Pete know I'm coming but I won't officially be representing the Nation."

"How long you be gone?"

"Couple days, three at the most. Depends on far along the case is."

"Case has gone to trial." She pointed to the folder she had laid on his desk. "Might be too late to do anything."

"Well, hell," he mumbled, flipping through the folder's contents. "Our two visitors this morning could've mentioned that." He paused, looking at a copy of a newspaper article about the court case. "Man-oh-man, would I like to sit in on that trial. Listening to the witnesses' testimony would save a lot of time."

"Why can't you?"

"Too chancy." He explained that he'd filled in for other lieutenants from time to time, including Pete Brody in District 4. "And because I'm not there officially, I can't flash my badge." He shook his head. "Badges make people more cooperative."

"Badges?" Jasmine said, a rare grin showing. "'We don't need no stinkin' badges.'"

Recognizing the line made famous in the old film, *The Treasure of Sierra Madre*, he smiled.

"Go as a spectator," she said. "Big case like this, be easy enough to get lost in the crowd. Just wear a Stetson and boots so you don't stick out like a sore thumb." She stood and began walking toward her desk.

"Hell, yeah," he said, laughing quietly. "Worth a try."

His focus shifting, he said, "Wait up, Jasmine." Catching up with her, he whispered, "You got time to do more research? I need to know about disputes dealing with the Arkansas River."

"Be still my heart," she said, her tone sarcastic. "That shouldn't take more than a year. Care to narrow the field?"

Chitto's thinking went to the phone call Bert Gilly received. "Those that happened ten to twelve years ago . . . and involving someone from the Nation."

"A Choctaw connection?" Her eyes narrowed. "Something tells me this doesn't have anything to do with the murder at Spiro Mounds."

"It doesn't," he admitted.

"Um-hmm." She gave a quick glance over her shoulder, then looked at him again. "The fact we're whispering mean Dan didn't sign off on you looking into that old case?"

"It does," he said, admiring Jasmine's perceptive abilities.

She paused briefly. "I'll see what I can do."

Back at his desk, Chitto picked up the round stone again and swiveled his chair toward the window. Since his conversation with Dan, his interest in his father's and Bert Gilly's murder had shifted from Vincent Messina to Bert's mysterious caller.

Who had betrayed them?

∞

Chitto left the office to take care of a couple of case calls he wanted to close before he left town. One involved a short meeting at the sheriff's department dealing with an assist he had made. The other was to drop off a report at the county social services department on a domestic disturbance he'd handled. While out, he grabbed a burger and Pepsi he ate on the drive back to the office. In a short meeting late in the day, he briefed Nate White on a half dozen cases still pending.

"Nothing you need to move fast on, Nine," he cautioned. "You have my cell number if you need to touch base on something."

Though he excelled at recalling the words of philosophers and other renowned people, Chitto encountered a problem dealing with names. When he first went to work for the department, he was given multiple-district assignments, which meant he was dealing with four departments—Tribal Police, Tribal Security, Casino EMS, and Dispatch—plus over 30 patrol officers. Adding to the confusion, more officers were stationed at the Choctaw Nation Hospital, and over 300 armed security officers were located in 18 gaming facilities. A dedicated police officer provided education to schools and communities, stressing the importance of staying off drugs, but to Chitto, it was just one more name to keep up with. As a result, he resorted to using associations as identifiers—a physical characteristic or a place, easier yet, a number—which led to using the district number to ID the respective field officer. The rationale made sense. People came and went but the districts remained the same. Ingrained now, he still referred to the field officers by their district numbers.

Seeming pleased with Chitto's confidence in him, Nine took on the added work without complaint. In appearance, the field officer was the antithesis of Chitto. Short in stature, light-colored eyes, fair of hair and skin—a walking example that being Native American was not a requirement for employment with the Nation.

Leaving the young field officer to look through the files, Chitto walked to Junior Wharton's desk. Sitting down next to Jake, the black German Shepherd ever present at Wharton's side, he let the K-9 Officer know he'd be absent a few days.

"Keep an eye on my boy, Junior," he said, pointing his chin at Nate. Chitto's one-and-only direct report, Nate was a bit green and a lot gung-ho.

"No sweat, man." Wharton nodded a head attached to a beefy neck. "I'll block for him." Not too many challenged the ex-football player, who was also a member of the Nation's SWAT team, especially when he was accompanied by the eighty-pound police dog.

It was after six o'clock when Chitto walked to the parking lot. Twilight. Though the day was cooling off, rain coupled with temperatures in the seventies made for sultry conditions. Air heavy with moisture was hard on the lungs. While he regularly longed for a cigarette, right then he was glad he'd given up the habit a few years before. He had substituted Doublemint chewing gum for cigarettes and went through several packs a week, but at least the new habit did not affect his lung capacity. Folding a stick into his mouth now, he keyed the ignition and headed his white Tahoe toward the house he'd occupied alone the last two years.

As he drove, he created a mental checklist for the trip. Decisions needed to be made and decisions led to consequences. Bunking in a cabin required food and that meant a stop at the corner grocery mart. An easy fix. He also owned a horse, a gray gelding named Blue that he used for both work and pleasure. The department relied on mounted patrols at large events and Chitto preferred riding a horse he knew. When he had time, he also hauled the horse to the Ouachita Mountains to camp out and do some rock hunting. He'd just laid in a supply of grass hay and a sweet-mix grain, so he was set in that department. He only needed to call the stable and arrange for someone to care for the horse. Another easy fix.

The big question dealt with Boycott, a yearling redbone-mix hound. Chitto's elderly neighbor, Hattie George, had discovered the scrawny pup on her back stoop several months before and adopted it. He and Hattie now shared ownership of the dog. Hattie made sure it got a good brushing and proper food each day, which showed in its gleaming russet-colored coat, but pups had a lot of energy. By the end of the day, Hattie was worn ragged, in need of a break, so Chitto took Boycott home nights and weekends.

He took the dog running in the evening when he could, from which both man and dog benefited. His wind had gotten better and Boycott now weighed a muscular fifty pounds. But taking the dog with him that weekend was out of the question. He would be traveling between towns, meeting with people, and attending the murder trial. A dog would complicate matters. Though he didn't like the idea, he would have to tell Hattie he couldn't take the dog.

The stop for groceries took fifteen minutes. He took care of the call to the stable between the store and his house. As he pulled his patrol car into the garage next to his Chevy pickup, he spied the locked gun cabinet that set along the back wall. Another decision to make. He would take his service weapon but would it be enough? First things first, he decided, postponing the decision until he went next door to tell Hattie about the upcoming trip.

When he knocked on Hattie's screen door, Boycott came running, squirming like a new-caught fish thrown on the bank. Hattie had named him after Cesar Chavez's dog. She admired Chavez, not only because he was vegetarian, as she was, but also an animal rights activist—a detail that caused her pioneer ranching family to shun her. But she had stuck to her guns. When push came to shove, principles won out. Family could go to hell.

Seconds passed. A minute. Chitto knocked again. When Hattie didn't appear, he stuck his head inside and called, "Hattie?"

"Back here . . ."

Following the sound, he walked down the hall to the kitchen. Hattie met him part way, pushing a walker and wearing an elastic back support, the kind that used Velcro straps for easy adjustment. Legs bowed from straddling a saddle from an early age made for a waddling gait in the best of times. Now, the effort of pushing the walker added a jerkiness that was even more unnatural.

"What the hell happened?" he asked, hurrying to her side.

"Fell off the back step. It was the rain, made the stoop slippery." She gave her head a shake, ruffling short, peppered hair. "Called the doctor and told him I'd thrown my back out. He sent out one of those EMT fellas to check me over. That's how I got this belly band and walker."

"You need someone to stay with you?"

"I can manage. Nothing's broke, just pulled some muscles. I need somethin', I'll call Angelina." She jerked the walker around, heading back toward the kitchen. "Got Boycott's dog chow all ready to go. It's back here."

On the way to the kitchen, Chitto adjusted his plans. It seemed consequences also lead to decisions. A perfect causal chain: a cause led to an effect and, in turn, the effect became a cause, precipitating another effect. No way around it, Boycott would have to go with him. Locating a brown paper bag in the broom closet, he emptied the dog's water dish and placed it inside. A dog bowl and bag of dog chow went in next. As he worked, he explained the upcoming trip.

"Not sure how long I'll be gone. Few days at the most." He hesitated, looking around. "I might need the long leash. Where is it?"

"Coat closet," she said, nodding toward the hallway. "A trip, you say. Business or pleasure?

"Business . . . sort've." He retrieved a leather leash from the coat closet and tucked it in the bag.

"Sort've," she grunted. "Anything need doin' while you're gone?"

"Yeah . . ." He paused a click. "Angelina's coming tomorrow. Let her use your key to get in. I'll leave her pay on the table. And tell her to check the fridge before she leaves. She's welcome to anything that looks like it won't make it."

It had taken a while for Chitto to give in to Hattie's urgings to hire her housekeeper, who she called Angelina Something-Or-Other. His resistance stemmed from a reluctance to have someone touching Mary's things, rearranging

33

them, cleaning them . . . eliminating her presence. He had finally been convinced he was not doing Mary a favor by keeping her from completing her journey, releasing her *shilombish* to the Land of Shadows.

In olden times, the Choctaw believed a person possessed an inner shadow, the *shiliup,* and an outer one, the *shilombish.* After death, the inner shadow began the long journey to the west but the outer shadow remained until the funeral ceremonies were completed. Sometimes, however, the outer shadow would not fade away until it felt everything was all right with its family or, in some instances, a violent death had been settled. This, according to his mother, explained those times when his father's spirit made itself known. Though it ran counter to his instinct, Chitto had to admit he felt his father's presence from time to time. He'd once felt Mary's spirit too, but not since he'd released it to the spirit world.

After a time, he'd hired Angelina. In addition to not using a last name, Angelina also required payment in cash. Both were indications she was a non-carded illegal from across the Rio Grande. He considered that fact inconsequential. The young woman was also a single working mother. To his thinking, food, clothing, and school supplies took precedence over the few bucks the government would get in taxes. She came every Saturday now.

"Be glad to," Hattie said. "She's also doing my place tomorrow. Don't worry, nothin' will go to waste. Those kids of hers are growing like weeds." She crooked a neck stiffened with arthritis, looking up at him. "Anything else comes up, give me a call. I'll do what I'm able."

As he walked back to his garage, Boycott racing ahead, Chitto moved to the last decision he needed to make. Weapons. His thoughts went to his dad and Bert Gilly, wondering what they had been carrying on that last trip. Since they were officially representing the Nation, they would've been armed. If nothing else, they'd be carrying their service weapons.

Why hadn't they used them? Could the answer be traced back to the mysterious phone call to Bert?

Forewarned was forearmed, Chitto decided. Prior knowledge of possible dangers gave one a tactical advantage. Setting Boycott's brown paper bag at the back door, he walked to the gun case. Unlocking it, he exchanged his duty belt for his IWB holster. A loose shirt or jacket would hide an inside-the-waistband holster easily enough. As he started to lock the cabinet, he paused, eying the Remington 879 and AR 15. If push came to shove, tactical advantages might need a bump, especially if there was a chance you'd be surprised or outnumbered. Quickly, he loaded both long guns into the gun rack of his Chevy dual-wheel pickup and his pistol and IWB holster in the glove box.

Retrieving the groceries from the front seat, he locked the truck, picked up Boycott's bag at the back door, and went inside to do his homework.

CHAPTER FOUR

Laying aside the folder containing information on the Spiro Mounds murder, Chitto walked to the coffee pot on the kitchen counter. The old-style percolator was one thing he'd insisted on keeping after he and Mary married. He liked the sound of the water as it came to a boil, the glass top that served as a gauge for the readiness of the brew, the gurgling sounds that emanated out the spout. Most everything else in the house spoke of Mary. Even though she'd been gone two years, he endeavored to keep the house the way she'd left it. She had good taste, leaning toward natural wood furniture, solidly constructed but not heavy, and earthy colors that complemented the Native American artwork she'd collected. A pragmatist, Chitto admitted that keeping things the same was an effort to keep her physically close. He'd only converted the kitchen into a makeshift office a few months before and that was because surprise office visits from FBI agent Ramon Rodriguez dictated he keep certain cases out of the spotlight. Those cases dealt with murders, all of which had been outside his jurisdiction.

Spooning coffee into the percolator's basket now, he eyed the *Tribal Jurisdictions in Oklahoma* map fixed to the wall. The Murder Map.

Multicolored sticky notes bearing initials indicated where recent murders had taken place across the big Check-

37

erboard, which included the Choctaw and other thirty-seven Nations. He had noted three murders initially, all occurring at ceremonial grounds. He'd added four more recently, all located in the Ouachita Wilderness area. Now another needed to be added. What initials would he print on the one destined for LeFlore County? He had yet to learn the name of the woman Bobby Taneyhill allegedly killed.

Thinking of the decade-old murder case, he wondered if he should add an additional two for his father and Bert Gilly. "No can do," he said to Boycott, who sat next to his empty food dish. "Can't chance the head honcho seeing them. He might think we were defying orders."

And you're not? taunted his conscience.

Boycott's tail thumped the linoleum as Chitto filled his dish with dog chow and freshened his water bowl. Turning to his own needs, Chitto resorted to his standby: crisp bacon and runny eggs with white-bread toast. As the bacon began to sizzle, the phone on the table rang. He frowned as he picked up the receiver, wondering who would be calling on a Friday night.

"Well?" Mattie Chitto said.

Chitto sighed. His mother had beaten him to the punch. "I'm heading up in the morning. I'll check into this Spiro Mounds thing but can't make any promises. You forgot to mention the case had already gone to trial."

"Oh. Well, it just started. Maybe you can find out something to prove Bobby didn't do it and take it to his lawyer."

"No promises," he repeated. "Look, I can't pursue this openly because it's out of my jurisdiction, so tell Mrs. Biggers not to blow my cover if she sees me around."

"I'll let June know," she said. "We had more work to do so she's spending the night here—"

The Horned Owl

A break coming on the line, Chitto listened to voices in the background.

"She says you can stay with her," Mattie said. "She lives in Poteau."

"Thanks, but I've made other arrangements . . ." He hesitated. "But it would be helpful if she let the boy's grandfather know I'll be by tomorrow to see him."

He listened to the sound of background conversation again. A minute later, Mattie came back on the line.

"She'll call him soon as we hang up. He'll be working at the Archaeology Center this weekend. He's the handyman. June says you also need to talk to the archaeologist there. Name's Mack Green—Dr. Mack Green."

"Why do I need to talk to him?"

"She didn't say. If you need anything, here's June's phone number."

He jotted down the number, then paused. "Why'd you save all that stuff, Mom?"

A pause. "What stuff?"

"Those drawings."

"Oh. I didn't. Your granny did. She said it was proof you'd been listening to her all those years—and you need to bring them back right away. She was real mad 'cause I came home without them."

"Can't. Left them at the office." He gave his head a slight shake, thinking about Dan Blackfox confiscating them. "Tell her I'll get them back to her soon as I can."

"*You* tell her," she said. "I don't wanna get chewed out again."

He sighed. "Gotta go now, Mom. Bacon's done."

"Wait up," she said. "What time should we look for you?"

Hesitation. "Wasn't planning to stop by. I don't have a lot of time and no clue where to start."

A grunting sound. "We were expecting you to come up this weekend. Since you can't make it for Sunday dinner, might as well stop on your way to Spiro. I'll tell her you'll be here tomorrow." *Click.*

Chitto shook his head, wondering when he'd lost control of his life. Setting his plate and the coffee pot on the table, he scanned articles from the *Poteau Daily News* as he buttered toast.

The murder victim was named Muriel Simpson. A recent article covering the trial featured a grainy picture of Bobby Taneyhill. A clip-on tie drooped at the neck. Heavy-rimmed glasses magnified dark eyes. A thick head of unruly black hair framed a thin face.

Typical-looking teenager, he thought. Boy on the way to becoming Man.

The article stated Robert Taneyhill, aka Bobby, had recently turned eighteen and was being charged with first-degree murder. If convicted, he could face a life sentence. A special judge had appointed the Oklahoma Indigent Defense System to represent him.

"Damn," he grunted. Indigent meant the family couldn't afford to hire an attorney. He wondered who had been assigned the case, if they were any good. In his experience, lawyers assigned to work pro bono didn't give their all.

The article reported the jury had been seated and gave details of the people who had already testified. The rancher who saw Bobby Taneyhill leaving the Archaeology Center. The manager of the Spiro Mounds Center who reported the body. The county sheriff who investigated the scene as well as the medical examiner. The teacher who had saved drawings Bobby Taneyhill had done in her class. Simpson's boyfriend she'd dined with that night and a neighbor she talked with outside her apartment. The trial was scheduled to resume on Monday.

"Damn," he grunted a second time, wishing the trial wasn't so far along. He picked up the coffee pot and watched the dark liquid stream into his cup, trying to come up with a strategy.

The words *Just follow the evidence* reverberated in his memory. They were the exact words he'd used with Dan Blackfox.

"*Right,*" he mumbled, reality setting in. Spreading apple butter on a piece of toast, he ate as he sorted the newspaper articles by date. Starting with a June issue published the day after the body was found, he began to read aloud.

"'The last night for LeFlore resident Muriel Simpson, age 33, began with her being locked out of her apartment and ended in murder outside the Spiro Mounds Archaeology Center where she worked. A deep knife wound to the back punctured a lung and fractured a rib. The medical examiner said she would have died from blood loss within 30 minutes after being stabbed. The victim had not been raped but her sexual organs had been mutilated . . .'"

Mutilated—

Appetite gone, Chitto pushed his plate away. June Biggers' words "heinous murder" echoing in his mind, he began to wonder what he'd gotten himself into? *Was* this a crime of passion as the psychiatrist said? A lust murder? A fantasy killing?

Picking up the article again, he focused on relevant details. Simpson worked late because a summer solstice tour had not ended until late that evening. After work, she'd met up with her boyfriend at a local tavern and left a little after eleven. From there, she had apparently driven straight home where she discovered she didn't have her apartment key. A neighbor who lived in the same apartment complex reported encountering Simpson a little before midnight. She told him she remembered leaving the key under the counter at the gift shop and was driving back out to get it. She had obviously done just that and died there. Stab wounds puncturing her lungs, she had died of blood loss.

The son-of-a-bitch let her bleed out . . .

Chitto's face contorted into a scowl. Only someone with a twisted mind would be that cold-blooded.

He turned his attention to pictures of the crime scene. A bloodstained path showed the body had been pulled away from the entrance to the building and left in tall grass next to a walking path. Captions under the photos indicated several sets of footprints were found at the scene but because of the solstice tour, incriminating prints were impossible to identify.

Chitto frowned, finding the killer's motivation puzzling. Why did he bother to move the body, and why to that spot? Calling Boycott to his side, he set his unfinished plate on the floor.

"What do you think, pup?" he said, watching the dog clean up the leftovers. "Did the killer drag the body to the trail to intentionally conceal his footprints? If so, the killer knew about the solstice tour."

Not only twisted, he reflected, but very smart.

Picking up the plate, he cleared the table and walked to the sink. Though the kitchen had a dishwasher, Chitto rarely used it. Now that he was the only one in the house, and prone to eating at fast-food places, he couldn't justify using the appliance. Dirty dishes would sit in the dishwasher so long, food remains dried to a shellac consistency. Pouring a capful of dish soap in hot water, he washed dishes as he sorted through other questions that came to mind.

Was the killer someone Muriel Simpson told about the tour or someone who had gone on the tour? Why had Bobby Taneyhill become the prime suspect? Working at Spiro Mounds, his grandfather probably knew the schedule. Had he mentioned it to his grandson?

Chitto recalled he was supposed to talk to the archeologist at the Archaeology Center, a man named Mack Green. Why? What connection could an archaeologist have with the murder? Something to do with the victim? The killer?

Setting the last dish in the drainer, he returned to the table, refilled his cup, and picked up another article. This one reported that no blood, fiber, or other concrete evidence was found linking Taneyhill to the crime, even after a search of the nearby home where he lived with his grandfather. Several knives were found in the home, which the grandfather said he used for skinning the animals he hunted as a food source.

"So," Chitto speculated aloud. "No hard evidence, just circumstantial . . . except for those graphic novels." He leaned back in his chair, staring into space.

"One thing for sure," he said, addressing Boycott. "Someone knew the woman was there, which means he either knew she was going there to look for her key or he followed her after she left her apartment . . ." He paused, another thought surfacing. "Or did he see her pull into the Center and go over to see what was happening?"

Leaning forward, he quickly sorted through the folder, looking for the map of Spiro Mounds and the location of Charlie Walker's house.

"Well, hell," he mumbled. "Right next door . . ."

He leaned back, imagining what might have transpired that night. If Bobby was awake enough to hear a screech owl, did he hear the car on the road, perhaps see headlights pull down the drive? Had he heard the woman scream and, dazed with sleep, attribute it to *Ishkitini*. Chitto rubbed his mouth, thinking that could explain why he visited the place the next morning.

Returning to his strategy about following the evidence, he wondered if others had been questioned. Thinking how he would have handled the case, he came up with three suspects: the boyfriend, the neighbor who saw her at the apartment complex, and Bobby Taneyhill.

Did the other two have solid alibis?

Dissatisfied, Chitto added the two men's names to Jasmine's research list. Picking up his mug, he finished off the last of the coffee and assessed the findings. The bottom line? There was no solid evidence against the boy, just those graphic novels. They were the prosecution's key to the case. Was there a good reason for thinking that way, he wondered.

He turned his attention to those who would provide important testimony at the trial. He could only come up with one for the defense: Charlie Walker, the grandfather, which the prosecution would destroy, accusing the old man of sleeping so soundly he didn't hear his grandson leave during the night.

The list for the prosecution was longer. The rancher who observed Bobby Taneyhill walking away from the Center the next morning. A hard fact. The teacher who informed authorities of the scary drawings the boy had done in school. Subjective, but she could probably provide supporting evidence. And the specialist in sexual homicides who was to provide expert testimony on the graphic novels. The wild card.

Unless . . .

Because there was a psychiatrist testifying for the prosecution, the defense attorney should have lined up another psychiatrist to refute the findings. There were two sides for every flip of the coin. Which side would the jury believe?

Chitto's gut told him the prosecution had a pat hand but he wasn't ready yet to fold his cards. He was putting his money on the long shot. Charlie Walker was an Elder, and honored men in the Nation didn't lie. That meant Bobby Taneyhill was innocent and the killer was still walking free.

Rising from the table, he tore a sticky note off a pad and printed MS on it, shorthand for Muriel Simpson. "Time to take the dive," he said, sticking it on the map near Spiro.

Boycott escorted Chitto to the bedroom and wriggled excitedly when Chitto pulled his duffle from the closet.

"Wipe that silly grin off your face, buddy," Chitto said. "We might be in over our heads on this one."

CHAPTER FIVE

Snugging a faded OU ball cap on his head, Chitto carried a coffee thermos and large zippered duffle to his pickup. He hauled a cooler out next, holding perishables packed in ice, and two brown grocery bags holding his and Boycott's non-perishables. Walking to a shelf in the corner, he pulled out two sleeping bags and a tie-out cable for dogs. Loading his gear and groceries in his pickup, he whistled Boycott into the passenger seat.

Though early, Saturday traffic was already starting to pick up. Durant was not a big town, between fifteen and twenty thousand regular residents, more when Southeastern Oklahoma University was in session. But Saturdays were always busy, with farm and ranch families in town to do weekly shopping and students from Southeastern needing a break from the classroom. Though he was a town dweller, Chitto escaped on weekends every chance he got. He was impatient now to trade paved streets and halogen lights for the natural world. When able, he took Oklahoma 69 north and felt his shoulders relax as the suburbs disappeared and the natural world emerged.

Folding a stick of Doublemint into his mouth, he settled back, beginning a three-hour drive to Spiro with a half hour stopover in Krebs to see his grandmother. Though the previous day's rain made it muggy, he rolled the windows down and breathed deep, enjoying the seventy-degree temperature, moisture-laden air, and smell of damp earth. Water stood in the ditches along the highway and creeks were running fast, leftovers from the thunderstorm. Boycott leaned out the passenger-side window, ears rippling, while Chitto took in the morning scene through the driver's side. Now and then, he glanced in his rearview mirror to see if anyone was following him, a habit he'd developed with previous undercover cases. But this day, he was traveling solo.

The highway ran north by northeast through a mix of savanna, prairie, and woodlands. Patches of sumac, leaves red now, daubed the hillsides, a counterpoint to alfalfa fields bright green from the rain. Black Angus, sleek and fat, fed on native grasses, watered in rivulets and creeks, and rested in shady cottonwood groves. Ranch country.

Forty miles into the trip, he poured coffee from the thermos into the cup that also served as a lid. With another forty miles to go to reach his hometown, he had time to think about his grandmother. Rhody Pitchlyn was highly respected in the Nation, some even considered her a mystic similar to old Sonny Boy Monroe. In truth, there were times when Chitto believed she did possess special abilities.

His grandmother asked little of anyone. She was content to work on her story quilt, comprised of colorful blocks capturing the old myths and legends of their people. The quilt was to be a gift to Chitto when complete, her way of ensuring the old stories did not die again. Because of the Removal and the priority put on survival, the Choctaw that were force marched to Indian Territory lost touch with their past. That lost past included stories that explained the people's beginning, their culture. A way to explain the way the natural world worked.

In recent times, Mississippi Choctaw had traveled to Oklahoma to teach the people those stories again. His mother

48

and grandmother were not the only ones who bought into the old teachings. A resurgence had taken hold. Now, not only were the stories being taught but also the language and culture, dances and rituals. A scientist by training, that resurgence had made a conflicted man of Chitto. Science dealt with facts, mythology with beliefs. Oil and water. He had taken the movement in stride for it would be disrespectful to do otherwise. Recently, however, that scientific veneer had developed cracks, as evidenced when he released Mary's spirit from the iron grip he'd held on it.

Would that it was so simple with his father's spirit, he thought. Maybe if he could find who the betrayer was, his father would complete the trip to the spirit world.

Forty miles later, he merged onto US-270N and was soon on the outskirts of Krebs. Once a coal-mining town, Krebs now served as a bedroom community to McAlester, the county seat of Pittsburg County and home base for District 11 tribal offices. It was also Chitto's birthplace and his father's former jurisdiction. Eli Clarence Bohannan had filled his father's empty position the last decade. He should stop by and see Eli, Chitto thought now, catch up on things with an old friend. He glanced at the clock on the dash.

"But first," he said to Boycott, "let's see what's on Grandma's mind."

Leaving the town behind, he drove down a country road. A few miles later, he turned off at a gravel drive winding through a natural tunnel of hickory trees. Listening to nutshells crunch under his tires, he drove toward a brick, ranch-style home. His mother's house. Noting a strange car parked in the drive, he exhaled loudly. That car indicated June Biggers was still there. He opened his car door reluctantly, not looking forward to another encounter with the sharp-tongued councilwoman.

Lu Clifton

Walking Boycott to the backyard, he said, "Take care of business. There's still a lot of road to cover." Not bothering to knock, he walked inside and called, "Anyone home?"

"In here," his mother responded.

Boycott was whining at the back door by the time he reached the kitchen. When Mattie saw the dog, she hiked her eyebrows at Chitto. He quickly explained Hattie's condition, which led to the need to bring the dog.

"Sorry to hear 'bout that." She glanced at the dog again, then at the table where June Biggers sat holding a cup of coffee. "June and me have lots of work to do . . ."

Papers were strewn across the tabletop, folders stacked on the floor. Another big project in the works. Chitto had no interest in what it was, only a hope that it did not involve the Choctaw police.

Reading the message in her words, he said, "I'm taking the dog with me."

She nodded, then glanced toward the table again. "You forget your manners?" she asked pointedly.

Chitto spoke courteously to June Biggers and though she responded in kind, neither greeting sounded heartfelt.

"Where's Grandma?" he asked.

"Front room, working on her quilt." She pointed her chin toward the stove. "There's coffee left."

"Tank's full," he said and walked to the living room where a large quilting frame had been set up in front of a flatscreen TV, the volume jacked up. Turning it down, he walked to where a stoop-shouldered woman sat, white hair twisted in a bun, and squatted next to her chair.

"You doing okay, Grandma?"

"Yeh." Rhody smiled at him. "I have been waiting for you. You bring those pictures back?"

"No, ma'am, but I will next time I come. It's this deal at Spiro, it got in the way."

She grunted softly, nodding.

He stood, taking time to look at the blocks laid out across the frame. "That's new," he said, pointing to one that portrayed a rabbit. "That *Chukfi*, the trickster?"

"Yeh," she said, looking pleased. "The story of how he lost his long tail."

He listened patiently as she told a story he'd heard many times before. How Fox had told Rabbit he caught fish by hanging his long tail through a hole in the ice. For Rabbit, however, the same plan backfired. He left his tail in so long it froze solid. To free himself, he had to jerk so hard his tail snapped off.

"The best-laid schemes of mice and men," he murmured. He searched the quilt again, frowning. "I don't see one about *Ishkitini*, the screech owl."

"It is here." She indicated a basket of embroidered squares next to her chair. Craning her neck, she looked up at him. "You ask about that one because of that boy you go to help."

He nodded. "Some believe that hearing its screech in the night is a sign of sudden death."

"Goes without saying," she said matter of factly. "*Ishkitini* is the Choctaw god that prowls at night, killing men and animals. Who would know best that someone had been killed?"

"Than the killer . . ." he said, letting the words trail off.

"You go now," she said. "Stop that monster that kills in the night."

Kissing the top of her head, Chitto walked back to the kitchen and told his mother he was leaving.

"I'll walk with you," she said, accompanying him to the back stoop. As soon as they were alone, she said, "I have a bone to pick with you."

"What now?" he sighed.

"Leslie isn't coming back next year. You have something to do with that?"

Leslie Anderson was a cultural anthropologist who had stayed with Mattie a few weeks to study adaptations made to old stories since the Removal. She and Chitto developed a friendship, one that Mattie hoped would lead to a second marriage and grandchildren. In truth, Chitto had wondered if something more could come of it. But Leslie had displayed a loyalty to an old flame, another anthropologist conducting a research project in the area, and left a goodbye note behind for Chitto signed, "Your friend." He'd expected her to stay in touch after she left. She hadn't.

As he took Boycott in tow, he said, "She say why?"

"She took a new job at that school in Washington, one with tenure. A graduate student is gonna finish the research." Mattie frowned. "But I think it was something else."

Chitto knew it was something else. Leslie had unknowingly influenced those who participated in a rebellious act. Feeling she had broken her word about not getting involved with the societies she worked with, she stopped her research early. Thinking she needed time to accept the consequences, he hadn't pressed.

Maybe he should have, he thought now.

Then again, maybe not, came the whisper in his ear.

"She might've got back together with that friend of hers," he said. "That other anthropologist she worked with."

"Back together?"

"They were a thing once."

52

"Oh." Mattie turned thoughtful. "I didn't know 'bout that."

He wrapped an arm around her shoulders and looked down at her. "It's time you stopped playing matchmaker, Mama. If something's meant to happen, it will."

She made a huffing sound. "And some people need a kick in the pants to get them going."

He raised his eyebrows. "You're criticizing me? You're still a young woman and Dad's been gone ten years now."

"*Me?*" Mattie Chitto's cheeks flushed. "I'm a one-man woman. No one will ever take Will's place."

"Well," he said, giving her shoulders a squeeze. "Maybe I'm a one-woman man." He stepped off the porch, grinning. "Blame yourself," he said over his shoulder. "I inherited your genes."

∞

At Krebs, Chitto took the exit for OK-31. The clock on the dash indicated he'd spent more time at his mother's than he had intended. The visit with Eli Clarence Bohannan would have to wait. Wanting to make up time, he pushed the speed limit.

Seventy miles later, he turned onto US-271 N. It wasn't long before he spotted a sign for Spiro. Reaching across Boycott for the folder Jasmine put together, he said, "Time to go to work, partner. But first, let's find our bunk."

Pulling off the highway, he searched a map for a back road that would take him to the cabin where he would be staying. "This should get us there," he said, taking a north-bound road.

Grassland had transitioned to a more heavily wooded terrain as he neared the Arkansas state line. Blackjacks and post oaks, hickory and walnut trees evoked a sense of closeness. Jasmine had found the perfect spot, just far enough away from populated areas to maintain privacy but near the Spiro Mounds Archaeology Center and the Walker home place.

And a stone's throw from where Dad and Bert were found, he reflected.

Spotting a cluster of pine log cabins at the base of a wooded ridge, he pulled down a hard-packed track. "You're kidding," he mumbled, passing a sign promoting *Bud and Birdie's Cozy Cabins* as the perfect romantic getaway.

Spotting the office, he drove toward it. A young couple wearing camp shirts, hiking shorts, and athletic shoes walked out of the newly varnished log building as he pulled up. Noting they were holding hands, he felt a sharp pain under his ribcage. Even as thoughts of Mary surfaced, he pushed them back into the quiet recesses of memory. She had completed her journey. He would ask no more of her.

Parking near the office door, he put Boycott on a leash and walked to the porch. "Mind your Ps and Qs," he said. Hooking the leash to a corner post, he walked inside.

"I'm Birdie," said a smiling woman behind the counter. A halo of white hair framed pink cheeks and a cherub mouth. Ample bosoms stretched the buttons on a blue-plaid shirt. "I figure you're Mr. Chitto. We've been expecting you."

"Sam will do," he said, admiring the interior of the room. The office was paneled floor to ceiling with golden-yellow knotty pine. Pine planks covered the floor. From the shine on the wood and lack of scuffs, Chitto figured the place was no more than a couple years old.

"Sam, it is," Birdie said. "If you'll just sign the register." She pushed a logbook toward him and pulled a key from a peg on the wall. "Got Number 4 all ready."

He looked up from the register. "Okay if I pay by the night? Not sure how long I'll be staying."

"Oh, for sure. This is our slow season." She paused, looking over his shoulder. "Your wife stay in the truck?"

"Not married," he said. "But I did bring a dog. Is that a problem? I'll stake him out, not let him run loose." He scooted the logbook back to her side of the desk.

"Not at all," she said, smiling. "People bring their pets all the time, except for the honeymooners. They don't have eyes for anyone except themselves. Just keep the dog on a leash when you're hiking and . . ." She pulled a handful of recycled plastic bags from under the counter. "Pick up after it. We get lots of city folk up here and they complain about dog poop on the trails. Always strikes me as funny they don't mention the squirrel and rabbit, deer and coyote poop."

She laughed, then walked toward the front window. "There's several paths along the ridges there." She pointed toward low hills. "On the creeks, too, if you plan to fish—"

Noticing her abrupt stop, Chitto went to see what had captured her attention. She was staring at his truck.

"We don't allow hunting," she said, the smile gone.

"I don't plan to hunt," he said, surmising the long guns she'd spied were the problem.

"I see." She eyed the truck again. "Do, uh, do you need help with luggage? Bud's in the backyard varnishing some furniture. I can get him—real fast."

"No, ma'am. I tend to travel light."

"Uh-huh," she said, eyeing his faded jeans and flannel shirt, the sleeves rolled to the elbow.

"Which way?" he said.

She stared at him blankly.

"The cabin?"

"Oh—that way." Pointing with her whole arm to Chitto's left, she mumbled, "I, uh, I hope you enjoy your stay."

CHAPTER SIX

For Chitto, a cabin translated to wood burning stoves with rusty grates, stacks of firewood infested with long-horned beetles, and no plumbing, electricity, or running water. Cabin 4 was a far cry from that expectation. It had been fitted out with the same knotty pine and planks as the office, the walls, floor, and cabinets radiating a golden glow. A small kitchenette and bathroom had been wedged along one side of the room; the rest served as bedroom and sitting area. Gingham curtains at the windows ruffled in a gentle breeze and a rag rug lay on the floor next to a knotty pine bed on which a handmade quilt covered a deeply tufted mattress. He shook his head, sighing.

"Hey, off there," he yelled as Boycott leaped onto the bed. Picking up one of the sleeping bags he'd brought inside, he unrolled it in a corner. "This is your bunk." He tossed the extra sleeping bag, meant for him, onto a chair.

Leaving the dog to settle in, he hauled his duffle and the grocery bags inside, along with battered cooler and gallon jug of bottled water. Setting the cooler on the kitchen table, he removed lunchmeat and cheese and placed them in a small, cabinet-high refrigerator. Chips and bread went on the countertop. His coffeepot and a can of Folgers went next to a two-burner gas stovetop. Dog food and water bowls were filled next and placed in a corner of the kitchen.

Deciding to check out the perimeter, he gave a quick look out a patio door leading to a covered porch. Seeing two rocking chairs and a swing, pots of red geraniums resting on tables and others filling window boxes, he shook his head.

When had cabins gone posh?

Looking beyond the porch, he saw the cabin was sitting in a wooded grove of mixed pine and hardwood trees. Walking to one of the brown bags, he retrieved the tie-out cable and whistled Boycott to the back door. Securing the cable in the ground, he secured the dog and returned to the porch. Pulling his cell phone from his pocket, he punched in a number. He waited through several rings before Jasmine picked up, in the interim noting other cabins scattered throughout the grove of trees. Undergrowth and grasses helped shield one from another, making for privacy.

At least the place had that going for it, he reflected.

A sudden movement in the tree shadows drew his eye. The figure of a man. And from all outward appearances, Shadow Man seemed to be watching him.

"Am I to assume you made it?" Jasmine said in his ear.

He turned his attention back to the phone. "Yep." He sat down in a rustic, peeled pine rocker. Freshly varnished. "Did you, uh, did you research this place before you made the reservation?"

"I did. What's it like?"

"Romantic."

"That's just how it was described. Pictures on the web page looked like it, too."

He hesitated. "And you chose it anyway?"

"Picked it deliberately. You're keeping a low profile, remember? No one would think to look for you there."

He grunted, finding it hard to fault her logic. "Found out anything new?"

"If you're referring to disputes along the Arkansas River, I found stacks. The ITC's pursued several settlements dealing with water and land rights." ITC was short for the Inner-Tribal Council of the Five Civilized Tribes, which included the Choctaw, Chickasaw, Cherokee, Muskogee, and Seminole. "Some of them have gone on for decades and been through many courts, one of them right up to the Supreme."

"Uh-huh," Chitto mumbled. "That the one dealing with the tribes rightfully owning the Arkansas riverbed within their territory?"

"Right."

"I'm more interested in land rights, not water."

"Hold on." The sound of paper rustling competed with static on the line. "Here's a case about a boundary dispute between the State of Arkansas and the Choctaw Nation. Seems this tax assessor for LeFlore County discovered Arkansas had annexed fifty-seven acres that originally belonged to the Nation. Funny thing is, even though those that lived there had mailing addresses in Fort Smith, they paid their property taxes in LeFlore County."

"You referring to Coke Hill?"

Chitto had read about the dispute years before. The Arkansas and Poteau rivers cut off the Choctaws from the fifty-seven acres of their land between the rivers and the western edge of Fort Smith. The piece became a refuge for riffraff and cocaine traders, the most notorious of which was called Cocaine Annie. A congressional committee eventually declared Coke Hill a menace to health and morals of Fort Smith and gave the town permission to police it. In the early part of the twentieth century, Congress, without consulting the Choctaws, gave Arkansas permission to extend its boundary.

It wasn't until the LeFlore County tax assessor discovered the discrepancy that the Choctaw Nation filed suit.

"Yes," Jasmine said, sounding hesitant. "Back then, it was called Coke Hill."

"The drug connection's interesting," he said, "but I'm more interested in cases pitting people against people." He listened to static building on the line, sensing more than technical problems.

"If you already know about those cases," she snapped, "why am I wasting my time? I have better things to do than go blind staring at my computer most of the night."

Chitto leaned back in the rocker, sighing. "You're right. I should've been more specific, but . . ." He paused, pitting prudence against urgency. "Look, Jasmine, I appreciate all the work you've done. It's just that I'm interested in something more recent and involving people, not governments. Maybe a dispute that would've gotten the attention of the Choctaw Police or . . ." He paused again, considering just how much to divulge. "Or involving Victor Messina."

"Victor Messina—"

"That's not for public proclamation," he said, noticing the man in the trees had moved to a new vantage point.

"Like I didn't know that? How's that old devil involved?"

Chitto rocked slowly, watching Shadow Man closely as he briefed Jasmine on the run-ins his father had with Victor Messina's drug operation over the years. He finished with, "Let's just say I'm trusting my gut."

"Ever consider a bowel cleanse?"

He chuckled, paused, said, "I think maybe I've been led here."

"Um-hmm," she said. "Sound like you took a spell of the fiery trivets." She quickly explained that one of her grandfathers took spells at being prophetic, which he referred to as the fiery trivets. During them, he believed he had influence over earthly matters.

"I don't think so," Chitto said. "More like a restless *Shilombish*."

"A ghost?" A mix of static and breathing came over the line. "Give me a minute," she said.

Chitto spent several minutes listening to unrecognizable sounds on the phone and watching Boycott strain the cable to its limit, his attention on the stranger moving about the woods.

"Okay," she said. "I found a few cases between individuals, mostly because the river flooded and changed the stream bed. What's now part of the defendant's property used to be on the plaintiff's. Messina's name isn't mentioned in any of them."

"Of course not," he sighed. "That would've been too easy."

"Speaking of easy," she said. "There has to be a better way to do this. Why don't you just check the address of the place where it happened? If your dad and Bert Gilly were going up there to meet someone about a land dispute, they probably met up with him there."

"Perfectly logical," he said. "But the bodies were found at Mayo Lock and Dam."

"*Mayo*? There's no way that place could be in legal contention. The Corp of Engineers runs that."

"Yep."

More breathing and static. "You think they were killed someplace else? That Mayo was the dump site?"

"Nope. There was too much blood on the ground," he said. "They bled out there."

A pause, then, "Color me dense, but why would they have been there?"

"Right, doesn't make sense." He paused, blinking. "I'm just speculating, but Dad and Bert were fishermen and their bodies were found alongside a boat ramp. They could've taken time to check out a new place, either before or after they met up with *whoever* they went up there to see, and got ambushed at Mayo."

"You're saying someone followed them and killed them there deliberately?" Jasmine's voice was barely more than a whisper.

Chitto rubbed a hand over his face, feeling tired. "Think about it. Being found on government property means the case would be handled by the feds. A slick way to keep other jurisdictions out of it."

"Okay . . ." A brief pause. "That would mean whoever did it would've known the area *or* were told where to do it."

"Right again." Chitto watched as Shadow Man changed his position, moving closer. Slowly, he reached under his shirt and placed his hand on the butt of his Glock.

"*But*," she said. "It doesn't answer the question of just who they went up there to see in the first place—which is why I'm plowing up the land transaction angle."

"Yep." He paused, eyes blinking. "When did those other cases take place?"

"Recent, as in the last few years, but . . ." The line went silent several seconds. "Sam, I couldn't unearth anything that seemed relevant during that time that dealt with the Choctaw, either tribal or individuals." The tenor of Jasmine's voice indicated the tension had not only resurfaced but was building. "What's more, I'm not seeing a thing that would need the involvement of the police in *any* jurisdiction. People don't resort to guns to settle boundary problems nowadays. Why would they? It wouldn't solve the problem. Those things are settled with paper. They let lawyers duke it out for them. *Moreover . . .*"

Chitto waited for Jasmine to complete her diatribe.

"I gotta be honest," she said. "I can't see where this is leading. It's like . . . like . . ." The line went to static again.

"Looking for a needle in the haystack?" he said, finishing her statement.

A weary-sounding sigh came over the line. "Leave it to the college guy to come up with a tired platitude. I was going to say, it's like being stuck in a revolving door or on a merry go round."

Chitto took a turn at being silent.

"A person on either one is constantly changing direction and getting nowhere," she said, sounding exasperated. "I could spend a year looking and find diddly-squat—and *you* could spend the entire week chasing your tail. You sure somebody isn't blowing smoke in your face? Who was your source for the land-dispute lead?"

"My source is solid," he said, not sharing that it was Dan Blackfox. "But you're right on one score. I have plenty of better things to do than chase my tail." Two council members were breathing down his neck and Blackfox would be expecting a report when he got back. "Okay, forget the land transaction angle."

"Gladly. See you when you get back—"

"Hold up. But maybe you could check into Muriel Simpson's boyfriend and the guy she ran into at the apartment complex that night."

63

Hesitation. "Why? You think the local authorities over-looked something?"

"Wouldn't be the first time, and the prosecution sure moved fast on this deal. You need names?"

"No, I made a copy in case I needed it. I find anything, I'll call you."

"All right then." Standing, he whistled Boycott to the porch. "I'll head over to see Charlie Walker now, the boy's grandfather."

"Good. Glad you're smarter than Custer was."

Chitto smiled. "Thanks, Scout. Any more advice for Custer?"

"Just this. Let your head lead you, not your heart." *Click.*

Jasmine wasn't one for dragging on a conversation. And she was proving to be right more times than wrong.

∞

Boycott let out a *woof,* staring into the line of trees and shrubs. Hand still on his gun, Chitto walked down the porch steps and waved the man in the trees to come forward. Shadow Man turned out to be a senior citizen, somewhat stooped, wearing a white painter's cap and carrying a paintbrush.

"Let me guess." Releasing his grip on the gun under his shirt, Chitto extended his hand. "Birdie's other half."

"That I am." The man gripped his hand. "I go by Bud."

"Call me Sam." He studied thin lines furrowing the man's forehead, the straight set of his mouth. "Something on your mind, Bud?"

"Well sir, Birdie sent me over. Said she forgot to mention that we provide a continental breakfast for our guests. She sets it out in the lobby 'bout six-thirty or seven, depending on how the dough rises. Nothin' special. Homemade cinnamon buns and coffee. Tea bags and hot water for the weak of heart."

"Beats the baloney and cheese sandwich I was planning on." Chitto took a minute, studying the man. Bud had more on his mind than homemade cinnamon buns, and clearly, he wasn't ready to broach it openly. Pointing his chin toward the gleaming cabin and deck furniture, he said, "You do nice work. Must've done it in your previous life."

"Before retirement, you mean?" Bud's laugh sounded like an echo from the bottom of a well. "Far from it. I was a dam safety inspector."

"Dam safety inspector?" Chitto gave a nod to the rockers. "Let's have a seat on the porch, Bud. I'd like to hear what that entailed."

Bud had retired from the OWRB, the Oklahoma Dam Safety Program, whose job was to ensure the safety of dams in the state, numbering in excess of 4,000. The biggest concern was the impact on life and property downstream.

"You do inspections on the Mayo?" Chitto asked.

Bud shook his head. "Professional engineers handled the big jobs. Button pushers mostly. Lot of automation with those big dams."

"That right . . ." Chitto paused, rubbing his mouth. "Those button pushers have a view of the boat ramps when they did inspections?"

Bud hesitated, forehead wrinkling again. "Not much. They leave that to the fish and game people."

Who wouldn't be around much in the winter, Chitto reflected.

"Mostly I checked earth dams on farms and ranches," Bud went on. "Didn't mind it though. Fresh air and exercise kept me fit."

"Still, it's a big responsibility. No matter how small, infractions are infractions."

"Aw, most people are honest," Bud said, shrugging. "You can always tell those that aren't."

"How's that?" Chitto asked.

"They give themselves away. You can tell a lot from body language."

Chitto nodded. He was a people watcher, too. "How'd you deal with them?"

"Applied a tried but true technique." Bud chuckled. "I shook the tree to see what fell out."

"Oh, yeah?" Chitto raised his eyebrows. "How's that work?"

"Well, see, for the most part, people live in the yesterdays or the today, few think of the tomorrows. So I'd start out giving them the what-ifs. You know, educating them on the consequences bad decisions would have on others, who in most cases would be neighbors. Altruism runs deep as a rule. Once they thought about it, most of 'em went to work fixing problems pretty quick."

Chitto took an immediate liking to Bud. He was a philosopher. "And those that didn't?" he asked.

Bud let loose one of his deep-well laughs. "I made 'em regret their decision."

Chitto grinned, then gave him a direct look. "I get the feeling you want to shake my tree, Bud."

A deep sigh. "Birdie's the one concerned." Bud pointed his chin toward the front of the cabin. "You pack a lot of heat in that pickup out there, lots more than our usual guests. And, uh, you don't look the part of someone into romantic weekends" He shrugged. "With so much in the news about terrorists and such, well . . ."

66

Chitto laughed quietly. So much for low profile.

Leaning forward, Chitto pulled his wallet from his hip pocket and flashed his Choctaw Nation Police ID.

"Sonofabitch—you're a cop?"

"Off-duty cop up here looking into something for a friend."

Just like Bert Gilly? asked the voice in his head.

Bud let out a hoot. "Wait till I tell Birdie."

"Did I mention I was off duty?" Chitto asked pointedly.

"What happens in Vegas stays in Vegas," Bud said, making a zipping motion across his lips. As he stood, he pulled a paintbrush from his hip pocket. "Like to stay and talk but I left a bench half done, and . . ." He lifted his eyebrows and grinned. "I don't report in soon, Birdie's liable to call the sheriff." He gave a wave as he walked toward the front of the cabin. As he rounded the corner, he called out, "Don't forget 'bout the continental breakfast. Birdie's right proud of her buns."

CHAPTER SEVEN

Chitto downed a ham and cheese sandwich for lunch, then loaded Boycott in the truck to begin his search for Charlie Walker's place. Weaving his way along back roads north of Spiro, he looked for something indicating he'd struck pay dirt: a number on a road sign or a name on a mailbox. On the decade-old visit he'd made before, he'd taken the Lock and Dam road north from Spiro to reach the Mayo boat ramp. On this trip, he was traveling unfamiliar roads in new country. The view suited him. Recently mowed hay bales were lined up in fields on the south side, round bales weighing upwards to a thousand pounds, whereas the north side was more private with homes nestled into wooded areas.

As the north side of the road transitioned from trees to grass, he slowed in front of a doublewide mobile home with the name *Walker* hand printed on the mailbox. Beyond the trailer to the east, he saw a cluster of buildings setting a quarter mile off the county road. The Spiro Mounds Archaeology Center.

Putting the truck in neutral, he studied the Walker place. An older model black Ford pickup sat in the drive, windows lowered. The front door of the trailer was shut and he saw no air conditioner on either side of the home. He made a grunting sound, thinking no one in his right mind would close up a place without AC in Oklahoma where summer temperatures often hit triple digits. Even this time of the year, highs in the 80s were common. Which meant no one was home.

It made sense, he thought. Charlie Walker would be working. With Spiro Mounds so close, he probably walked to work. And unable to post bail, Bobby Taneyhill would be in a holding cell in the county lockup.

Chitto leaned forward, fighting the urge to pull down the drive and look around, but just because the place was temporarily untenanted didn't mean there weren't eyes on it. There was a clear view of the trailer from Spiro Mounds and though at work, Walker would be keeping a close watch on things. The murder had gotten a lot of attention with the press the year before. Now, with the trial in progress, it would get even more. The reason for closing up the place became clear: to keep snoopers out.

Proceeding down the county road, Chitto stopped in front of the sign for the Spiro Mounds Archaeological Center. Though not large, the sign was riveting. A painted circle in the middle displayed a man in war paint. The face had been painted white and a black eye mask covered the eyes. An eared headpiece, painted red, was centered atop a shaved head. Large red discs filled the earlobes.

Scary bastard, Chitto thought, an image of *Ishkitini* popping into his head.

Scanning the site, he saw two single-story buildings sitting at the edge of a cottonwood grove. Several cars sat in the parking lot and people were visible outside the buildings and on walking trails. Grassy mounds resembling beached whales lay scattered about the grounds. On the periphery of one mound, a section of ground had been laid out in squares and marked with flags. Dirt was piled along the outside edge of the squares, where people worked in clusters. An archaeology dig was in progress.

The clock on the dash read three-fifteen. Sorting through the file Jasmine put together, he learned the site's hours were Wednesday through Saturday, 9 AM to 5 PM, and Sunday, noon to 5 PM. Councilwoman June Biggers was supposed to alert Walker that he would be by today. She had also recommended Chitto talk to a Dr. Mack Green, an archaeologist that worked there. Curiosity mounting, he pulled down the drive.

He parked in front of the two buildings near the cottonwood grove, debating whether to stake Boycott under a tree or take him along. Betting Charlie Walker was working somewhere on the grounds and the archaeologist would be near the dig site, he clipped the leash to Boycott's collar and locked the pickup. Boycott led the way, nose to the ground.

Chitto scanned the grounds as he walked, hoping to catch sight of his intended targets or someone looking official that could direct him. Noticing people entering one of the buildings more frequently than the other, he followed the crowd. A sign identified the building as the Interpretative Center.

Walking inside, he entered an octagonal-shaped room with a vaulted ceiling. Walls had been painted ochre red and a dark, plank ceiling was coated with shellac. Displays on tables or in cases stood against walls, above which hung pictures showing the ancient mound builders performing various activities. A warrior in war paint with bow drawn. A woman and child in front of a thatched hut. Pottery makers and weavers at work.

Standing displays in the center of the room contained artifacts and replicas of tools and utensils the mound builders would have made. Noting displays of bone and chert used to make tools and weapons, Chitto's interest piqued. He had given up a career in field geology but that didn't mean his interest in origins, of either people or planet, had diminished.

"Donations are appreciated."

Chitto turned toward the voice. An attractive woman wearing cotton Dockers and blue polo shirt stood behind a counter on which a donation jar sat. Chitto noticed tourist items for sale in the glass case beneath. Miriam Simpson's replacement, he decided.

"I can hold onto your dog here while you look around." Walking from behind the counter, she held out her hand for the leash. "Dogs like me," she said, smiling.

He took in the woman's blue eyes, sun-streaked brown hair, light sprinkling of freckles across her nose, and lack of wedding band. He also picked up on something in the way she spoke. A light drawl. East Texas, perhaps. Maybe the hill country.

How had the all-American-girl ended up in this far-flung corner of the Choctaw Nation?

"Something wrong," she said, eyes quizzical. "Or did the cat get your tongue?" A teasing smile made a showing.

Does she think I'm coming on to her? Taking a step back, he said, "Nope, just thinking." Removing his wallet, he slipped a bill into the jar. Boycott took the opportunity to sit down on the woman's feet, his head resting against her knee.

"Told you," she said, scratching the dog's head.

"Get over here, you pervert." Chitto pulled Boycott to his side. "Sorry," he said to the woman. "He has the manners of a Texas warthog."

Her laugh was full, unpretentious. The laugh of someone comfortable in her own skin. But as he resumed his police-trained scrutiny, that skin began to flush.

"Any questions?" she said, lifting a hand toward the displays. "You, uh, you look like you have questions."

"Matter of fact, I'm looking for Charlie Walker."

"*Oh.* Charlie's our jack-of-all-trades. He keeps the place greased and running. I saw him go into the utility room after lunch. Plumbing problems, I think." Motioning at the door, she said, "Go around this building and look for a metal door. Warm as it is, he'll have it propped open."

Chitto followed the directions she had given. Peering into an open doorway on the backside of the building, he saw a man lying on the floor next to an oversized water heater, a collection of wrenches within arm's reach. He had found the honorable man.

"Mr. Walker," he said, stepping inside. "I'm Sam Chitto. June Biggers said I should look you up." An all-angles-and-bone man stood slowly, wiping his hands on a rag.

"Saw a white pickup checking out my place a bit ago, figured it was you." Walker extended a hand roughened with time and work. "Mighty glad you're here." A thin smile stretched cheeks as leathery and wrinkled as his hands. "Want some coffee?" He motioned toward a large black thermos and stack of Styrofoam cups.

"Would I ever." Chitto hadn't had a cup of coffee in hours. "I'm feeling a bit caffeine deprived right now. Okay if I stake my dog outside here?"

"Sure thing. Just let me clean up. I'll bring the coffee out there, nice breeze today."

Chitto retrieved the tie-out cable from the truck. Driving the stake into the ground under a cottonwood, he clipped Boycott to it just as the handyman walked out, the thermos and two Styrofoam cups in his hands.

Charlie Walker was not the feeble old man Chitto had envisioned. He guessed the man was in his seventies but he moved with the agility of a man much younger, and a ramrod straight back and muscular shoulders indicated he was far from weak. Recalling the picture of Bobby Taneyhill in the paper, Chitto found it hard to believe the boy had been spawned from the same gene pool.

"Have a seat," Walker said, nodding toward a cottonwood. Sitting with his back against another tree, he poured two cups of coffee and handed one to Chitto. "You take sugar? Whitener?"

"Black and strong," Chitto said, taking a seat across from him. Though not as hot as he liked, the coffee was fresh brewed and tasted as if it had been made using a grind, not the instant powder. He remained silent as Walker took two packets of sugar from his pocket and watched as he rotated the cup slowly to dissolve the grains. Though knuckles were knotty as an oak burl, both hands were steady.

Walker took a sip, appeared satisfied with the outcome, and looked at Chitto. "Appreciate you coming all this way to prove my grandson's innocence."

"*Whoa*—" Chitto held up a hand. "I don't know that I can do that. I just said I'd look into it."

"You're the one to do it, anyone can." Walker swirled the cup again. "I've been hearing things about *Hatakachafa*."

"*What*—?"

"That's what they're calling you," Walker said.

Chitto slumped against the tree trunk. It wasn't the first time the moniker had been pinned on him. *Hatakachafa* meant the Nameless One in Choctaw. According to old legends, *Hatakachafa* was a war chief and great hunter that destroyed monsters doing harm to the People.

Word about that last undercover operation must have leaked out, he thought. The tribal telegraph was efficient—at times, too efficient.

"Look, Walker, I'll do what I can," he said. "But I'm just an off-duty cop, operating off the grid and in the dark. Now, what can you tell me?"

Walker leaned forward slightly. "Bobby didn't do it. He was home all night."

"I read that in the paper, but . . ." Bending one leg, Chitto rested the Styrofoam cup on his knee. "I need more than your word."

Walker stared at Chitto, eyes narrow slits.

"Look, *I* know you're an Elder and wouldn't lie," Chitto said. "But we're not dealing with the Tribal Council here. This is a whole other ballgame."

Walker thought a bit, then nodded. "I need to fix that heater before I leave," he said, indicating the utility room. "How 'bout we meet up at my place. I get off work at five, later if I have to go to town for parts."

"Deal." Chitto drained the coffee cup and stood. "June Biggers said I should look up an archaeologist named Green while I'm here."

"Give me a minute and I'll make your acquaintance."

Walker carried the thermos and empty cups back into the utility room while Chitto retrieved Boycott. When Walker returned, he followed him around the corner of the building.

"I'm keeping my place locked these days," Walker said over his shoulder. "Keys in one of those magnetic holders under the eave. You beat me there, go on in. Coffeepot's ready to plug in."

Chitto waited outside the Interpretative Center, watching Walker motion to someone inside. Seeing the woman he'd met earlier exit the building, his jaws went slack.

"Mack," Walker said. "Mr. Chitto here needs to talk to you." He turned to Chitto. "Meet up with you at the house later."

Chitto watched Walker disappear behind the building, then turned to stare at Mack Green. She looked up at him, the teasing smile appearing again.

"Looks like the cat's still got your tongue," she said.

"I was told to look up a Mack Green. It's just, I thought you'd be a . . ." He lifted a hand, let it drop.

"Man? Fools lots of people. My given name's Mackie, it's a family name. But some people shorten it to Mack."

"Right, a man," he said, which was only half the lie. The other half dealt with the fact she didn't fit the image of an archeologist who spent long hours working in the sun and weather.

"So, what did you need to see me about?" she said.

"I guess we need to talk."

"'Bout what?"

"Damned if I know but it deals with Bobby Taneyhill."

"*Bobby*—" The teasing smile was long gone.

Noting the U-turn in behavior, Chitto wondered what prompted the change. He had obviously struck a nerve. Waiting for her to gather her thoughts, he watched her closely.

"Well . . ." She paused, giving a quick glance toward the Interpretative Center. "Now's not a good time. Where are you staying? Maybe I can meet you there after I get off work."

He hesitated. "Place called Bud and Birdies. But today's out. I'm meeting with Walker later."

"Bud and Birdie's," she repeated. "I've heard of it. Supposed to be romantic."

"Could be," he said. "But I'm here with a dog."

Her eyebrows hitched a notch. "Hope you're talking about *this* dog," she said, looking down at Boycott, who was again sitting on her feet.

"*Boycott*," he said, giving the leash a tug.

"Boycott?"

He quickly explained how Hattie had given the dog its name based on dietary choice and how it had rankled her pioneer ranching family.

"A rebel," she said. "I like that." She glanced toward the Center again, then back at him. "Tell you what. How 'bout you come by in the morning? We're only open a half day on Sundays and don't open till noon, but I get here early to check things out."

"That'll work."

"Say, nine o'clock? That'll give us an hour or so before others start showing up."

"That'll work," he said again. Fishing a card from his pocket, Chitto wrote his cell number on the back and handed it to her. "In case something comes up."

"Detective Sam Chitto, Choctaw Police," she said, reading the card aloud. Retrieving a card from her hip pocket, she handed it to him and said, "In case something comes up on your end. See you tomorrow, Detective Chitto."

"Sam will do," he said, reading her card. "See you 'round nine o'clock, Dr. Green."

"Ditch the title," she said. "I prefer Mackie."

Chitto watched the archaeologist until she disappeared inside the building. Her demeanor had definitely undergone a transformation when he mentioned Bobby Taneyhill. Why? he wondered, frowning.

Pocketing the card, he led Boycott to the pickup and considered his findings. The archaeologist had not lived up to his expectations, but then neither had the grandfather. As he turned the key in the ignition, he couldn't help but wonder what else he'd let slip by him.

∞

Chitto pulled to a stop where the Spiro Mounds drive intersected the county road. The clock on the dash now read four o'clock. He had an hour to kill before he was to meet Charlie Walker. He could turn right and kill that hour at Walker's place. Fix a fresh pot of coffee. Do some snooping. Or . . .

The place where his father and Bert Gilly died was a couple of miles away—a place that he'd been told to avoid.

No, he reflected. *Ordered* to avoid.

"Screw it," he mumbled, turning left.

Within minutes, he was parked at a Mayo Lock and Dam boat ramp. He stared through the windshield, comparing the scene before him with one from his memory. Changes had taken place in those ten years, the effects of progress. More asphalt. More boats. More noise.

He listened to the sound of people yelling to each other. The clank of metal, the rev of boat motors. A *lot* more noise than before. It was because of the time of year when the murder happened, he decided. It was winter then, not fall, and a different time of day. Daylight would be longer now, too, unlike when his dad and Bert Gilly had been there.

The medical examiner had determined his dad and Bert had been killed a little after dusk, which meant the place would've been deserted for the most part. What few fishermen that had been there would've gone home to a hot supper, maybe fried fish, French fries with catsup, a six-pack of Bud.

Was the timing for the murder *that* carefully planned, he wondered.

78

A nudge from Boycott pulled Chitto back to present day. Putting the leash on the dog, he opened the door and got out. The hound needed to stretch his legs—and *he* needed to stretch his mind.

Walking along the side of the boat ramp, he ran his eyes over the ground, looking for a place he'd stood a decade before. Even though time had erased visual clues, he knew when he reached the exact spot.

Ten years now . . .

Squatting on his heels, he studied the ground, willing it to speak. Several FBI agents had investigated the case, why hadn't any of them learned anything? Regardless of his personal opinion of them, FBI agents were well trained. And regardless of jurisdictional ties, no cop wanted a cop's killer to go free.

But the killers had gone free. Why?

His forehead rutted with lines, Chitto stood. It didn't stack up, he thought, looking around the site. Logically, *something* should have been discovered.

A niggling started up at the base of Chitto's skull. Was it possible a piece of evidence had been overlooked? *Had* someone blown smoke in their face, misled them intentionally? *Or* had someone deliberately withheld a critical piece of information?

Chitto immediately thought of Dan Blackfox who had only divulged the reason for Will Chitto and Bert Gilly being in LeFlore County the day before. A nighttime phone call. But Blackfox's reason for withholding that information made sense. Chitto was still a college student at the time, not a member of law enforcement. He wasn't on the need-to-know list.

He paused, wondering if Blackfox also withheld the missing piece from the FBI.

As soon as the thought crossed his mind, Chitto dismissed it. He didn't know anyone more thorough than Dan Blackfox, or more trustworthy. And just like Blackfox, Chitto would bet his life on their own people being trustworthy.

That left the FBI. With so many agents involved, pointing a finger at any one of them would be damn-nigh impossible. Still, the Bureau pursued the case. That fact alone said they still considered it an ongoing investigation.

And yet, they continue to come up empty-handed. Why?

Removing his ball cap, Chitto ran a hand through short-cropped hair. So many unanswered questions were frustrating. Even more frustrating, he didn't know where to go to find the answers. With his father and Bert gone and Wanda dying last year, Dan Blackfox was the one closest to the case.

Could Blackfox have forgotten something? Research had shown memory was fallible.

With a sigh, he replaced his cap. Not that man, he thought. This case was as imprinted on his brain as it was his own—as was the need to solve it. They had both made a promise to Wanda on her deathbed that they wouldn't let up until justice had been served. Was it possible they might not fulfill that pledge?

Giving in to Boycott's persistent tugging, Chitto followed the dog down to the riverbank. The Arkansas was a typical Great Plains riverway, with wide, shallow banks subject to seasonal flooding. The McClellan-Kerr Arkansas River Navigation System made it navigable for barges and large river craft to Muskogee because of a series of locks and dams. Right then, the river was busy with not only human traffic but natural as well. Birds swooped and insects buzzed. Fish jumped, silvery streaks that glistened in the sunlight. The smell of live bait—worms, minnows, chunks of carp— permeated the air.

Stooping to pick up a round, flat stone, he flung it across the river's surface. Following its path, he silently counted the skips. Just when he thought it would sink, it made one more.

No, he thought, studying the concentric circles where the stone finally sank from sight. As long as I can draw a breath, I won't quit.

Glancing at his watch, Chitto pulled on the leash and began the walk back to his truck. His steps were slow but his mind was active. It kept circling back to the one piece of new information he'd learned. Bert Gilly had gotten a phone call in the night to come to LeFlore County, a three-hour drive and out of his district. Wanda had never mentioned the call, but then neither had Pete Brody. Why not? Other than Blackfox, Brody was the only one who knew that Bert Gilly and his father would be in the area. Was Pete Brody as true-blue as Blackfox thought he was?

A saying of Ronald Reagan's suddenly came to mind: "Trust, but verify."

CHAPTER EIGHT

Chitto arrived at Charlie Walker's place a little before five. Staking Boycott near the fence line, he decided to take advantage of the time to survey the premises. A scattering of ordinary debris was piled at the back corner of the lot: scrap lumber, engine parts kept handy for repair jobs, metal fence posts and spare wire. The door on a single-car garage sat open and a quick glance inside indicated the building was used as a workshop and storage shed. An older model John Deere riding lawn mower was parked on one side of the building. On the other side, a doghouse, with *Shug* painted above the door, looked unused. A 55-gallon open-head burn barrel sat in an open spot, a light spiral of smoke drifting upward. Looking inside, Chitto recognized the curled edges of newspapers, colored advertisements, and household trash.

The backside of the home bordered thick woods. Owl habitat. Pretty much the *only* place an owl would be, Chitto thought, as he completed his tour of the place. The front area was a rutted gravel drive spotted with oil. Treeless. No shrubbery. Owls, especially small owls, would inhabit places where wildlife and birds were abundant and cover provided protection. All of which raised a question: was the sound Bobby heard real or imagined? He looked toward the trailer, wondering which side Bobby's bedroom was on: front or rear.

Proceeding to the front stoop, he spotted Walker walking across the field separating the home site from the Archaeology Center. Over the years, foot traffic had worn a trail through the grass leading straight from the Center's parking lot to the trailer house.

Walker nodded as he stepped over a three-strand wire fence. "Find anything interesting when you was snooping around?"

"Cops are curious by nature," Chitto said, grinning slightly. "Only interesting thing was what I didn't find. Where's Shug?"

"Died last year." Walker ushered Chitto into a combination living and dining room. A small kitchen sat on the other side of an eating bar, on which sat a slow cooker smelling of meat and herbs. Another door in the kitchen led outside.

"Sorry to hear that. Old age?"

"Little more than a pup. Got off her chain somehow. Bobby found her on the road yonder, figured she was hit by a car." He pointed his chin toward the back door. "He buried her in the woods back there."

Looking through a back window, Chitto spotted a bare spot at the edge of the woods and small wooden cross, denoting a gravesite. The boy had cared deeply about Shug.

Walker washed up with dish soap at the sink, then opened a cabinet. Removing plates and bowls, he handed them to Chitto. "Set the table. I'll make coffee, warm the bread."

"I could stand to wash up, too," Chitto said, depositing the dishes on a Formica-topped table surrounded by chrome chairs. "Bathroom?"

"First door on the right."

Chitto paused midway down the hall, looking toward two rooms at the end of the trailer. The bedrooms. Which side of the house was Bobby's on? Though seemingly minor, it could be a major point. If it was on the backside, the boy might have heard an owl. If on the front . . .

Other than *Ishkitini*, what might Bobby have heard?

The unobstructed driveway and open field would funnel traffic noises to the house, from both the county road and the Archaeology Center. If Bobby had heard cars driving into Spiro Mounds—Muriel Simpson and her killer's—the defense could cast doubt on the prosecution's case. Reasonable doubt led to innocent verdicts and hung juries.

That question still preyed on his mind as he returned to the kitchen. Nodding across the living room towards the window facing Spiro Mounds, he asked, "You get a lot of noise from that place over there?"

Walker eyed him, eyebrows knotted. "I'm not here when it's open."

Chitto shook his head slightly. He'd made a rookie mistake, asking a question when the answer was obvious. If he was going to help this man, he needed quit screwing around and shoot from the hip.

"Tell me about Bobby?" he said, setting the table with mismatched dishes and tableware. "What did he do when you were gone, when he wasn't in school, that is?"

"Chores mostly." Walker continued his kitchen duties as he talked. "Cleaning, laundry, cooking. Summers, he kept the yard picked up. Cut the grass and pulled weeds, took care of any varmints that came around, kept the culvert running clear. Irrigation clogs it when the farmers water their fields, backs up the driveway." He took two heavy mugs from the cabinet. "Winters, he shoveled what snow we got, burned tree limbs ice storms brought down. More ice than snow 'round here."

Considering this, Chitto wondered if Bobby was, in fact, the weakling he appeared to be.

Walker handed Chitto a steaming mug. "At night, he made up his stories." He cocked his head toward the hallway. "There, in his bedroom."

"I'd like to see those stories," Chitto said, sipping coffee.

"They took 'em."

"They . . . The police?"

Walker nodded. "You like rabbit stew?"

"Hell, yeah. It's a big step up from what I had planned."

Remembering the newspaper article that mentioned the grandfather kept knives for skinning, Chitto was struck with a sense of relief. In the next instant, the feeling faded. Had Walker taught Bobby to be proficient with a knife? Did Bobby have a reason to kill Muriel Simpson?

Or did Walker have a reason to want her dead? asked the voice in his head.

Chitto paused, considering the question that had surfaced. As a cop, he was trained to suspect everyone. Even though Walker was an honorable man, was he taking too much for granted?

"Sit down," Walker said. "We can talk as we eat." Setting the slow cooker on the table, he dished up bowls of a thick meat-and-vegetable stew. Returning to the kitchen, he pulled a cast-iron skillet holding cornbread from the oven and set it on a potholder next to the stew pot.

"You do a lot of hunting?" Chitto asked, taking a seat. "Those woods back there would have plenty of game."

Walker shook his head. "Not so much anymore. Eyesight's failing. Bobby's the one kept the freezer stocked."

One question answered. Both Walker and Bobby were skilled with a knife.

Taking a chair at the end of the table, Walker scooted a butter dish toward Chitto. "I don't mess with grace," he said. "Dig in."

"How well did you know Muriel Simpson," Chitto asked, buttering a wedge of cornbread.

"Didn't," Walker said. "She worked inside. I worked outside."

"So your paths never crossed?"

"'At's right." Walker looked across the table. "She got there after I started work, left before I got off. Why you ask?"

"Like I said," Chitto said. "Cops are curious by nature. Back to Bobby, where are his parents?"

"Gone."

"Gone where?"

"Just gone."

Watching Walker crumble cornbread into his stew, Chitto decided "Gone" was as much as he was going to get from this tight-lipped man.

"Okay," he continued. "That must be how Bobby came to live with you." He looked across the table again. "When was that exactly?"

Walker looked toward the front window, staring at something only he could see. "He was real little, barely walking. Maybe two, three years old." He made eye contact with Chitto. "He's always been small, had weak eyes. I don't think he got enough to eat and . . ." He shook his head. "My daughter and her husband were no good. They left the baby alone a lot. I think that's what turned him inward."

Inward, Chitto repeated silently, a gamut of possibilities running through his mind. Typically, a generic description

87

spoke to a deeper problem. Malnourishment could cause growth retardation. Abandonment issues might have long-lasting psychological effects. Alcohol fetal syndrome could cause physical and mental defects.

"Did his parents do drugs?" Chitto asked. "His mother drink alcohol?"

Walker paused a beat, then said, "Not here." A hardness in his eyes indicated he knew where the line of questioning was going. "Bobby's a healthy boy. I take him to the clinic for regular checkups. Dentist, too. And he's smart. Never got below a C on his report cards." He paused, rubbing the back of his neck." He just didn't get the right kind of food when he was little, didn't grow like he should. And being alone so much turned him inward."

Chitto nodded, thinking it was enough to turn anyone inward. Prisoners of war suffered the same symptom.

Walker refilled the coffee mugs from the pot on the counter, then walked to a breadbox in the kitchen. He returned with a package of store-bought cookies. "I don't bake much," he said.

"I live alone, too," Chitto said, taking two crème-filled sandwich cookies. "Tell me about Bobby's friends."

"Didn't have none." He looked across the table at Chitto. "When he was little, I took him to work with me. Couldn't leave him here alone. I set up a card table and chair in the utility room, bought him coloring books. He liked to draw better'n anything. He was always a good boy. Quiet. Happy with paper and a box of crayons. He learned to read young, then . . ." He rubbed the back of his neck again.

Chitto waited, giving the man time to sort his thoughts.

"When he started to school, the other kids were bigger, liked to roughhouse. And when he got older, sports was big.

Basketball. Football. Bobby wasn't good at any of 'em, so those kids, they pushed him around. Called him names."

Chitto nodded. "Bullies learn tricks of the trade early."

"Yeah, bullies." Another pause. "Even when he got older, he went with me. Winter, summer, didn't matter. Then Mack started working there a few years back and Bobby took to her right off. Followed her 'round like a puppy, wanting to do things for her. She took to paying him a little salary. Made him feel real good that he could buy his own paper and pens."

"That archaeologist gave him a job?" Chitto wondered if that was the reason June Biggers wanted him to talk with Mackie Green, if she was thinking the archaeologist would make a good character witness. He frowned slightly, recalling the witnesses listed in the newspaper that had been called to testify. Mackie Green had not been on the list.

"Yeah, Mack Green." Walker looked at him, brows knotted. "But you'd know that. You talked to her today."

Chitto shook his head. "Just like you, it wasn't a good time. I plan to meet with her tomorrow. What kind of things did Bobby do at the Center?"

"Helped me out time to time. You know, carrying things, cleaning up, hauling trash to the dumpster out back. As for the work he did for Mack, better you ask her. I fix bad pipes and scrape paint."

Chitto nodded, then glanced toward the hallway. "Okay if I look at Bobby's room?"

Without a word, Walker rose and walked down the hall.

Bobby's bedroom was on the same side of the house as the Archaeology Center. Chitto walked to the window, noting it was the kind made of aluminum with removable panes for cleaning. With no air conditioning, Bobby would've had the window open in mid-summer when the murder happened.

Which would make it easy to hear vehicles pulling into the Center's parking lot, perhaps mistake a woman's scream for an owl's screech.

He turned to Walker. "June Biggers said that Bobby knew someone had been killed because he heard *Ishkitini.*"

"Told me that when he got up."

"Did you ever tell him the old story of the Horned Owl?" Chitto asked, looking out the window again. "Maybe others?"

Mostly grassland, there were few trees around Spiro Mounds. About the size of a pint jar, the screech owl preferred treed areas where it could hide out in nooks and crannies. He glanced beneath the window to the gravel drive, six to seven feet below. Not even a weed grew in the sterile ground. He paused abruptly, studying a rectangular impression more closely, then glanced toward the doghouse next to the garage. He turned to face Walker as the man answered his question.

"Did tell him old stories from time to time. But as he got older, he preferred books." Walker nodded towards a corner bookshelf.

Remind you of anyone, the internal voice taunted.

Hearing Boycott bark, Chitto turned back to the window. The dog was looking toward a car pulling out of the Mounds parking lot. A silver SUV.

"Shug must've died before the murder happened," Chitto said, walking toward the bookshelf.

"How's that?" Walker looked at Chitto, frowning.

"With her doghouse right below the window there, she would've heard the commotion and barked. A hound's hearing is second to none."

"That'd be right," Walker said. "She didn't miss much."

Chitto ran his eyes along the rows of the bookshelf. Most of the books were old ones the libraries had pulled off their shelves and sold cheap. The collection indicated Bobby Taneyhill liked science fiction and fantasy, imaginary worlds that exist in the mind only.

For most people, said his internal voice.

Turning to Walker, he said, "Mrs. Biggers said Bobby went looking for a body the next morning."

"Soon as he got up. He slept in because of the tour he went on."

Another question answered. Bobby *had* been on the solstice tour. "And he told you he found Muriel Simpson when he got back that morning?"

"A body, didn't mention a name. Guess the woman's shirt was pulled up over her head. As he was walking back here, he saw Gordon Osgood driving up to the Center."

"Osgood." Chitto frowned. "Haven't heard that name before."

"The big boss over there. Runs things. He's the one reported the body. It made more sense to let him handle it since . . ." He hesitated. "Most people don't believe in things like *Ishkitini*."

Chitto nodded. "Did you hear it? The screech owl, I mean."

Walker shook his head side to side.

"How about cars driving down the road?"

"I don't pay no mind. People drive back and forth to the dam all the time."

Chitto grunted softly, wondering what else Walker didn't pay any mind. "According to the papers, you were certain Bobby was here all night."

"That'd be right. The elbow on the kitchen sink rusted out. I went to town and bought one after work, put it in that night. Fought with a slow leak a long time but finally got it to seal. Had a clear view of both doors. Bobby was in bed when I turned in."

Chitto hesitated. "Your head would've been under the sink."

Walker stared at him. "I'm not deaf."

"Right, right." Chitto exhaled slowly. "What time was it when you went to bed?"

Walker paused, blinking. "Must've been 'round midnight."

"And you told the defense attorney about the plumbing problem?"

"Gave her the receipt from the hardware store."

Her. The defense attorney was a woman.

"The receipt show you bought the part the same day?"

Walker nodded, jaws clenching. "Cops said I could've replaced it after the woman's body was found."

"Contending you fabricated the story as an alibi for Bobby."

Walker nodded again.

Chitto looked around the spare bedroom. Brown paneled walls. Brown carpet. A single bed. A student's desk in the corner with pencils and pens in jars, bottles of ink lined up in a row. He walked to the desk and opened the drawers. Empty, as was the wastebasket. The police had taken everything.

He checked the closet next. Shirts and jeans hung neatly, shoes and boots lined the floor, stacks of drawing paper lay on the shelves. No board games or old toys. None of the electronic gadgets teenagers accumulated: cell phones, iPods, earplugs.

Inward, Chitto repeated silently, wondering how he was going to get into the head of Bobby Taneyhill.

"Too bad they took all the stories," he murmured. "Might've helped to look at them."

Walker took a minute. "Didn't say they took all of them all," he said quietly. "Just those that were here."

CHAPTER NINE

Chitto left Charlie Walker's place close to seven and drove straight to his cabin. The shadows were lengthening and lights in neighboring cabins glowing when he arrived, but it wasn't fully dark and he had energy to burn. Walker had dealt him a card he wasn't expecting. To work off charged energy, he changed into sweats and his running shoes and took Boycott down one of the trails. When the cabins disappeared from view, he unsnapped the leash and let the dog run free.

Doing a slow jog, Chitto let the night enfold him. The racket of katydids, crickets, and frogs bombarded his ears. Fireflies hovered in low places along a creek bank, looking like flickering specters. Standing water and rotting oak leaves gave off the smell of a sweet-sour mash. A glance at the dial on his watch indicated he'd been on the trail a half hour. Whistling Boycott to his side, he reversed his route. In all that time, he didn't spot or hear a single owl.

It was pitch black when he made it back to the cabin. Filling Boycott's food dish, he turned on the small TV. Reception poor, he turned it off and pulled a yellow pad from his duffle along with the newspaper articles on the Muriel Simpson murder. He laid the articles aside about eleven o'clock and checked his notes. He had jotted down the time the trial was to begin on Monday and the names of two people: Baxter Littlejohn, Muriel Simpson's boyfriend, and Bernard Wasilewski, the neighbor at the apartment complex.

Glancing at his watch, he wondered why Jasmine hadn't called. Was it a sign she hadn't found anything on the two men? Or a sign that she was still angry about the wasted research she'd done? Fighting an urge to call her, he picked up his cell phone and looked up someone else's number. Hitting Dial, he sat quietly, waiting for voicemail to kick in.

"Sam here, Pete," he said after the requisite beep. "I'm planning to attend the Simpson murder trial on Monday. Thought I'd run by the office and bend your ear about a couple of things first. Look for me early."

Tired to the point of exhaustion, he undressed down to his undershirt and shorts, threw open the windows for air, and stretched out on the tufted mattress. Closing his eyes, he willed sleep to come. It was a lost cause. His subconscious was standing guard, alert for the call of an owl.

∞

Chitto's cell phone rang at six o'clock Sunday morning. Checking caller ID, he smiled.

"Morning, Scout." Stuffing pillows behind his back, he pulled himself into a sitting position and retrieved the yellow pad from the nightstand. "Am I to assume your research this time was more to your liking?"

"My *liking*?" A snort came from the line. "Let's just say it wasn't as mind-numbing as those land disputes. Who you want first? The boyfriend or the neighbor?"

"Which one you like the least?"

"The boyfriend," she said and began reeling off what she'd dug up.

Quickly, Chitto jotted down Baxter Littlejohn's age, address, current place of employment, and arrest record.

"Sounds like the guy's got a drinking problem," he said, reviewing incidents of drunk and disorderly, driving under the influence, and barroom brawls. "You get the name of that place he and Muriel Simpson went to that night?"

She had. Jotting it down, he said, "The drinking why you don't like him?"

"That, and . . ." A long pause came over the line. "What was it Shakespeare said about the guy who was dangerous because he thought too much?"

Chitto hesitated. "You mean, 'Yond Cassius has a lean and hungry look, he thinks too much'?"

"I love it when you get erudite," she said. "But yes, Cassius. Seems to me this Littlejohn is working overtime to divert attention away from himself. I bet he was wagging like a dog with two tails when that teacher brought in those pictures."

Chuckling, Chitto asked, "What else you find on him?"

"Nothing to write home about. He's a local. Born in Spiro and went through public school there. Wasn't motivated to go beyond high school. Work history's erratic, mostly at ranches around the county."

"Probably the drinking," Chitto said. "Tell me about Bernard Wasilewski."

"Nothing much on him, not even a speeding ticket. Born in Detroit forty-two years ago, joined the Navy soon after high school. He's an ex-corpsman who now works at the Veteran's Clinic in Fort Smith."

"Fort Smith, and he lives in Spiro?" Chitto ran through possible reasons someone would make the twenty-five-mile commute from Fort Smith to Spiro and came up with hunting, fishing, and hiking. But those same activities were readily available on the Arkansas side of the state line.

"He's lived in Spiro about two years," Jasmine said, "which is how long he's been at the Fort Smith clinic. Prior to that, he was in San Diego and Corpus Christi, plus a couple places in South Carolina."

"Duty stations," he said. "Did he stay in the Navy long enough to draw a pension?"

"Don't know." A pause followed, accompanied by sounds of paper rustling. "He's worked at hospitals and clinics on both coasts the last few years, as a civilian but always in veteran clinics. Guess that's where he feels comfortable."

Chitto sat quietly, digesting the information.

"You're not talking," she said a minute later.

"Sounds like he's moved around a lot," Chitto said.

"Maybe he wants to see the world."

"We're talking Spiro, Oklahoma," he said.

"Maybe he's tired of seeing the world."

Chitto chuckled again. "His military records show he pull any overseas duty?"

"Don't know. Why?"

"Sometimes vets search out a place to unwind." Chitto thought of Chickasaw Sergeant, Frank Tubbe, who retreated to the Colorado mountains for a time following his discharge from the service.

She sniffed loudly. "You'll have to get his military records from someone else. I don't have that level of clearance. Let me see what else I dug up." Static filled the line as she reviewed her notes. "Appears he fills in on weekends at the clinic there in Spiro occasionally. The Fort Smith clinic's closed on weekends, which frees up his time. Also found a few pictures of the two men. Want me to fax them to Pete Brody?"

"No," he murmured. "Something tells me I'll be seeing both these guys close up. Thanks, Scout. You done good."

With her typical abruptness, Jasmine hung up. Wasting no time, Chitto hooked Boycott to a porch post, sat a full food dish next to him, then showered and dressed. Slipping into a clean shirt and the jeans he wore the day before, he snugged his ball cap on his head and his holster at his waist. Loading Boycott, his notes, and the file on the Simpson murder into his pickup, he pulled away from the cabin. Yesterday, he didn't know what he and Mackie Green needed to talk about. Today was a different story.

CHAPTER TEN

Chitto stopped for coffee at the office on his way to the Archaeology Center to meet with Mackie Green. Birdie and the smell of freshly baked yeast rolls welcomed him. All smiles, she ushered him to the coffee pot.

"You want, you can eat with me and Bud in the kitchen," she whispered, eyes gleaming. "You know, since you're working undercover."

"Thanks," he murmured, "but I have to meet someone. Maybe I'll just take a couple of those rolls with me."

"You betcha!" Fetching a box of waxed paper, she wrapped up two packages of rolls as Chitto filled his mug. "For your police dog," she said, giving the second package a discrete pat.

Suppressing a laugh, Chitto walked to his truck. As he was backing out, he saw Birdie giving him the zippered-lips sign through the front window.

He finished off two of Birdie's cinnamon rolls on the way to Spiro Mounds. Police Dog made short work of the other two. He pulled into the parking lot at five minutes to eight and set to work. An hour later, Mackie Green drove in.

"You're punctual," she said, smiling broadly.

"So are you," he said, eying her closely. Her outward demeanor displayed confidence but dark circles under the

101

Lu Clifton

eyes signaled a less-than-restful night. "You replace Muriel yet? I noticed you were working the gift shop yesterday."

"I was filling in for Anna, the new girl. One of her children took a bad fall on her bike and she wanted to check on her." She motioned toward the front door. "Ready for a tour? You've already given a donation." She scratched Boycott's head. "Might be a good idea to keep this guy on leash. Wouldn't want him to mistake a relic for a hambone."

"Already took a tour, at least of the grounds."

Since arriving earlier, Chitto had spent most of his time visualizing the night of the murder. He'd studied the parking area, the kill site, the route to the walking trail where the body was found, and the proximity of Charlie Walker's home. As he'd looked around, he created a mental list of questions needing answers. Were there any signs the victim had struggled? What was the condition of Simpson's clothing? Had any DNA material been collected?

Her smile faded. "Sounds like you've been here a while."

"A bit." He nodded toward the dig site. "You involved in that dig?"

She glanced at the site. "On my days off. It's a joint project between the universities of Oklahoma and Arkansas but they let me hang around." She looked at him again. "Reminds me of when I was back in college."

"Where'd you go to school?"

"Austin as an undergrad, finished at OU." She nodded at the dig site. "What do you think?"

Chitto shrugged. "Not much to see. I am curious about the spot they picked. Some of the other mounds appear more promising burial sites and most of them look undisturbed."

"Very observant," she said. "Only one's been dug into, that big one there." She pointed to one of the larger mounds. "But the team's not looking for burial sites. They're interested in understanding the nature and extent of the non-mound habitation here. You know, the nuts and bolts of life. How the people lived, did day-to-day things. They started a couple of years ago, using remote sensing to identify anomalies that look like prehistoric structures. That site they chose was the most promising." Opening the door to the Interpretative Center, she waved him inside. "Ready for that tour you paid for?"

"Tell you what," he said, locking eyes with her. "How about we look at Bobby Taneyhill's drawings instead."

"Wow," she said, exhaling slowly. "Charlie must trust you a lot." Pushing through the door, she murmured, "Okay, follow me."

"Walker said Bobby helped you out," he said, falling in behind her. "What'd he do?"

"Different things, but mostly he made posters for the various events. I was trying to steer him toward a career in graphic design after he finished high school. Art school, then maybe a job with an advertising agency."

Hearing him grunt, she turned to look at him. "What?"

"Just seems a lot to take on, given what this job requires. You've got a tough schedule. After hour tours, rotating exhibits . . . Your plate's plenty full."

"It is," she sighed. "But Charlie's worried what will happen to Bobby after he dies. The kid doesn't have anyone else, so . . ." She let the sentence hang midair.

"He also cleared the trails before a tour," she said, picking up where she left off. "Trash, sticks and debris." She swiveled her head to look at him. "Sometimes handicapped people attend. You know, wheelchairs and walkers."

Chitto followed quietly, assessing the information. "I can't see him working for an ad agency. Haven't seen anything yet but his work sounds pretty dark."

She laughed softly. "So was Ralph Steadman's in *Rolling Stone*." A pause, then, "Maybe you aren't familiar with him."

"Hunter S. Thompson's cartoonist pal."

"Right," she said, sounding pleasantly surprised.

"Possible, I suppose, but still a long shot. How about the tours? Did he go on all of them?"

"Not all. Just those he had an interest in."

"But he did go on the solstice tour last year."

"Matter of fact, he did." She stopped in front of a door on the back wall. "Why do you ask?"

"It's my job to ask questions."

She flipped through a ring full of keys, found the one she was looking for, and unlocked the door. Engaging a doorstop to hold the door open, she said, "This is where we store those exhibits not in use."

Through the doorway, Chitto saw dark silhouettes of unidentifiable objects. As Mackie flipped the light switch, the objects took on form and meaning. Display tables. Glass cases. A replica of a canoe. He paused to admire a tray of chert of various sizes and colors, some embedded with small shells.

Noticing Mackie watching him, he said, "I'm a geologist by training. OU's my alma mater, too."

"Oh, yeah?" The broad smile appeared. "You didn't filch anything from the dig site, did you?"

He grinned slightly. "I was tempted, but first and foremost, I'm a cop. Stealing's against the law."

"Darn it," she said, eyes twinkling. "And I was looking for an excuse to frisk you."

"That's my job," Chitto said, the smile gone.

"I was teasing," she said, shaking her head slightly. "Apparently you're all business."

"I am when I'm working."

Lifting her chin, she motioned toward the back of the room. "The drawings are in there." She walked toward a file cabinet in the corner. Opening the bottom drawer, she reached to the back and pulled out a tan portfolio with a button and string closure. A drawing on the front of the folder resembled the warrior at the entrance to the Center. Indicating two chairs in the corner, she sat down in one of them and rested the portfolio on her lap.

"I guess Bobby was working on illustrations for this story when the hullaballoo started over the ones the cops found at home," she said, indicating the folder.

Chitto noticed the protective way her hands lay folded on top of the portfolio. "Why wasn't this one with the others?" he asked, pulling a chair around so he faced her.

"I don't know," she said, blinking. "Never occurred to me to ask."

"How'd you get hold of it?"

"Charlie found it in the utility room and brought it to me. He . . . well, *we* decided the police had all they needed."

The two had colluded about concealing evidence? Chitto rocked back in the chair, attempting to reason through their decision. He could understand Walker—he was the boy's grandfather and naturally protective—but Mackie wasn't family. Moreover, as a scientist, she should have remained objective, made rational decisions.

"And you *both* looked at the drawings," he said.

"That's right." A pause. "Why?"

"Depends on what the drawings show," he said, thoughts going to incriminatory evidence. "Why'd Bobby do them here? From the looks of his bedroom, that was where he worked."

"Not always. See, this place had become his home away from home, his refuge. Charlie kept a table and chairs in the utility room. Bobby's hung out there since he was little, and pens and paper are easy to carry."

She waved an arm toward the exterior room. "I personally think this place was his inspiration. The mounds people were an artistic civilization. Keep in mind this was a center for trading. Obsidian from Mexico, colored flint from New Mexico, copper from the Great Lakes, mica from the Carolinas, conch shells from the Gulf Coast. They did a lot of engravings on conch shells."

Chitto cocked his head, blinking. "Engravings of what?"

"Anything and everything," she said, shrugging. "People and animals, geometric designs and symbols, all manner of things. The ancient peoples who inhabited this place were an important leadership group. And because they traded so extensively, they developed a picture language to communicate."

"Which is how languages everywhere started," he murmured, turning pensive. "What do you think Bobby's pictures are saying?"

"I'm an archaeologist, not a shrink." Fine lines creased her brow. "What I do know is the people that lived here led exciting lives and Bobby's was anything but. He was very familiar with the history of this place, though. How it was the intellectual hub for a national confederation of Mississippian tribes." She sighed, head shaking slightly. "I always figured he was making up for his own life through the stories he invented."

"Any of those engravings deal with violence?" he asked.

She lifted a hand, let it drop. "What society doesn't have violence? There's the need to protect one's territory, one's beliefs. And, of course, dignity and pride get wrapped up in it—that proverbial sense of right and wrong. That led to the need for warriors."

"Like the guy on that sign out there?" Chitto pointed his chin in the direction of the entrance."

"And you," she said, the hint of a grin showing.

He snickered. "Hope I don't look that damn scary." Sobering, he said, "I was thinking how some of the old Choctaw rituals involved things like beheading, scalping, various forms of mutilation." He paused, forehead creased. "According to the newspaper, the Simpson woman was mutilated. I don't know the specifics—"

"Her nipples were cut off and she was stabbed in the genitals."

Mackie Green's candor surprised Chitto until he considered she wasn't just a woman. She was also a scientist whose job was to pull back the veil and look close in order to make sense of what was confusing and strange. Or disturbing.

Sounds like your job, whispered the voice in his head.

He nodded at the portfolio she still clutched. "Could there be a connection between what the boy's been exposed to here at the Center and the novels he does?"

"Possibly," she said thoughtfully. "They're extremely graphic in places, but teenagers are impressionable and . . ." She hesitated. "Well, he wasn't popular with his peers."

"That's what Walker said."

"Peer acceptance is so important at that age. It had to hurt."

"Don't overlook the hormone factor," he added.

"Hormone?" she repeated.

"Testosterone. Did Bobby have a girlfriend, date anyone in particular?"

She snorted. "I doubt he ever went on a date—" She looked away suddenly, then back again. "There was this one girl . . ."

He leaned forward. "I get the feeling you're trying to prepare me for something."

"No—it's probably nothing . . ." She paused, swallowing. "I, uh, I came by my office one day and overheard Bobby on the phone. He had a bad crush on this girl that sat next to him in some of his classes. She'd been nice to him, as in being his partner when they had to team up on projects. So I encouraged him to call her, ask her out." She shrugged. "My motto is nothing ventured, nothing gained."

Another misconception, Chitto thought. Scientists were generally the Spartan type, not good-time girls.

"And you told him he could use your office?"

"No . . ." Her forehead wrinkled in a frown. "That was a surprise. But I just figured he didn't want Charlie to overhear him." She waved a hand dismissively. "Anyway, he must've gotten up his nerve that day and . . ." Anger flashed in her eyes. "The little bitch *laughed* at him. I mean, she was laughing so loud, I could hear her from the hallway."

"Did he see you?"

"Regrettably. He bolted from my office and almost ran me down. He was so embarrassed, so humiliated." She looked at Chitto, expression sober. "He avoided me for the longest time. Even now, there's times when he won't look me in the eye."

"Is that when he started working on what's in there?" He indicated the portfolio again.

"I don't know." She frowned again. "But see, for Bobby *this* would be normal." She tapped the portfolio. "The novels were his way of venting."

Excuses, he thought. Why's she trying so hard to make allowances for him?

"Sounds like he held grudges. He have a temper, too?"

"Temper—" She snickered. "Look, I've worked here four years. Never once have I seen Bobby act out like other kids do. Even when the police talked to him—and they did several times before they arrested him—he was always cooperative. What does that tell you?"

Chitto paused, considering her assessment of the boy. "What about Muriel Simpson?"

"Muriel?" She shook her head, looking confused. "What about her?"

"He show an interest in her?

"Unequivocally, *no* . . ." Abruptly, her voice faded to silence.

"Now is not the time to hold anything back, Mackie."

"Well, it's probably nothing, but . . ." She drew a breath. "See, we had to talk to Muriel a few times about the way she dressed. Some of her blouses left a little too much to the imagination, if you get my drift. What male of the species wouldn't notice something like that?"

Chitto paused, rubbing a hand across his mouth. "Maybe it's time to open that portfolio."

∞

Mackie Green took Chitto to her office in the adjacent building where he could look through the portfolio's contents in private. She carried in a bowl of water for Boycott, then went to check the Interpretative Center before it was time to open it to visitors.

Chitto turned the pages slowly. As in comic books, written copy was limited and highly punctuated. Balloon tails pointed to a character's mouth. Burst balloons and bold type indicated someone was screaming. Question marks in combo with exclamation marks showed a shouted question. Sound effects were shown with hollow, see-through letters. The drawings carried the plot of the story: a bizarrely dressed main character shown in stealthy pursuit of an enemy, the final chase when he caught up with and subdued the person. In this case, a person lying on the ground with low scraggy branches hanging overhead.

Mackie Green stuck her head around the doorframe. "How's it going?' she said, taking a seat across from him.

He leaned back, letting out a sigh. "I can't decide if the protagonist fits a hero archetype or villain. In appearance, he looks like a Goth version of that warrior out there on the sign. And because this is a work in progress, we don't know how Bobby planned it to end." He tapped a finger on the stack of pages. "Suppose the drawings the prosecution have are anything like these?"

She hunched her shoulders. "I didn't see them, but probably."

"So other than Bobby, Walker was the only one to see the others?"

"I guess, until the police took them."

He tapped the drawings again. "You said you'd looked at these."

"I did."

He paused, looking her in the eye. "As a woman, what would you think seeing a woman spread eagle on the ground?"

"Keep in mind that I'm not your typical woman," she said. "Antiquity's full of this kind of thing, so not much shocks me. The more important question is what would jurors think?"

"Right." He glanced away, then back at her. "Why aren't you a witness for the defense? Your understanding of how picture languages develop, and knowing Bobby the way you do, could prove helpful."

"Or I could bury him. The first thing the prosecution would ask is whether I've seen any of Bobby's work. And when it came out that I have, they'd want to know how. And before you know it, I'd be explaining those." She lifted her chin toward the drawings on the desk. "You can bet the prosecution would want to know what I was doing with them—especially when they found out I'd been hiding them all this time."

"Good point." He paused, thinking his suspicions of Mackie may have been premature. She had given the matter some thought so her actions were logical, especially given her fondness for both Bobby and Walker. "Still, I'm surprised the defense attorney didn't ferret you out."

She let out a grunt. "Have you talked to that defense attorney?"

"No. Have you?"

She shook her head. "I went to the trial the first day, just for a couple of hours. I wanted Charlie and Bobby to know they had someone pulling for them." She looked at him, blinking. "Why haven't you talked to her?"

Chitto folded his hands behind his head, debating how much he could trust this woman who, in essence, was not only a stranger but a possible suspect. Deciding he didn't have a choice, he leaned forward.

"See, this case is outside my jurisdiction, which means I'm not here officially." Briefly, he related the visit from his mother and June Biggers. "It's not like I can waltz into the attorney's office in open daylight and ask to see the evidence—or confer with Bobby." He watched her lips tighten to a flat line, then her head began to nod.

"Why'd you ask about the attorney?" he said.

"She's young," she sighed. "I doubt she's handled many cases, much less a murder trial."

"Just what I was afraid of." As the room grew silent, he looked at her. "You think Bobby did it?"

She paused briefly. "I believe Charlie's telling the truth. If he says Bobby was there all night, he was."

Chitto paused, giving her a piercing look. "Is this all of it?" he said, indicating the portfolio. "The *only* evidence you've been concealing."

"That's *it*," she snapped, her face flushing.

"Had to ask," he said, rising. "Okay if I take the portfolio with me? I'd like to look through it again."

She shrugged. "If Charlie wanted you to see it, I don't see why not. I can give him a call—or maybe you can let him know when you see him tomorrow." She glanced at him. "You *are* going to the trial."

"If I can figure out how to sneak a hound dog into the courthouse."

"Boycott?" She turned thoughtful. "Leave him with me. I have tomorrow and the next day off so I'm free. I'll be working with the archaeology team."

"The archaeology team," Chitto repeated slowly. "Well, see, he likes to dig."

"So do we," she said with a laugh.

Chapter Eleven

Chitto was on the way to Spiro when his cell phone rang. Checking the number, he pulled onto the shoulder and said, "Hey, Pete. What's up?"

"Wife's at church, thought I'd drive up to see you. That trial starts early tomorrow."

"That would work. I was heading to Spiro to check out the last place Muriel Simpson went that night. Also want to get the local scoop on the boyfriend and that neighbor who saw her last. Where you want to meet up?"

"Dorothy's Donuts on Broadway. Be there in thirty."

Chitto pulled a map of Spiro from the glovebox. Broadway was the main street through town. Within fifteen minutes, he'd found a quiet parking place on a side street where Boycott would have plenty of shade. Taking his long guns from the rack, he laid them in the rear floorboard and covered them with a tarp. Filling a bowl with bottled water, he lowered the windows a crack for circulation, locked up, and headed for Broadway. A car horn got his attention as he turned the corner He returned Pete Brody's wave and walked to where he parked.

"Appreciate this," he said, shaking Brody's hand. "Let me buy you a cup."

The District 4 Field Lieutenant was in his mid- to late-fifties, graying at the temple, and showing some overhang in the middle. Being it was the weekend, he had opted for a cotton shirt and khaki pants. A straw Stetson shaded his face.

"Might cost you a couple of donuts, too," Brody said, pushing through the door of the donut shop. "This place makes 'em from scratch."

Chitto followed Brody to a booth by the front window where they would have privacy. A middle-aged woman in a gray uniform and white apron was at their table within seconds, two menus in her hand.

"Mornin', Dot," Pete said, sliding into the booth.

"Mornin' Pete. What'll it be?"

Brody ordered coffee with half-and-half and two jelly-filled donuts. Chitto resorted to black coffee and white-bread toast and jelly. As she walked away, Brody turned to face him.

"I gotta say, you're gettin' a late start on this case, Sam. Soon as Dan called to say you were coming, I gathered what I could but this thing's been moving at the speed of light."

"I noticed. There a reason for that?"

"Glory hounds. It's an election year." He paused as Dot set two mugs of coffee and a carton of half-and-half on the table. "Local officials are chomping at the bit," he added as she walked away, "thinking this trial's gonna put this place on the map."

"I figured it had something to do with politicians." Chitto looked at Brody. "What's your take? You think the boy did it?"

"Damned if I know," Brody said, stirring cream into his coffee. "Kid sounds a bit off center to me, but I'll leave that determination to the psychiatrist they're bringing in."

116

That wild card again . . .

"Any suggestions on who to talk to? Someone who might've interviewed the witnesses?"

"Did that before state jurisdiction took control." Brody pulled a well-thumbed notebook from his hip pocket, corners of certain pages folded down. "Apartment manager described Muriel Simpson as a 'loose woman.' Seems Simpson dated a lot of different men, brought them back to her apartment, some of which stayed the night."

"Oh, yeah?" Chitto frowned suddenly. "How come this Baxter Littlejohn she had dinner with didn't accompany her home that night? He was her boyfriend."

"*Ex*-boyfriend. According to some I talked with at the roadhouse, she dumped him that very evening. Guess he was so drunk, he fell down—and talking loud, too. Several overheard them arguing."

Chitto lifted his eyebrows. "Sounds like motive to me."

"Don't it though."

Chitto paused, rubbing his mouth. "He must've had an airtight alibi."

"Didn't leave the bar right away. Bartender wasn't sure of the exact time but said it was almost closing time, which is around one o'clock. Bartender also said Littlejohn was a loud-mouthed drunk but all talk and no action. Didn't think he was sober—or clever—enough to do what was done to that woman and hide his tracks."

Chitto let out a grunt. "But then, we both know anger can be a great motivator."

Brody checked his notebook again. "Also looked at that neighbor, Bernard Wasilewski. Apartment manager described him as 'a shadow.' Quietest tenant she's ever had. Never saw anyone come to visit or him leave with anyone.

Works at a clinic in Fort Smith weekdays, fills in here at the Spiro clinic on weekends when need be." He looked up at Chitto. "In the military, he'd be called a hospital corpsman. Guess he'd be called a nurse now."

Chitto nodded. "And not only know how to use medical instruments, such as scalpels, but have access to them."

"Yes indeed." Brody turned back to his notebook. "Good work history, pays his bills on time, doesn't raise cane." He sucked the spit from between his teeth. "It's the quiet ones that worry me."

"Bobby Taneyhill sounds like one of those."

"He does at that."

Chitto drummed fingers on the table. "The thing is we know what the Taneyhill boy did in his spare time. Nobody seems to know about this Wasilewski." He looked at Brody. "He have any hobbies?"

Brody resorted to his notebook again. "Apartment manager commented she saw him leave on weekends wearing hiking boots and carrying a backpack. Guess he's a lover of the great outdoors." Closing his notebook, he looked at Chitto. "So, there you have it. The three primary suspects. Which one you like?"

Chitto laughed humorlessly. "Right now, I don't like any of them." He paused, making eye contact. "What's your opinion of the grandfather and that archaeologist at the Center."

Brody's eyebrows hitched. "You considering them suspects?"

"Right now, anyone who breathed the same air as Muriel Simpson is a suspect."

"We're paid to be cautious." Brody shook his head side to side. "Don't know much about either of them. Keep in mind, my office is in Poteau. But from what I hear, the grandfather was a straight-up citizen. Hard worker, kept his nose clean. Member of the local tribal council, too." He paused a few seconds, blinking. "Know even less about the archaeologist lady. No incidents involving the law . . . no rumors to speak of."

"To speak of," Chitto repeated.

Brody shrugged. "She's a single gal, the liberated kind."

"Meaning?"

"She's seen at the local bars from time to time. Anyone who isn't the church-going type makes those that are wag their tongues, building something out of nothing." He lowered his voice as Dot walked toward them. "Also made the acquaintance of the defense attorney, thinking you might want to bend her ear. Name's Susan Dayton."

"Hell, *yeah*." As Dot set their food on the table, Chitto looked up at her. "We'll need refills on the coffee."

"Another one of these donuts, too," Brody said.

"What's your opinion of this attorney?" Chitto asked as they started on the food.

"Green as a gourd. That Taneyhill kid doesn't stand a snowball's chance in hell unless someone with street smarts can guide her thinking. I made you an appointment with her today 'bout one o'clock."

"Where?" Chitto glanced at his watch. It was a quarter of twelve.

"My place. Seemed the most logical rendezvous point. We live a ways out, thought it best for you to follow me there."

Chitto hesitated, rethinking the decisions he'd made for this trip. "I, uh, I brought a dog. He's in the truck."

Brody shrugged. "No problem. Our place is fenced. Wife doesn't set dinner on the table till three or so on weekends, which allows plenty of time for a confab with the defense attorney. She can't join us but I told Molly to set a plate for you."

"I owe you, Pete."

"So . . ." Brody broke a donut in half and looked at Chitto. "Let's finish up here and head to my place for the rest of this conversation, which deals with your daddy and Bert Gilly. If anybody can find out who those sons of bitches were that murdered our boys, you can."

Chitto smiled. Verification had been achieved. Pete Brody was, indeed, as true-blue as they came.

∞

The drive to Pete Brody's place took a half hour. Chitto took time to admire the place as he pulled up a long drive. The house was a modest two-story with vinyl siding and red metal roof, but the land around it made it appear grander. A shade boundary of ancient oaks and bristly pines surrounded the home and the adjacent pastureland was clipped as clean as an English manor. He put Boycott on his leash before exiting the truck.

"How much land you got here, Pete?"

"Nineteen acres all told. C'mon, let's put your pup in the backyard. He can chase those damned rabbits eatin' Molly's flowers."

Chitto put Boycott into a heel position and followed Brody. They walked through a gate leading to a spacious backyard enclosed with a six-foot chain-link fence.

"Tall fence," he commented. "Deer problem?"

"Yep, and still they clear it." Brody walked toward a covered patio on which sat a covered barbeque grill and wooden deck furniture with plush pillows. "Thought we'd talk to that lawyer out here. Don't like to talk work in front of the wife."

"That was Dad's policy, too."

"It's a good one. Keeps harmony in the house." Brody eyed Boycott. "What is he? Redbone?"

"He didn't come with a pedigree but I'd bet a Redbone figured prominently."

"Turn him loose. He'll be all right."

A door off the patio opened as Chitto let Boycott off leash. A short woman with graying hair and round face walked out carrying a pitcher of tea and several glasses. Brody introduced her as Molly, his wife of thirty-five years.

"Please to meet you, ma'am," Chitto said, removing his ball cap. "Sorry for my appearance. I would've changed but I was on the road when Pete called, and . . ." He pointed his chin toward Boycott. "I have my dog with me but I'll pick up after him." He pulled a wad of plastic bags from a hip pocket.

"Relax, Lieutenant Chitto. We had dogs when the kids were growing up."

"Sam," he said. "I go by Sam."

"All right, *if* you'll call me Molly instead of *ma'am*. Besides, Pete needs to work off those donuts he had earlier." She looked at her husband, gray eyes twinkling. "Must've been a three-donut day. I was worried you weren't gonna make it back before that woman got here."

Pete glanced at his watch. "Made it with time to spare."

"Time to spare, my ass." She cocked her head toward the door. "That's the doorbell now."

∞

Susan Dayton had a lot of schooling under her belt. Her Juris Doctor degree took seven years, including four years of undergraduate work and three years of law school. That's all she had under her belt. Her shirt and slacks hung on her like she was a wire coat hanger. That, combined with round eyeglasses and a pixie haircut, gave her the appearance of an orphaned waif.

"Where'd you go to school?" Chitto asked after introductions were over.

"Oklahoma City U School of Law. It's the same school the judge graduated from." She straightened her shoulders. "Graduated in the top ten percent of my class."

He looked duly impressed, then followed with, "But this is your first murder trial."

"Yes," she sighed, sounding tired. "And I wish people would stop bringing that up. I participated in a lot of mock trials at school." She checked the time on an expansion-band watch. "Look, can we get on with this? I need to review my case notes this afternoon. Mr. Brody said you were a tribal policeman looking into this case as a friend of the family."

Chitto's laugh sounded hollow. "Not sure *friend* is the right word. The important thing is I need to stay under the radar. I've missed the trial so far. How's it looking?"

She shrugged. "Preliminaries are over. You can read about it in the newspapers." She pulled copies of the *Poteau Daily News* from her briefcase.

Chitto waved them away. "Thanks, but I've seen them."

She pushed her glasses up her nose. "Then why'd you want to see me?"

"You miss a lot when you're not in the courtroom." He paused, then repeated, "How's it looking?"

She sank back into plush cushions, her eyes following Boycott's meandering around the yard. "That psychiatrist Monty's bringing in has me a little worried."

"The prosecutor for the state is named Monty?"

"That's what he goes by, but his name's Montgomery. Montgomery Powell."

"You line up another one to refute his findings?"

"Of course," she replied coolly. "But the prosecution's has done this kind of thing for police departments all over the country. Mine's not nearly as . . . impressive."

"I see." Chitto eyed thin clouds scudding across the sky. "What was it Paschal said? 'People arrive at their beliefs not on the basis of proof but on the basis of what they find attractive.'"

"In other words," Brody said, topping off the tea glasses. "You're screwed."

"I didn't say that," Dayton snapped, glaring at Brody. "I just said I was a *little* worried."

"Better than being overconfident," Chitto said. "According to the papers, robbery wasn't a motive. Simpson's wallet was still in her vehicle and nothing else was missing."

"That's right. The prosecution's hanging its hat on it being a fantasy killing. Both psychiatrists received copies of the novels the police found, so . . ." She paused. "It's a wait-and-see game."

He nodded, not divulging there was another manuscript that neither the prosecution nor defense had seen. "Tell me about those other manuscripts. I'm assuming you didn't bring copies as that would violate attorney-client privilege."

"I didn't." She looked away, lacing and unlacing her fingers absentmindedly. "The, uh, the main character's this weird-looking superhero that wears Shaolin leg wraps and no shirt. He pulls his hair into this topknot . . ." She made a wriggling motion above her head. "And wears black makeup on his mouth and around his eyes."

"Sort of a modern-day Goth monk," Chitto mused aloud, thinking of the drawings that Mackie Green had shown him.

"Yes—*exactly*. Apparently, this superhero's mission is to wipe out the bad guys. He singlehandedly battles and defeats entire gangs, most of whom look like *normal* teenagers. You know, tee shirts and jeans, crew cuts and ponytails—except for their faces." She exhaled, shook her head slightly. "No eyes, nose, or mouth. Just a blank space."

Chitto frowned, thinking of the victim in the book hidden away at the Center. The woman on the ground also had a blank face but he'd assumed the drawing was unfinished. Defining features revealed a person's fundamental nature. Is that how Bobby sees everyone, he wondered. A body without essence?

Dayton looked at Chitto and Brody. "And, of course, lots of knives, spears, and blood—pools of blood . . ." She inhaled, exhaled.

Chitto read the signs. As a junior attorney, the case had been dumped on her and she didn't think she had a chance of winning it. A hard pill to swallow for someone who finished top of her class.

Noticing Chitto exchange a look with Brody, she said, "What?"

"Interesting word choice, 'normal,'" Chitto said. "Whether you think Bobby's guilty or innocent, your job's to get him off."

A scarlet flush crept up her neck.

"You mentioned ponytails," Chitto said. "So girls are depicted, too?"

"A few." She brushed a fly away from her tea glass.

"Are you putting Bobby on the stand?" he asked.

"No." She made another swipe at the fly.

"Probably a good move," Brody said. "From the pictures in the paper, he wouldn't stand up under a cross-examination."

"Look," she said, sighing loudly. "I know my job."

"Okay, how do you explain this?" Chitto said. "This thing happened at night. How the hell can someone cut off a woman's nipples in the dark?"

Dayton shrugged slightly. "Muriel Simpson apparently left the car lights on so she could see the front door more clearly. The police turned them off the next morning to prevent the battery from completely running down."

"Uh-huh," Brody grunted, looking thoughtful. "Well, if you're good with a knife, I suppose that'd be enough light. Hell, I gutted a deer once using a helmet-mounted flashlight."

Making a throaty sound, Dayton took a sip of tea.

Deciding it was a good time to move on, Chitto said, "Are these graphic novels all the prosecution is presenting as evidence?"

"No," she said hesitantly. "The investigators also found a candy bar wrapper at the scene. A Hershey's chocolate bar. They're saying Bobby dropped it when he killed her."

Chitto stared at her. "His fingerprints were on it?"

"Yes, but . . ." She looked at them "I'm *not* worried about it. Bobby said he ate it when he was on that tour the previous evening and the wrapper must've fallen out of his pocket." She brushed a hand through the air dismissively. "It's inconclusive evidence—which I've already covered."

Chitto paused, wondering how many times inconclusive evidence had swayed a jury. "And the only motive presented thus far is the one from the psychiatrist. A fantasy killing."

"That's right."

He thought a bit. "So, what's your strategy?"

She stared at him.

"Create reasonable doubt with the witnesses," he said, responding to his own question. "It's all you can do." He looked at her directly. "You *did* reserve the right to recall witnesses."

"*Of course*," she snapped, "but I see no reason to do so." She turned away, then swiveled her head around to look at him. "Do you?"

"Depends. Fill me in on a few details. Were Simpson's nipples cleanly removed or hacked off?"

She flushed again. "I don't remember the medical examiner commenting on that. Why?"

"It could indicate whether the attacker was adept with a knife or had an unsteady hand. If they were hacked off . . . Well, Buster Littlejohn was falling down drunk that night— and his story doesn't ring true. There were those at the bar who heard Simpson break it off with him, yet he's waxed poetic about being Simpson's boyfriend."

"In other words," Brody said. "He's lying through his teeth."

"He had an alibi," she countered quickly. "The bartender said he was there till he closed."

"Remind me," Chitto said, looking at Brody. "What day of the week did the murder take place?"

"A Saturday night. Awful busy at that place on a Saturday night."

Dayton wrapped a paper napkin around the sweating tea glass. "So you're suggesting Littlejohn could've left, followed Simpson, killed her, then returned to the bar." She shook her head. "You just said he was too drunk to drive."

"People drive drunk all the time," Chitto said. "But that doesn't mean their hands are steady enough to perform a surgical maneuver."

She let out a grunt. "For God's sake, he's a *ranch hand.*"

Chitto and Brody exchanged another glance.

"What?" she snapped, glaring at them.

Pulling his notebook from his pocket, Brody tore out a page and wrote down a name. "Check with this man," he said, handing it to her. "He's been ranching in these parts half a century."

She glanced at the name on the slip. "And why would I do that?"

"Just ask him to tell you what a stockman's job entails."

She drew a long breath and exhaled slowly. "Okay, I'll recall the medical examiner."

"While you've got the ME on the stand, verify whether it was a frontal or rear attack."

"No need. It was in the back. Knife between the ribs. The, uh, the mutilation occurred later."

"So, *after* she was dragged to the walking trail, where she died . . ." Chitto paused. "Blood spatter?"

"A bloodstain pattern expert testified that there wouldn't be significant blood transfer to the assailant because he dragged the body, didn't pick it up. If they'd found him on the scene, there might've been a little blood on him." She fanned the air dismissively again. "They didn't find anything on Bobby's clothes when they checked."

"With a punctured lung," Brody commented, "most of the bleeding would've been internal."

"Drowned in her own blood . . ." Chitto exhaled slowly, then looked at Dayton again. "Were there signs she fought back?"

Lu Clifton

She shook her head. "There wasn't anything under her nails and none were broken."

"Okay," he said, blinking slowly. "So Muriel Simpson not only knew her attacker but she trusted him. No woman I know these days lets a stranger walk up to them, and most would be holding a key between her fingers to use as a weapon." He doubled his hand into a fist, his thumb through two fingers as a demonstration.

"Yeah," she nodded. "I do that."

Chitto paused, frowning. "Thing is, this apartment key business doesn't fly for me. She obviously had a key to the door at the Center and she drove her car there. Why wasn't the apartment key on the key ring along with the others?"

She waved the air again. "When she ran into the neighbor at the apartment complex that night, she told him she'd had a spare made at the hardware store and was in the process of putting one of them back on her key ring when she got distracted. Her key and the new one were on one of those metal rings the store gives you. Both keys were found at the scene, still on the metal ring. The police tracked down the key shop, which confirmed she had a spare key made and picked up both it and the original late in the day."

Brody grunted. "In other words, the story pans out."

Chitto nodded aimlessly. "Except she trusted someone enough to let them walk up to her in the middle of the night." He craned his neck around, looking at her directly. "Who'd she know that well?"

She arched her eyebrows. "Bobby Taneyhill, of course. They both worked at Spiro Mounds. Look, I thought you were on his side—"

"And who else?"

"What?"

"Who did she tell she was going back to Spiro Mounds to get her key?"

She looked away, eyebrows knotted. "The neighbor."

"Why'd she feel comfortable sharing that information with him?"

"I . . . don't know."

"Well clearly, she didn't consider him a stranger. And what was he doing outside at that time of night? What was it, almost midnight?"

"Taking out the trash," she replied quickly. "There's a Dumpster out back for the residents. He said he was cleaning his apartment and went right back inside to finish up."

"Any witnesses to that? Sounds like the manager there at the complex keeps a close eye on things."

"I drove by the place right after it happened," Brody said. "That's a fourplex, two up and two down. Manager lives in one of the downstairs apartments."

"Which one Wasilewski live in?" Chitto asked, looking at Dayton.

Raising a hand, she mumbled, "Don't know."

"And who's a trained medic with access to medical instruments?" Chitto said.

She set her tea glass on the table with a *thunk*. "You're suggesting Bernard Wasilewski followed Muriel Simpson and killed her." She lifted her hands, palms up. "What would be his motive? He works at saving people's lives, not taking them. Good God—he was a Navy corpsman. Care to venture how many servicemen he's saved?"

"Plenty, I imagine. But that doesn't explain why he's moved around so much since he mustered out."

She frowned. "How do you know that?"

129

"A better question is how come you don't?"

She leaned back, jaws slack. "You think *he* did it?"

"I don't know," he said. "But that's not the point. If you can create enough doubt in the jury's mind, you might get Bobby Taneyhill off." He held up two fingers. "Motivation and opportunity equals reasonable doubt, Counselor."

She blinked. Stood. Said, "I need to go."

Chitto stood, too. Extending a hand, he said, "Go get 'em, tiger."

Walking to the corner of the yard with a view of the front, Chitto and Brody watched a beige sedan plummet down the driveway.

"What'd I tell you," Brody said.

"Green as a gourd about covers it."

Brody let out a grunt. "Bet that woman doesn't weigh a hundred pounds soaking wet."

"Yeah, but good things come in little packages. She was thinking long and hard there at the end."

Brody chuckled. "You rattled her cage pretty good."

"Hopefully she'll do the same with the jury."

"Hell," Brody said, giving him a sideways glance. "You almost had me convinced one of those other guys is the guilty one."

"Almost?" Picking up a small stone, Chitto rubbed it between his fingers. "Why almost?"

Plucking a blade of grass, Brody chewed on the stem end. "I noticed you said she *might* get Bobby Taneyhill off, not prove him innocent."

The corners of Chitto's mouth turned up. "Your memory's slipping, Pete. In our business, people are entitled to the presumption of innocence."

"Damn it, Sam. Would you just say it like it is for once?"

"I'm only sure of one thing," Chitto said, hurling the stone over the fence. "Few of us are what we seem."

CHAPTER TWELVE

"This magnolia's Molly's pride and joy," Brody said, stopping next to a woody shrub. "It's something to behold when it's in bloom." Leaning close to examine a yellowing leaf, he said, "Tell me about this *federales* that's been giving me the third degree."

"*Federales*?" Chitto turned slowly to face him. "You talking about Ramon Rodriguez?"

"That would be him." Pulling a stick from the flowerbed, Brody tossed it to Boycott. "It's been the Spanish Inquisition 'round here. Questions about how long I've been on the job. How long Wayne Drumright's been field officer here. When did Ruth Bledsoe leave—*why'd* she leave? I even saw him at the courthouse last week going through records. Police chief said Rodriguez gave him the third degree, the sheriff said the same thing."

"And?"

"*Nada*. They're as in the dark as I am." He paused, eyeing Chitto. "Can you shed any light on the matter?"

"Maybe." Chitto exhaled slowly. "Rodriguez was in the office a while back and I rode him hard about the FBI's failed effort on Dad and Bert Gilly's murder. Seems he'd just been assigned to the case." He paused. "Sounds like he's playing catch up, looking at things from the get-go."

Brody let out a grunt. "Well, that would explain why there's so many cops up here that don't belong up here."

Chitto rubbed the back of his neck, eyeing Brody. "That's what I wanted to bend your ear about, Pete. Just this last week, Dan told me Bert got a call at his house the night before that trip, from a friend up here."

Brody paused, blinking rapidly. "Hell yeah, that's right." He looked over the fence, studying a distant line of trees. "Dan mentioned that when he called to tell me those boys would be in the neighborhood."

"Did they check in with you when they got here?"

"For a fact, they didn't. But I just figured they'd taken the northern route, bypassing Poteau."

Chitto nodded slowly. "That makes sense, would cut off some time." He looked the older lieutenant in the eye. "I've been chasing my tail on this thing, Pete. Wondering why Bert got the call and not you."

"Wondered about that myself," Brody said. "Made me feel like I wasn't doing my job. All I could figure was it must've been my family circumstance at the time." He paused briefly. "You see, I was in and out of the office quite a bit back then. That oldest daughter of mine was having a baby, a difficult birth. Didn't think she was gonna make it, child either."

"How'd it turn out?"

"They both pulled through." As Boycott ran up, Brody wrestled the stick from his mouth and gave it another toss. "Only grandchild that daughter will give me, but that's okay. I feel lucky to have 'em both."

Chitto stared through the galvanized wire fence, hands resting on the top rail. As the autumn sun had burned off the morning haze, the air was crystal clear. Warmed by temperatures bordering on eighty, the smell of new mowed hay and alfalfa was enough to make you heady. "Another thing I can't figure out is this land dispute business," he murmured.

"Hell, yeah," Brody said again. "Since when do we get mixed up in that kind of thing—or have the time for it? I spend my days dealing with drunk and disorderly calls, abusive husbands, domestic disturbances, shoplifting, rape . . ." His voice trailed off.

"Sounds like my day."

"Something else I found puzzling was where they were found," Brody said.

"Dan had a theory about that." Chitto briefed him about the trip being partly personal, to check out a new fishing place.

"Hmm . . ." Brody paused briefly, then turned his gaze to the distant tree line. "Sam, you do realize those guys that pulled the trigger probably weren't even from around here."

"Doesn't matter who pulled the trigger," Chitto said. "I know Victor Messina was behind it."

"How?" Brody said, facing him.

Chitto leaned against the fence, arms crossed. "Last year, Wayne picked up Victor Messina's grandson, Leon, in connection with a dogfighting ring in the county. The kid had blown through a stop sign causing a hay truck to clip his rig in the rear."

"I remember that," Brody said. "Put that Messina kid in the ditch and spread stuff used in dog-fighting operations everywhere. Chains, wooden sticks, buckets . . . And inside his car was a pit bull wearing a studded collar."

"Right. Wayne tied it to another incident that a sheriff's deputy had just called in dealing with an older pit bull that had been found less than a mile away. A bait dog so far gone, it was left tied to a fence post to die. Wayne hauled Leon in and called me to assist with a lie detector test."

Brody nodded slowly. "Wayne talked to me about it. Heartbreaking how cruel some people are to animals."

"The lie detector test didn't show much," Chitto continued, "so we pushed Messina hard to see if he'd let something slip." He paused. "The kid let something slip all right, but not about dog baiting."

"Go on," Brody said, his mouth a straight line.

"I, uh, I laid pictures of a torn-up dog in front of Messina and asked him what he thought the one who was responsible deserved. He asked 'What?' And when I told him a bullet in the head . . ." Sweat beaded on Chitto's upper lip, his forehead. "The bastard laughed." Chitto paused, turning away.

"Take your time, Sam."

"Anyway," Chitto said. "Wayne asked him if he found that funny and Messina said, 'Coming from him, I do.'" He paused, looking at Brody. "Wayne didn't get it, but the kid had let slip that he knew dad and Bert were killed with a bullet to the head." He shook his head slowly. "That was confidential information not shared beyond a few and never to the press or public."

"Uh-huh," Brody murmured. "In short, how would the Messina kid have known how they were killed?"

"Right."

Brody grunted softly. "Old Messina's holed up most of the time now, somewhere over in Fort Smith. He's seeing some kind of specialist, not sure what kind. Figure it can't be good but if you're thinking he's ready to make a deathbed confession, you're delusional." He glanced at Chitto. "Maybe you and the *federales* should team up. Two heads are better than one."

"Rodriguez?" Chitto snorted. "Now who's being delusional?"

"Feds can open doors we can't."

"In your dreams. I'm assuming he was driving standard FBI transportation, a black SUV."

"Couldn't say," Brody said with a grin. "But probably. Black's supposed to be intimidating."

Chitto's snort was followed with a frown. "What about that grandson? He still around?"

"Leon? More or less. Supposed to be running the show but according to the grapevine, he's taken a liking to the stuff his grandfather pushes."

"Dope?"

"Ironic, isn't it? Since Victor's son was killed, he's raised that boy. Mother died when he was just a little guy." He shook his head. "His grandson taking up the habit has to be a hard pill to swallow."

"I call it righteous justice." Chitto paused, blinking. "Dad was hell-bent on putting Messina out of that business. You think that had anything to do with what went down?"

Bert plucked another blade of grass and chewed it slowly. "Then why'd Bert get the call? Your dad and I talked now and then about Messina's operation, but not Bert."

"Well . . ." Chitto took a minute, considering the question. "Dad was in charge of District 11. He was a lot closer to Messina country than Bert was and probably more impacted."

"Exactly my point. Bert had your job back then, way down in Red River country." Hearing a call from Molly to come to dinner, Brody motioned Chitto toward the back door. "See, that's what's confusing to me about that fishing story. There's all kinds of fishing places on the Red River and lakes galore between there and here—*big* ones. Hell, Lake Eufaula was right in Will's backyard." He looked at Chitto. "You've seen the Mayo lock and dam. What's it got that those other places don't have beat four ways to Sunday?"

Chitto glanced away, blinking. "You know, I got pretty close to Bert's wife over the years and she never mentioned that phone call once. You think Bert had the same policy as you and Dad about not involving the wife in police business?"

Brody chuckled. "Wanda was *in* the police business. She worked for the department over thirty years." He opened the door and waved Chitto inside. "Matter of fact, if the call came through on the home phone, Wanda would probably have answered it. That's the way it works around here."

Chitto followed Brody up a flight of stairs. "If that's the case, the call must've been made to Bert's cell phone."

"So? Hell, I give my number out all the time. Bet you do, too." Pausing on a landing, he turned to Chitto. "What'd Mattie say about it?"

"Mattie— My mother?"

"Think about it." Brody continued up the stairs. "Will and Bert would've been gone a couple days. Your dad might not've given Mattie the reason he'd be gone, but he would've told her something."

"Hell, yeah," Chitto mumbled. "He would have."

"Maybe Will mentioned the call to her."

"If not him . . ." Reaching the top of the stair, Chitto looked at Brody. "My mother and Wanda Gilly knew each other since grade school and were good friends up to the day Wanda died."

"Well now, that's interesting," Brody said slowly. "Seems curious neither of those gals mentioned anything about that call. Coincidence, you think?"

Chitto glanced away, an old saying coming to mind. If you believe in coincidence, then you aren't paying attention.

∞

Chitto left the Brody place a little after five with a plastic container of leftovers, compliments of Molly, and a head full of questions, compliments of Pete. He'd cautioned Brody about mentioning their conversation to Dan Blackfox, explaining the extra scrutiny the department was under. He'd left with a promise to keep Brody informed of anything he learned.

He bypassed the town of Spiro again, taking the back route to the cabin in the woods. Forty-five minutes later, he was sitting in a rocker on the back porch, listening to Boycott slurp water and staring at the number he'd pulled up on his cell phone. He knew he had to make the call, for he was out of options. The debate in his head revolved around how much to reveal, what to conceal. He pushed the Dial button.

"Hey, Mama," he said, hearing the voice on the line. "How's the reception?"

"A little staticky, but okay." Pause. "What's wrong?"

"Something doesn't have to be wrong for me to call," he said.

"Oh." Another pause. "That means you've figured out a way to get Bobby Taneyhill turned loose."

"Hold on now. I called to talk about someone else, not him."

"Who?"

"Dad." Even with crackling on the line, he recognized a sharp intake of breath.

"It's his *shilombish* again, isn't it," she said. "You're up there where he got killed and your father's ghost is trying to tell you something."

"No, it's nothing like that. It's just . . ." He exhaled slowly. "Okay, I did go to the place where it happened and it got me thinking about a couple things."

"Like what?"

"Like what he told you about the reason he and Bert came up here."

An annoyed sigh. "You know Will wouldn't talk about work stuff at home."

"But he was going to be gone a couple days this time, so he had to tell you something. Where were they planning to stay overnight? Did Dad mention the name of the person they were coming up here to see?"

Hearing nothing but static, Chitto became worried the connection had been cut. "Mom? You still there?"

"I was thinking," she said. "All Will said was he'd call me when they got settled in, but he didn't say where and he didn't mention a name."

"And he didn't call."

"No. And his cell phone was missing when they brought him home."

Chitto paused. "What about Bert's cell?"

"Was it missing, you mean? I don't know. Why?"

"Just fishing." Chitto hesitated, hoping the next question didn't open up a can of worms. "Did Wanda mention a call Bert got just before the trip?"

"No." Another pause. "How'd you know he got a call?"

Sighing, Chitto relayed the Blackfox story about the land dispute and his theory about checking out a new fishing place, cautioning her to keep the information to herself.

"Will didn't take any fishing stuff with him," she said.

"Well, he wouldn't have if they were just checking out a new place." A throbbing started up behind Chitto's eyes. "And Wanda never mentioned it."

"No . . . Now, why would she do that?"

Can of worms. "Let's start over. Tell me what you remember about that day." The line went to intermittent dead air and static. "Mama?"

"I was thinking again. Will told me about the trip when he got home from work the night before. So the next morning I packed a change of clothes for him in that little blue zipper bag he carried. Remember?"

"I do. Did he wear plain clothes or his uniform?"

"His uniform, but Bert didn't. I remember because Will was watching for him at the front window and laughed when he pulled up. He said Bert looked like a barber pole."

Chitto paused. "I don't understand."

"Bert got out of the car to clean the windshield and he was wearing a bright red windbreaker with blue and white stripes down the sleeves. Looked like one of those bargains you find at a going-out-of-business sale."

"Did Dad wear that old black jacket he'd had a coon's age?"

"Of course." A sigh came on the line. "They were a pair that day. A peacock and a crow."

"Was he wearing his service weapon?"

"Your dad? Never went without it. It was missing, too. When they brought him back, I mean."

141

"You think Bert was wearing his?"

She hesitated. "I would imagine. Even if he wasn't in uniform, he was still on duty."

Who would know a cop's routine better than a cop's wife? Chitto thought. "What time did Bert get there?"

More static, then, "About mid-morning. Will left his car here and rode with him."

Chitto rubbed his forehead as he digested the information. "What'd Bert have to say? He probably came in for a cup of coffee."

"Not this time. He just waved at me, and then . . ." The line went to dead air again.

"Mom?"

"I need a minute . . ."

Hearing the strain in her voice, Chitto swore under his breath. What had he been thinking, making this call?

"Okay, I'm back," she said. "Then Will kissed me and he was gone."

Chitto looked away, swallowing. "Sorry I brought it up, Mom."

"I'm not," she said. "That last part's the memory I hold on to. Are we through talking about Will?"

"Yeah. Let's talk about Wanda. Did you and she ever discuss things?"

"About what happened? No, we both got busy with other things. It was that or go crazy. She had her job and I decided to run for council." She paused briefly. "Wonder why she never mentioned that phone call."

"Just let it go. Blackfox probably got the story mixed up. A lot of time's passed and memories are fallible."

"Not all of them," she said softly.

He drew a breath. "I need to go now."

"Wait a minute. Tell me about the Taneyhill boy. What are you doing to help him?"

Two cans of worms. "I talked to the defense attorney today, made some suggestions. That's all I can do now that the trial's underway. It's up to the lawyers and the jury."

"What's your opinion?"

He hesitated. "Of what?"

"The outcome."

"Too early to say. The psychiatrists are testifying this week. Both the prosecution and the defense are bringing one in."

"That sounds hopeful."

He didn't respond.

"What are you thinking, Sam?"

He drew a breath. "Why don't we wait until all the evidence has been presented?"

Static again, then, "Okay. We'll talk later."

"Wait—one more question. When both you and Dad were home at night, which one of you answered the phone when it rang?"

"I did," she said. "And when I was gone, he'd let it go to the answering machine." Laughter mixed with the static came over the line. "He didn't like having to write down messages from my friends. He said they talked too much." A brief pause. "Why did you need to know that?"

"Not sure. I have to hang up now."

"Okay. Call before you leave, let us know when to look for you. I want to know about the Taneyhill boy."

Chitto stared at the dead phone in his hand, wondering what the call had accomplished.

Changing clothes, he led Boycott to the hiking trail. As he jogged behind the dog, he silently ticked off what he'd learned that day.

His father was in uniform and Bert in plain clothes, but both were armed.

They left mid-morning and did not stop in Poteau; the northern route would've gotten them to Spiro around noon, barring stops on the way.

The ME estimated their time of death early evening. In the winter, sunset occurred around five-thirty or six.

Wanda had not known about the phone call, which in all likelihood meant it had been placed to Bert's cell phone.

His father's service weapon was missing. Though not verified, Bert's gun was probably missing, too.

The findings only added other questions to a long list. What happened in those missing four to five hours? If the caller was a friend of Bert's, why didn't he call the house phone? How did he know Bert's cell number? Did Bert have his phone with him when the bodies were discovered? Missing guns were understandable, but why the phones?

Frustrated, Chitto whistled to Boycott and raced him back to the cabin. He reached the door drenched in sweat, out of breath, and out of ideas. Grabbing a bottle of water from the refrigerator, he made for one of the rockers on the back porch. Pulling the chair toward the railing, he propped his feet on the top rail and considered his options. He came up with the same one he'd been dealing with since the beginning.

And around and around we go . . .

CHAPTER THIRTEEN

Chitto looked up as a two-door silver Jeep pulled into the Spiro Mounds parking lot on Monday morning. A glance at his watch indicated it was 8:05.

"You beat me again," Mackie Green said, joining him at Interpretation Center's front door. She wore a blue ball cap, cargo shorts and baggy tee shirt, scuffed hiking boots.

"I was hoping to get a tour," he said, thinking that Mackie finally looked like an archaeologist. He'd worn clothes he hoped would help conceal his identity at the trial: boot-cut jeans, western shirt with pearl snaps, and square-toe Justin boots. His windbreaker and Stetson were in the pickup.

"Sure thing." She glanced at the unoccupied dig site. "Most of the dig team goes home on the weekends. They get back here about nine or so. I'll get the door."

"Not the Interpretation Center," he said. "Let's do the solar tour instead."

Her smile faded. "When does the trial start? The tour usually takes about two hours . . ." She paused, blinking. "Or I can give you the highlights in thirty minutes."

"That'll work. I'm more interested in the lay of the land, not details. But maybe you should lock this up first." He handed her the portfolio containing Bobby Taneyhill's latest work. "I looked through it again last night. Safer in that locked room of yours than with me. I'll wait out here with Boycott."

Taking the portfolio, she disappeared inside the Interpretative Center and returned a few minutes later. "This brochure will fill you in on the tour," she said, striking out down one of the trails. "The solar alignment occurs about sunset."

Mackie was in good shape. Chitto had to walk fast to keep up with her.

"The route's only about a mile long. It starts at the Center and winds around points of interest—like that." She pointed to a hut with a thatched roof. "It's one of the old dwellings we managed to save. We had to rebuild part of it but it gives you an idea of how the people lived. They were humble folk, but learned."

Chitto surveyed the grounds as they wound their way down walking trails. "How much land you have here."

"About 150 acres all told." She veered down another trail. "I usually talk about the Caddoans, who have been identified as the mounds builders. Then I give a little history of the place, how twelve of the mounds form a giant calendar for tracking the seasons. Those mounds were constructed to create alignments when the sun rose and set on solstice and equinox days, marking the key seasons."

"Their version of the Old Farmer's Almanac," he commented.

"Right," she said. "Their survival depended on it. It's how they knew when to plant in the spring, when to harvest in the fall, and when to begin stocking up for the dead months."

"I like their version better," he said. "How many were on the tour."

She paused, blinking. "Not sure of the exact number but quite a few There was a high-school class here, a summer science class." She glanced at him. "Maybe twenty all told?"

"And Bobby went along."

"That's right."

"He mix with the high-school kids?"

She shook her head. "He stayed at the back of the group, like always."

"Did you notice him eating a candy bar?"

"Candy bar?" She gave him another sidelong glance. "I don't remember. Why do you ask?"

He briefed her on the assumption the investigators made after finding the candy bar wrapper and Bobby's fingerprints.

She made a scoffing sound. "What does that prove? Wouldn't be the first time someone brought a snack and dropped trash on the ground." She slowed, pointing to an irregular shaped mound. "That's Craig, the burial mound. A mining company got the right to dig here some years back and tore the hell out of it. Sold off a lot of the artifacts but we've managed to get some returned. Regrettably, many others were destroyed." A deep sigh. "They used a backhoe."

"You said the tour ended at sunset. In June, that would be about eight, eight-thirty?"

"Sounds about right, but that doesn't mean it's over. There's always a few stragglers with questions—and that was especially true with that particular tour. The science teacher and students were an inquisitive bunch. It was nine or after when I left."

"What about Muriel Simpson?"

"Muriel?" Another pause. "She usually stayed till all the people were gone. Sales are good after a tour." She slowed her steps. "But I *do* remember she left before I did that night.

147

Seemed in a hurry, like she was late for something—" She glanced at him. "A date, the papers said she met her boy-friend."

He nodded. "That could help account for her leaving her key behind."

"Yes, it could," she said, nodding slowly. "She was prac-tically running when she left."

"And when did Bobby leave?"

She looked away, blinking. "I honestly don't know. He must've slipped away while I was talking to the science class." She came to a stop. "Here we are." Pointing to one of the mounds, she said, "In summer, the sun sets right over this mound."

As a tourist attraction, the mound would be considered unimposing, but as a trained scientist, Chitto admired the so-phistication behind the feat.

"It's a lot more impressive at sunset," she said as if read-ing his mind. "The light's beautiful, the sounds, too. Birds and bats are active then. And bugs, of course."

"What kind of birds?"

She hunched her shoulders. "The usual. Mockingbirds. Whippoorwills. Sometimes a heron."

"Ever hear any owls . . . screech owls?"

She frowned slightly. "A little early in the evening for owls, but yes, occasionally." She turned quickly, facing him. "You're thinking of what Bobby said."

"Right." He looked across the grassy meadow toward the Walker place. "I've spent a lot of time outdoors, including camping out nights, and I have to say I don't remember hear-ing a screech owl more than once or twice. Most people wouldn't even know one when they heard it."

"I don't know, it's pretty distinctive." She paused, blinking. "To me, it sounds like a horse's whinny. Easy to identify if you're lucky enough to hear one, but they are elusive little buggers. We hear hoot owls mostly."

Hearing a vehicle, Chitto glanced toward the parking lot, which was filling up with people. "Looks like the dig team's here and I need to get to Poteau." He paused, rubbing the back of his neck. "Not sure when the trial will end today. I'll pick Boycott up soon as I can."

"No hurry. Want to grab a bite later? I'd like to hear how the trial went."

"Yeah . . ." He nodded, looking thoughtful. "That just might work."

"Work for what?" she said, her brow creasing.

"I need to check out that place Muriel Simpson met up with her boyfriend."

"The Four Corners Bar?" She laughed. "*Great.* There's a small dance floor and it's Monday—Karaoke night."

Pete Brody's words about Mackie Green being a liberated woman echoing in his ears, Chitto raised his eyebrows. His surprise, however, came from learning she frequented the same bar as Muriel Simpson.

A coincidence? he wondered.

You don't believe in coincidences, whispered the voice in his head.

"Thing is," he said. "I don't dance and I definitely don't karaoke."

"Then you can fill me in on the trial." She held out a hand, palm up. "I need something to write on."

Awkwardly, he fumbled a pen and business card from his pocket. As she wrote down her address, he asked the question that was now needling him.

"Where were you the night Muriel Simpson was killed?"

"What—" She looked up at him.

"The night of the murder," he said. "Were you at the bar that night?"

"No," she said slowly. "I wasn't."

He waited.

Exhaling loudly, she said, "Jeez, you cops— I had an alibi, okay? A date, who I would rather not involve. We, uh, we stayed close to home that night. I learned about Muriel the next morning at work."

He lifted a hand. "Just doing my job."

"I know," she grumbled. She returned the card and pen to him." Pick me up at my place. After digging all day, I'll need to clean up." She gave him a quick up-and-down look. "No need to change. What you're wearing is good. The boys around here don't take to dudes."

She turned, glancing at the group walking toward the dig site, a scruffy-looking, sun-baked bunch led by a man wearing a floppy hat. "I need to catch up with Frank," she said, taking Boycott's leash. "He's the professor in charge."

Chitto watched as she joined the others, assessing her comments. He was satisfied her alibi was solid, for he'd seen through the elusive-sounding response she provided. In short, she'd had an overnight guest the night Muriel Simpson was killed.

One suspect crossed off the list.

Quickly, he returned to the Interpretation Center where Muriel Simpson was attacked. Studying the contour of the ground, he followed the direction the body would've been dragged and stopped between two large cottonwoods where low branches hung over the walking path. Native grasses grew on either side, one and two foot high but not tall enough to completely hide a body.

Conclusion? The body wasn't dragged there to hide it. It had been deliberately moved to shield the killer's tracks.

As Chitto walked toward his truck, his eyes were drawn to the worn footpath leading across a grassy field. He paused at a vantage point, following the path across the meadow to the fence line separating Spiro Mounds from the Walker place. On the other side of the fence, a tall man stood watching him. Charlie Walker didn't miss much, he thought as he continued to his truck. For some reason, that thought made him uneasy.

∞

Chitto let out a low whistle as pulled into the courthouse parking lot in Poteau. Recently renovated, the facility was impressive. Pete Brody had told him it now measured a 100,000 square feet and was comprised of a 190-bed detention center, the sheriff's office, and an expanded three-story county office annex. The annex housed the county offices, including the County Commissioner, District Attorney, Clerks Office, a county courtroom, and a hearing courtroom. Justice was big business in LeFlore County.

He spent several minutes looking for an empty parking space. Though he passed several SUVs, he did not spot a black one, the FBI's vehicle of choice. That absence made him breathe easier. Maybe Rodriguez had left town.

Finding an empty space on the last row, he locked his waist holster in the glove box and fitted his Stetson low over his eyes. Assessing the wisdom of leaving a rifle and shotgun in a vehicle so close to the sheriff's department, he'd left them locked in the cabin. Hurrying inside the building, he lined up to go through security check. Noticing a posted sign about turning off cell phones, he pulled his from his pocket and shut it down. Once through security check, he followed signs to the courtroom and pushed through the door.

The courtroom was typical. A wooden barrier, called the bar, divided the large room. On one side was the judge's bench, bailiff and recorder's tables, the jury box, and the defense and prosecution tables. An open space in front of the bench and jury box, called the well, could not be crossed without permission. The spectators' gallery occupied the other half of the room, in this case, an elevated tier of rows lined with padded seats.

Surveying the gallery, Chitto identified reporters near the front, wearing professional dress and holding pens and notebooks. Stetsons and western boots filled the other sections. The locals. A man on the aisle with a military haircut and wearing a button-down shirt drew his eye. Bernard Wasilewski. Because Susan Dayton had reserved the right to recall witnesses, the former Navy corpsman would be in court until the trial ended. As would Buster Littlejohn, Muriel Simpson's boyfriend.

Chitto looked around as he started up the steps, trying to identify Littlejohn, but the number of men in Stetsons made it impossible. Reaching the top row, he took a seat where he would be inconspicuous yet have a clear view of the action, and especially Bobby Taneyhill. Sitting down, he perched his hat on one knee and listened to the nervous hum of whispers. Spotting a boisterous man in western gear backslapping his peers, he smiled.

Cassius was present and accounted for.

The room grew quiet as Charlie Walker entered. He wore a suit coat with oversized shoulder pads, wide tie, slacks that bagged at the knee, and an expression that said he felt as out of place as his outfit. Looking neither right nor left, he proceeded to a seat near the defense table that had been reserved for him. He paused before sitting, looking over the spectators in the gallery. Finding Chitto, he nodded.

That nod spoke reams. Chitto nodded in return, deducing that defensive attorney Susan Dayton had briefed Walker on the meeting at Pete Brody's the previous day. Chitto was now considered a part of the team. Feeling curious eyes of others on him, he was glad the defense and prosecuting attorneys chose that moment to enter the bar.

Dayton had worn three-inch platform heels to increase her height and a navy blue suit to project a professional image. Montgomery Powell—Monty, for short—didn't need an aid to height or image. The attorney was tanned, around six foot two, and fit. That much was evident in the way a dark suit fit broad shoulders and slim hips and the way he lounged in his chair at the prosecution table. All smiles and sunshine.

A bantam hen and the cock of the walk.

Chitto turned his attention to Bobby Taneyhill. He had trailed Dayton into the courtroom wearing the same garb he wore in the newspaper picture, right down to the clip-on tie. About five foot seven or eight and of slight build, the teenager stared straight ahead as if not seeing anything around him. The look on his face was unreadable.

A blank face . . .

The seat he'd chosen allowed Chitto to see the boy's profile and, to a degree, his facial expressions. No matter how brief, facial expressions appeared in response to emotions experienced.

As do microexpressions, he thought.

These expressions occurred when a person was consciously trying to conceal signs of how they were feeling, but they were difficult or impossible to hide. They typically occurred when people had something to lose, and this trial was definitely a high-stakes situation for Bobby Taneyhill. Unable to see the boy's full face, he would have to study the minutest of changes, but he had experience with such situations. He had instigated lie detection tests in the Nation and not only watched when they were administered but often assisted with the interpretations.

Chitto studied the boy now, eying his posture. His body was stiff and his head erect but there was no sense he was breathing. Like a scared rabbit, he reflected. When rabbits were threatened, they froze in place. A defensive move.

What are you, Bobby, he wondered. Predator or prey?

It was going on ten o'clock by the time the jury was seated, an even mix of men and women and a decent combination of white, black, Latino, and Native American. As the bailiff's voice shattered the hum in the room, Chitto stood with the others when ordered to rise. With aplomb, Alonzo Knapp, District Judge for the 16th Judicial District took the bench. A gray-haired man in imposing black robe, Knapp quickly reminded the jury of its responsibilities, then got things rolling.

Immediately, Susan Dayton took the floor. "If it pleases the court," she said. "I would like to recall the medical examiner." She checked her notes. "Mr. Wallace Murdock."

"Objection," the prosecution responded. "He's provided all relevant testimony."

Walking as close to the judge as was permitted, Dayton said, "There are facts that need to be clarified, your Honor."

"I'll allow," Knapp said.

A middle-aged man in a rumpled suit made his way down the tiered steps and took the stand. As there was no need for him to be sworn in again, Dayton moved briskly to her point.

"You've already established that you're an experienced medical examiner, Mr. Murdock. You've examined hundreds, if not thousands, of bodies and wounds perpetrated on those bodies. Would you please describe the way in which the nipples on Muriel Simpson were removed." A buzz filled the courtroom.

The ME stared at her. "They were, uh, they were cut off," he stammered. The buzz in the courtroom morphed into laughter.

Unfazed, Dayton pushed ahead. "Yes, you've testified to that. My question deals with exactly how that was achieved. Was it done using a hatchet . . . a pocket knife . . . a scalpel?"

"Leading the witness—" Monty Powell jumped to his feet. "And I fail to see the relevance of the question."

"Everything's relevant in a murder trial," Judge Knapp said. He looked at Dayton. "Rephrase your question, Counselor."

Dayton centered herself in front of the ME. "Would you describe the *appearance* of the wounds?"

Wallace Murdock paused, thinking. "Well, the skin wasn't badly torn or the cuts that jagged, so I'd say a sharp instrument was used."

"Take your time," Dayton said patiently. "Be as explicit as possible."

Murdock paused again, eyes squinting as if he was calling something to mind. "Small cuts encircling each nipple, severing the flesh and connective tissue underneath."

"What would be the purpose of making that kind of incision?" Dayton said, pacing the open space in front of the well.

Murdock turned thoughtful again. "I'd say it was so the nipples would come off easy."

Dayton stopped in front of the witness again. "What kind of proficiency would be required to do that?"

The ME committed more time to thinking. "Someone accustomed to using a really sharp knife, like a . . . a scalpel."

"Thank you." She turned to the judge. "That's all for this witness at this time."

"Care to redirect, Mr. Powell," the judge asked.

"No, sir. Not right now."

Chitto watched Bobby Taneyhill as the ME returned to the gallery. Hands folded in his lap, the boy stared straight ahead. Throughout the questioning, he'd remained deadpan and his body language displayed little to nothing about what was going on in his head.

Scared to death? Chitto wondered. In a state of shock?

After Murdock returned to his seat in the gallery, Dayton addressed the bench. "Permission to approach." When Knapp granted the request, she walked a document to him, then delivered a copy to Monty Powell at the prosecution table. Turning to face the bench, she said, "I now request that Dewey Poindexter be called, testifying as an expert in his field"

"*Object*," Powell said, flipping through the document. "Why wasn't I informed of this witness?"

"You just were," Dayton said briskly. She turned to the judge again. "Mr. Poindexter's expertise is critical to arriving at a fair and just decision."

Chitto smiled. Banty Hen was showing Rooster she had spurs, too.

Adjusting his bifocals, the judge began scanning the document she'd handed him. As the minutes passed, the crowded gallery began to fidget, then murmur.

"Quiet," the judge yelled, looking across the room. "This court's still in session."

Another minute passed as he resumed reading. When done, he looked over his glasses at Monty Powell. "I'll allow. I'm interested in seeing where this is going."

Dewey Poindexter's bearing alone demanded respect. He was probably better than six foot in his youth, but age and injury had robbed him of a few inches. He strode to the witness stand wearing a dark brown shirt buttoned to the neck, a western sports coat, and khaki pants. His boots were square toe Tony Lamas and he carried a brown felt Stetson. After the swearing in, he sat down in the witness chair, crossed one ankle over a knee, and perched the Stetson on the bent leg. He nodded politely as Susan Dayton approached.

Chitto smiled, the little defense attorney had followed up on the lead Pete Brody had given her. The man in the witness chair was a stockman.

Dayton took time to establish that Poindexter's family had been pioneer settlers in LeFlore County and that he had run a ranch for the last fifty years.

"Would you describe the tasks you perform as a stockman, Mr. Poindexter?"

The rancher brushed thinning hair off of a forehead a wide-brimmed hat kept pale. "The usual things when it comes to livestock," he said. The list included feeding, watering, herding, grooming, weighing, catching, and loading cattle and horses.

"A big job." Dayton paced as she talked. "What about personal care of the animals?"

"Well, ma'am, we clip 'em, trim 'em, shoe 'em. Castrate those that need it, dock ears and tails, and mark 'em to identify ownership and grade."

"What about caring for sick animals? Your ranch is a long way from the vet."

157

"'Bout forty miles as the crow flies. We treat minor ailments ourselves, administer medications, vaccinations, insecticides as needed."

She came to a stop before him. "Describe the treatment of a minor ailment."

"Minor?" He thought a minute. "I guess removing bots would fall into that bucket."

"Bots?' she said, frowning.

"Larvae," he said. "Botflies lay eggs under the skin, the eggs hatch into larvae and leave a pocket that can get infected."

Observing the shocked expression on Susan Dayton's face, Chitto chuckled. She'd had no idea what a bot was. Now, she did.

Recovering quickly, the petite defense attorney asked, "Do you surgically remove these larvae?"

"No, ma'am. As a rule, we squeeze 'em out. They're nothing more than a big maggot, you see. The larva needs to come out so it can finish developing into a botfly. To do that, it makes a hole in the skin of the animal. If the time is right, you can squeeze the larva out the hole." He used his fingers to demonstrate the squeezing method, and finished with, "Then we squash 'em."

The gallery erupted in laughter, which Judge Knapp quickly brought to order.

"Your Honor—" Monty Powell jumped his feet. "This is nothing but a ploy to delay the trial."

Knapp peered at him over his glasses. "I'll be the judge of that, Mr. Powell." He waved a hand at Susan Dayton, giving her permission to proceed. She did.

"Let's move on to marking. How's that accomplished?"

Poindexter blinked a few times. "Variety of methods. Brands, tags, paint, tattoos."

"Tattoos," Dayton said, pausing. "How are those done? Are they cut into the skin—"

"Leading the witness," Powell yelled, jumping to his feet.

"Sustained," the judge said. "Rephrase, Counselor."

Dayton faced Dewey Poindexter again. "Describe the manner in which a tattoo is applied to an animal."

Poindexter complied, describing how a pair of pliers was used to make sharp, needle-like projections into the skin. Tattoo ink forced into the punctures remained visible after the puncture wounds healed. "On cattle and horses, tattoos are usually letters or numbers on the ears," he said, fingering an earlobe.

"Thank you," Dayton said. Walking to the defense table, she glanced at her notes, then faced the witness again. "You mentioned castration. Would you please describe how that procedure is done?"

Monty Powell jumped to his feet again. Alonzo Knapp beat him to the punch.

"Sit down, Mr. Powell. You keep interrupting this witness, and we'll be here all day." He looked at Dayton. "Proceed."

"Would you describe how castration is done, Mr. Poindexter?" she said, repeating the question.

"Depends on whether you band, use a Burdizzo pincher, or cut."

She nodded. "Which method do you use, Mr. Poindexter?"

"I prefer cutting," he said. "It's the most dependable."

Dayton stopped dead center of the witness stand. "Would you describe what's involved in that method?"

Poindexter hesitated, looking at the judge. "There's ladies present, Judge."

Alonzo Knapp smiled at Poindexter. "I appreciate your concern but ladies aren't the delicate creatures they once were. Please answer the question."

Resettling his Stetson on his knee, the rancher went into a detailed description on castrating a bull calf. The first step involved restraining the animal, followed by ensuring conditions and instruments were sterile.

"The whole area's washed in antiseptic soap," Poindexter said. "When you're sure everything's clean as you can make it, you remove the lower third of the scrotum, exposing the testicles." Using both hands, he demonstrated the slicing method. "Then you slit the membrane covering each testicle and pull out the testes."

"I see," Dayton said coolly. "Is it safe to say that you make small cuts encircling each testicle, severing the flesh and connective tissue for easy removal?"

The gallery as a whole caught its breath and Chitto gave Susan Dayton a look of admiration. She had just paraphrased the medical examiner's words. With the others, he awaited Poindexter's answer.

"Yes, ma'am," he responded. "I'd say that about covers it."

Dayton paced some more. "You mentioned sterilization of the instruments was critical. Tell us what those instruments are."

Poindexter rubbed a hand across his mouth. "Sharp knife or scalpel's the tool of choice, though some use an emasculator."

"Scalpel," she repeated. "And do you personally attend to this procedure on your ranch?"

Poindexter chuckled. "Ma'am, I run hundreds of heads of cattle. My ranch hands take care of it."

She stopped abruptly, looking at him. "*Any* ranch hand can do it?"

"Nope, not all. But if he's worth his salt, he can. If he isn't, he doesn't work for me."

Nodding, she walked toward the jury box. "And tell us, Mr. Poindexter," she said, talking to the witness over her shoulder. "How long has Buster Littlejohn worked for you?"

A loud murmur rose from the gallery.

"Quiet in the court," Knapp said, giving his gavel a bang. He turned to the witness. "Answer the question, Mr. Poindexter."

The rancher rubbed his bottom lip, thinking. "Off and on, I'd say fifteen years."

Dayton stood before him again. "And can you verify that Mr. Littlejohn knows how to use these instruments."

"Yes ma'am, I can."

"And have you witnessed him performing this . . . delicate procedure."

"I can," he repeated.

Facing the judge, she said, "No more questions for this witness."

Turning to the prosecution, Knapp said, "Care to cross, Mr. Powell?"

"Not at this time," he sighed.

"You're dismissed, Mr. Poindexter," the judge said. Glancing at a clock on the wall, he looked at both attorneys. "After that stimulating testimony, I'm inclined to break for lunch." He looked at Susan Dayton. "Are you planning to introduce any more *surprise* witnesses, Miss Dayton?"

"No sir," she said. "But I will be recalling some who've been on the stand."

"We'll resume at one-thirty," Knapp said, dismissing the jury. As he rose and left the room, the spectators were given their leave.

Chitto stood aside, avoiding the rush of people hurrying toward the door. The nervous hum in the room had become a low roar. The gallery wasn't the only place buzzing. Pushing his way to the front, Buster Littlejohn now leaned over the bar, huddling with the prosecuting attorney. Still, his voice carried like he was using a megaphone.

"She's making me out to be a *monster*," Littlejohn hissed, pointing to Susan Dayton. Monty Powell wrapped an arm around Littlejohn's shoulder, trying to quiet him.

A life in ashes, Chitto thought.

The reverse was taking place at the defense council's table. Walker and Susan Dayton were involved in a confab of their own but Dayton was doing the talking. Walker, looking much relieved, nodded now and then.

Chitto turned his attention to Bobby Taneyhill. The teenager had risen to his feet, waiting for the guard to escort him back to the holding cell. His face impassive, the boy stood with hands hanging loosely by his side, eyes darting between the defense and prosecution's table. It was the only observable movement he'd witnessed in the boy.

Like his grandfather, Chitto thought, Bobby didn't miss much,

CHAPTER FOURTEEN

Chitto glanced at a wall clock as he exited the courtroom. Judge Alonzo Knapp had set a time of one thirty for the trial to resume. It was now a quarter to twelve. Rather than give up his parking place, he decided to walk to lunch. For advice on local eateries, he checked in with the security guards at the courthouse entrance.

"The Warehouse," the male guard replied immediately. "They make a mean burger."

Chitto gave a quick nod. "My kind of place."

"Except they're closed on Mondays," said a young female guard. "But the drive-in right around the corner's a local fave. It's not a chain and their specialty's deep-fried green beans. There's some tables outside where you can eat."

"I'll give it a try."

With directions firmly in mind, Chitto walked toward Broadway, which happened to be the name of the main street in Poteau just as it was in Spiro. A few turns later, he found the place. The drive-in was a Sonic knock-off but shaded picnic tables in the back offered fresh air and privacy. Walking to the window, he ordered a cheeseburger, the fried green beans, and a large iced tea. Sweet.

Within minutes, he was handed a plastic basket containing burger and fries, a waxed cup with a straw protruding

163

from the top, and a handful of sugar packets. Dodging incoming and departing cars, he made it safely to the outermost table. Setting his hat down crown first on the table, he sank onto the bench seat. He was unwrapping the burger when a shadow fell across the table. Remembering he'd left his revolver in the truck's glove box, he tensed.

The wiry man that looked down on him was a shade under six feet, wore an unbuttoned shirt over a black tee, and stonewashed jeans. A straw Stetson allowed a forelock of straight dark hair to straggle down. Ray-ban sunglasses hid his eyes.

"Well hell, Raymond" Chitto said, ripping open a sugar packet. "I heard you were in town." He noticed a gold chain around Rodriguez's neck, the shape of a cross clearly recognizable under his T-shirt, and a bulge at the waistline that wasn't belly fat. "That's not your usual outfit. Working undercover?"

"Been up here a while," Rodriguez said. "Clothes are at the laundry."

Chitto gave him another up and down. "I gotta say, Raymond, these suit you."

He considered the FBI to be a cult of self, having observed over the years that most agents held themselves above those who worked in local, state, or tribal jurisdictions. Ramon Rodriguez epitomized that attitude to a T. Casual dress for him was a sports coat, tie, and shoes buffed to a shine. And always, the Ray-bans.

Rodriguez set a plastic basket and waxed cup on the table. "Can we skip the name game?" He was referring to Chitto's habit of deliberately mispronouncing his first name, Ramon, just to goad him. "How about we settle for Ray. I figure it's the least you can do since I'm busting my *pompis* trying to solve your father and his partner's murder." Placing his Stetson next to Chitto's, the Ray-bans next to it, he plopped down across from Chitto.

Chitto took in the sweat under the FBI agent's armpits, the scar along the side of his cheek, the weary look in his eyes. "I go by Sam," he said, sampling the fried green beans.

Rodriguez paused, eying Chitto's basket. "What the hell are those things?"

"French-fried beans." He scooted the basket across the table. "Go ahead, live a little."

Rodriguez declined with a headshake. "I'll stick to fried spuds."

Chitto grinned. "I figure anything breaded and deep fried can't be bad. I bet fried green caterpillars would even taste good. Go on, give 'em a try." Again, he shoved the basket toward Rodriquez.

Unamused, the agent shoved the basket back to him. "Who told you I was in town?"

"Pete Brody. Sounds like you're plowing old ground. Turn up anything new?"

Rodriquez answered with another headshake.

Chitto made a grunting sound. "*Nada?*"

"So far, but I'm still checking. Lots of turnover in this business." He eyed Chitto. "I suppose you're pursuing your own investigation, even if it's not your jurisdiction. Seems you like to do that."

"Nope. Here on another matter."

Rodriguez stirred a packet of sugar into his tea. "That trial that's going on?"

"Yep." Chitto paused to chew a mouthful of burger. "I hear you checked out the local boys. Tribal police, the county and town cops." He looked at Rodriguez. "What about your own kind?"

"Lots of turnover," Rodriguez repeated. Fingering French fries into his mouth, he mumbled, "That mean you're not checking into *my* case?"

Chitto looked away, rubbing grease off his mouth with a paper napkin. "Sorry to say, it does." He looked at Rodriguez directly. "But I've been wondering about a few things."

"Such as," Rodriguez said, fingering more fries.

Chitto drummed his fingers on the table, wondering if Rodriguez could get him off the merry-go-round he'd been riding. The way things were going, he wasn't going to get off it by himself.

"Here's the deal, Ray." Chitto made eye contact. "I tell you what I know, you don't mention I'm your source . . . and you keep me in the loop."

Rodriguez paused long enough to take a swig of tea. "Deal. What do you have?"

"A phone call. I have it on good information that a call from someone up here is what set up that trip my dad and Bert made. Something about a land-transaction dispute. And the call probably came through on Bert's cell phone. Any mention of that in the files?"

Rodriguez looked away, blinking. "What kind of land transaction?"

"Don't waste your time. It's a dead end."

Rodriguez let out a snort. "Thought you weren't sticking your nose in my case."

Chitto grinned, then turned serious. "It's this phone call that's got me puzzled. No one seems to know anything about it."

Rodriguez finished off his burger. "I'll check the files. That all you've got?"

"Only thing solid."

The FBI agent stared at him. "Talk about what's not."

Chitto wadded napkins and greasy wrappers into a ball. "Missing weapons—at least my dad's was missing so I'm assuming Bert's was, too. And my dad didn't have his cell phone on him when he was found. Not sure about Bert's."

Rodriguez shrugged. "You sure your dad had it with him?" He followed suit, balling up his soiled napkins and greasy wrapper.

"He was supposed to call and let my mother know where they'd be putting up for the night. He didn't."

Rodriguez paused, blinking. "My guess is weapons and phones ended up in the Arkansas. That river's deep there by the dam . . ." He paused again. "And awfully convenient."

Chitto ruminated on this as he finished his tea. "Too late to drag it, I suppose. Sure like to locate Bert's phone."

"Hell, if anything's down there, it's buried in mud so deep we'd never find it. Even if we did, probably wouldn't reveal anything. All kinds of ways to disable a cell phone. Remove the GPS chip to avoid your location being tracked, take out the battery and SIM card so you can't be found . . ." He waved a hand, indicating there were too many to enumerate.

Chitto nodded slowly. "But was Bert Gilly enough of a nerd to know those things?"

Rodriguez considered this, then reached for his hat. "Trial's resuming soon. You've got my number."

Picking up the trash he'd balled up, Chitto made a mark on the ground, took a pitcher's stance, and threw it toward an open trash barrel. The ball landed in the dirt.

"Low and outside," Rodriguez said, eyeing the throw. "How long you be in town?" Toeing the mark on the ground, he assumed a similar stance and landed his ball dead center of the barrel.

"You've pitched," Chitto said, eyeing Rodriguez. "Where?"

"Sandlot, then UTPA."

Things fell into place. The rumor was that Rodriguez had been part of a gang along the Rio Grande. Chitto had doubted the rumor because it made no sense. Gang members didn't change affiliations if they valued their lives. But the University of Texas-Pan American was a state school in the Rio Grande Valley. Deep South Texas. Maybe someone had been a positive influence. A coach or . . . He eyed the gold chain again. A priest.

"Let me guess," he said. "Criminal Justice."

Rodriguez replied with a half-smile. "You?" he asked, slipping on the Ray-bans.

"OU. Criminal Justice and Geology." He grinned. "I like options." Retrieving his trash from the ground, he deposited it in the barrel. "Don't know how long I'll be here," he added, replying to the FBI agent's previous question. "Depends on how long this trial lasts. Couple more days, I expect."

"Need a ride?" Rodriguez nodded toward a black SUV across the lot. "I'm spending my afternoon in the sheriff's department. Courthouse is on the way."

"Thanks, but walking clears my head."

Rodriguez nodded. "Keep it out of the dirt," he said over his shoulder.

Chitto smiled at the comment. The coach of his baseball team used to give him the same advice. He suspected Rodriquez's meaning was entirely different. Still, as he began the return walk to the courthouse, he had the sense the merry-go-round he'd been riding just might've slowed a little.

∞

Afternoon temperatures and a shoulder-to-shoulder crowd hiked the temperatures in the courtroom ten degrees. A hard-working air conditioner failed to dispel the aroma of body odor and manure embedded in the soles of boots. By the time the first witness was called, the back of Chitto's shirt had stuck to the chair. The only person who appeared unaffected was Bobby Taneyhill, who projected the same frozen face and posture as before.

The bartender, Chitto thought, watching Mick Weddle take the stand. Susan Dayton was going down the list they'd discussed on Sunday at Pete Brody's place. Again, the prosecuting attorney, Monty Powell, protested. Again, Judge Knapp overrode the protest.

Weddle was a barrel-chested man with dark hair and five-o'clock shadow, the kind that was permanent on some men. Eyeing the square, blocky man, Chitto ventured he also doubled as the bouncer at the Four Corners Bar.

"In your previous testimony," Dayton said, "you mentioned Muriel Simpson and Buster Littlejohn got into a confrontation that night they met at your place. Is that correct?"

"'At's right. Got so loud, couple at the next table moved away."

"So, the two were talking loud."

"'At's right."

"What was the cause of their disagreement?"

Weddle hunched beefy shoulders. "Couldn't say."

Dayton looked at him pointedly. "Do you have a hearing problem, Mr. Weddle?"

Weddle blinked a few times. "I can hear just fine."

"Good," Dayton said, smiling pleasantly. "Then what did you hear?"

Weddle squirmed in his chair. "Well, seems Muriel was late and . . ." He shrugged. "It's a bar, so Buster started drinking. By the time she got there, he'd had a few. He was mad 'cause she was late and she was mad 'cause he'd been drinking."

She paused briefly. "Did you witness Mr. Littlejohn fall at any time that night?"

Weddle glanced toward the gallery, eyes settling on Littlejohn. "Yeah, Buster did take a fall."

"From alcohol consumption?"

"Naw," Weddle said, shaking his head. "Buster can hold his liquor. I think maybe he just stood up too fast or tripped."

Dayton pursed her lips. "So, he wasn't what you'd term falling-down drunk?"

"Objection," Monty Powell called out. "Calls for an opinion."

After Knapp sustained the motion, Dayton faced Weddle again. "Part of a bartender's job is to know when to cut customers off. Is that correct, Mr. Weddle?"

"'At's right," The bartender said. "If they're regulars, we know when they've hit their limit."

"Was Mr. Littlejohn a regular customer, Mr. Weddle?"

He hesitated slightly. "Comes in once or twice a week after he gets off work. Weekends, too."

"A regular customer," she said. "And did you cut him off the particular evening we're discussing?"

Weddle blinked a few times. "Not as I can remember."

"Inconclusive, Judge," Powell said, sounding tired.

"I withdraw the question," she said, resuming her pacing. "What are your busiest nights of the week, Mr. Weddle?"

Weddle paused, blinking at the sudden change in direction. "That'd, uh, that'd be Friday and Saturday."

"I believe that argument took place on a Saturday night." She checked her notes. "Yes, it was." She looked at him again. "And you also testified that Mr. Littlejohn was there at closing time."

"One of the last ones to leave," Weddle confirmed.

"And did you have eyes on him the *entire* evening?"

Weddle sat back in the witness chair, staring at her. "Well, I wasn't looking right at him the whole time, if that's what you're asking."

"I'm asking if you can say with absolute certainty that Buster Littlejohn could not have slipped out on one of the busiest nights of the week and return before closing time . . . without you seeing him."

Weddle swallowed. "Well, no, not absolutely."

"No more questions, your Honor."

Chitto eyed the jury. Cages were starting to shake. Bobby Taneyhill, on the other hand, seemed as unfazed as ever.

The judge looked toward the prosecution's table. "Mr. Powell? Do you wish to cross-examine or shall we move on."

Powell waved a hand through the air. "Move on," he muttered.

The judge turned at defense table "Your move, Miss Dayton."

∞

171

Bernard Wasilewski was the odd duck in the pond, in deportment and appearance. Susan Dayton's redirect served to underscore the obvious.

"I believe you're originally from Detroit," she said, glancing at a packet of papers she held. "And in the last few years, you've also lived in Seattle and Houston."

A frown etched Wasilewski's forehead. "That's right," he said slowly.

He's not comfortable with her digging up his past, Chitto thought. Why?

"You're a long way from home for a city boy." She smiled amiably. "How long have you lived in Spiro?"

He turned aside briefly, thinking. "Little over two years now."

"And you've lived in the same apartment building that entire time, the same one that Muriel Simpson lived in?"

"It's the only place I've lived since I moved here," he said. "And yes, Miss Simpson lived there, too."

"Miss Simpson?" Dayton took a spot in front of him. "Seems unusual to use such a formal address for a friend."

The frown reappeared. "I wouldn't say we were friends."

"No?" Dayton began to pace. "And yet, Miss Simpson felt comfortable confiding to you that she was going back to the gift shop to retrieve her keys." She gave him a quick glance. "You testified that you ran into her when you took out the trash that night, then went back inside to finish cleaning your apartment. Is that correct?"

"That's right."

"Can anyone confirm that, Mr. Wasilewski?"

Wasilewski followed Susan Dayton as she continued her incessant pacing. "I'm, uh . . . ." He paused, rubbing his mouth. "I'm not understanding the question."

Like hell, Chitto thought, studying the ex-corpsman. He understood the question perfectly. He just didn't like what it was implying.

"Did anyone else see you and Miss Simpson talking?" Dayton stopped in front of the witness chair. "See you go back inside the apartment building?"

Wasilewski raised a hand, let it drop. "I didn't see anyone else."

Dayton began pacing again. "Is your apartment the only place you ever saw Simpson?"

Noticing Wasilewski wipe sweat from his upper lip, Chitto frowned. Wherever it was, he didn't like where Dayton was taking him.

"Uh, no," Wasilewski said. "She came into the clinic a couple times for treatment. I work there part-time."

Dayton stopped to look at him again, head cocked slightly. "What kind of treatment?"

A long pause. "Well, as I recall, a sprained ankle once . . . a scrape on her arm another time."

"And you treated her?"

"They were minor problems. A doctor wasn't required."

"And you were able to provide treatment because you retired out of the Navy as a hospital corpsman . . ." A quick look at her notes. "Between two and three years ago."

He concurred with a nod.

"And where did you serve?"

Almost inaudibly, Wasilewski listed places both stateside and overseas.

"You left out the Middle East," Dayton said, checking her notes. "So you administered medical aid to those serving

173

in Afghanistan and Iraq." She frowned. "But don't corpsmen serve in hospitals or on ships?"

"I was attached to the Marines."

"Meaning you were on the ground with the troops."

He nodded again.

Pausing, Dayton removed her glasses and looked him in the eye. "Before we proceed, I'd like to thank you for your service, Mr. Wasilewski."

An apology? Chitto inhaled quickly. Oh, hell. She was going to crucify him.

Donning the glasses again, Dayton checked her notes. "According to records, you retired before you reached your fortieth birthday." She set her notes aside. "You must've joined young."

Wasilewski shrugged. "I was about twenty-two."

She paused, blinking. "And you drew a full pension?"

"No . . . partial."

Chitto noticed a sheen on Wasilewski's forehead. Why did this line of questioning have him sweating?

"*How* partial? I believe twenty years is required for a military pension."

"I was short a couple years."

"Why was that?"

Wasilewski rubbed back of his hand across his mouth. "Hypertension."

She frowned. "I'm not a medical expert, but I believe that's extreme psychological stress." A question phrased as a comment.

He nodded.

"And how does one get a disability from psychological stress?"

He rubbed his mouth again. "It can cause high blood pressure, which can result in dizziness, palpitations . . . headaches."

"And was this hypertension so severe you were unable to perform your duties?"

He licked his lips. "I was shipped back to the states for some R&R."

"R&R?" Tilting her head, she said, "Wouldn't therapy be more accurate?"

He swallowed. "I, uh, I did go to some therapy sessions. After that, I . . . Well, I decided it was a good time to retire."

"I see." She began to pace again. "Is that why you moved to Spiro? Because you needed more R&R?"

"I liked the place. It's . . . it was quiet."

"Much quieter than big cities and war zones, I imagine. Tell me, did you suffer these symptoms before you entered the service?"

"No."

"So basically, you mustered out early and received a partial disability . . ." She stood in front of him, hands clasped behind her back. "Because you were unfit for duty."

"*Object*," Monty Powell shouted.

Alonzo Knapp looked between Dayton and Powell. "Approach the bench, Counselors."

As a body, the gallery leaned forward. Chitto shook his head, amazed that judges and attorneys thought these sidebar conversations would go unheard.

"Where's this line of questioning going, Miss Dayton?" Though little more than a whisper, Judge Knapp's words were clearly audible.

Dayton's response was no less private. "I'm attempting to clarify opportunity and motive for the jury, your Honor. Mr. Wasilewski has suffered bouts of mental instability. In addition, he has expertise with medical instruments—such as scalpels—and he was privy to the fact Muriel Simpson left her apartment key at the Spiro Mounds gift shop." She paused. "In other words, in all likelihood, he was the last person to see Muriel Simpson alive."

"Other than the killer," Powell snapped. He jerked his head toward Bobby Taneyhill.

"*Councilors*—" Judge Knapp hissed. Sighing, he rubbed fingertips across his lips, then turned to Susan Dayton. "I believe you've made your point, Miss Dayton. Dismiss the witness."

Dayton's sigh reverberated around the room. Returning to her table, she faced the bench and said, "No more questions for this witness."

"*Cross-examine*," Monty Powell said, jumping to his feet. Facing the jury box, he talked to the witness over his shoulder. "Were you honorably discharged, Mr. Wasilewski?"

"Yes, sir. I was."

"He was honorably discharged," Powell said, making eye contact with the jurors. Walking toward the prosecution table, he said, "No more questions."

Knapp looked at the witness. "You're dismissed, Mr. Wasilewski. And may I voice Miss Dayton's sentiment about being grateful for your service."

Too late, Chitto thought, reading the jury. Cages had been rattled.

Turning to the prosecutor, Judge Knapp ordered the next witness called.

Monty Powell took his feet, looking apologetic. "The psychiatrist that's to testify has been delayed. His flight from California was late into Fort Smith. He won't land for another thirty, forty minutes."

The judge looked at Dayton. "And your next witness is the other psychologist?"

"That's correct," she said. "He's to testify *after* the prosecution's witness."

Knapp looked at the clock on the wall as he considered the situation. "That being the case, this court is adjourned until nine thirty tomorrow morning." Without delay, he dismissed the jury and left the bench.

Again, Chitto waited for the flow of people to ebb. As before, a person in the gallery rushed to the bar to bend the prosecutor's ear. This time, a woman wearing an olive-green pantsuit. Chitto frowned, watching the exchange. Whoever she was, she had Monty Powell's ear. A similar scene was playing out at the defense council's table. Walker had his head bent toward Dayton, in all likelihood getting her assessment of the prior testimony.

Proceeding down the steps, Chitto's attention was drawn to the only calm person in the room. Bobby Taneyhill stood quietly, observing the stampede of bodies from the gallery and the hushed activity at the prosecuting and defense attorneys' tables. Then, for mere seconds, a smile played at the corners of his mouth.

Chitto grunted softly. Rabbit wasn't scared anymore.

∞

Chitto waited outside the courtroom, watching for Susan Dayton to appear. To avoid attention, he stood in front of one of the lobby signs, giving the appearance he was there on business and unfamiliar with the building. He was also on the

177

lookout for Charlie Walker. He didn't want to chance an encounter with the man right then.

Seeing Walker exit through the front doors, he relaxed. As Susan Dayton came out a few minutes later, he fell into step beside her.

"Your job sucks, Counselor," he said quietly.

"Chitto—" Her shoulders slumped as she recognized him. "You're not happy with how I'm doing . . . *again*."

"Not at all. You're doing a hell of a job. A tad rough on Wasilewski."

Her eyes popped open. "May I remind you that you're the one who led me down that path? What is it now?"

"*Touché*." Taking her elbow, he walked her to the side of the corridor where they could talk more privately. "One question. Was Bobby given a lie detection test?"

"No." Her eyes widened. "Why?"

"Let's just say, I like it when no stone's been left unturned. So, Bobby refused to take a test?"

She shook her head. "Actually, his grandfather was the one who put his foot down, saying there was no need." She lowered her voice. "You see, Walker was working on the kitchen sink that night and had a clear view of both doors. He insisted Bobby couldn't have left the house without him seeing him. He also produced proof."

"A copy of the receipt from the hardware store."

Her eyes widened again. "Seems Walker's confided as much to you as he has me." She paused, brow creasing. "Why didn't you ask him about the lie detection test?"

He exhaled slowly. "Respect for an honorable man, I suppose. I notice the two of you confer at the breaks. He seems to be dogging your tracks pretty close."

"He is," she sighed. "I feel as if he's my client, not Bobby." Her shoulders drooped slightly. "And I have an obligation to keep my client informed." She shook her head, fatigue showing. "But let's face it. Bobby doesn't have a grasp on how serious this is. For God's sake, he thinks *owls* talk." Pushing her glasses up her nose, she said, "Is that all?"

He paused. "If it wouldn't violate your code of ethics, maybe you could avoid telling Walker I asked about a lie detection test."

She stared at him. "You're making me uncomfortable, Sam."

He smiled. "I'm a cop, Susan. It's my job to make people uncomfortable." Noticing a woman in a business suit watching them, he said, "She looking for you?"

She glanced the direction he indicated. "My research assistant."

"If she's the one who dug up the dirt of Wasilewski, she's doing a bang-up job."

Thin shoulders slumped. "Yeah, I know. It sucked, but . . ." Dayton lowered her eyes. "Look, I have to go. I need to prepare for tomorrow."

Chitto noticed dark circles under her eyes. The banty hen was keeping late hours.

"Just keep on doing what you're doing," he said, turning toward the exit door. "You've got Monty looking over his shoulder."

CHAPTER FIFTEEN

"Now there's a surprise."

Chitto eyed the Harleys and made-in-the-USA pickups in the gravel parking lot. Deciding to check out the place he and Mackie Green planned to go that evening, he'd driven to the Four Corners Bar. Mick Weddle had gotten creative in naming it. The low, cinderblock building sat at the intersection of Highways 59 and 271, creating four corners. Given the locations, bikers and cowboys would make up the clientele.

Shifting into drive, he continued to his cabin at Bud and Birdie's where he changed into a chambray shirt and his grungy running shoes. He'd be recycling his western garb the next day at the trial and didn't want them smelling of beer and smoke. Pulling on his light windbreaker, he slid behind the steering wheel and pulled his Glock from the glove box. Undoing his belt, he fitted the IWB holster under his shirttail, which he'd let hang loose. Tugging the jacket low, he pulled on his faded ball cap and headed for Mackie Green's place.

The house was an older Craftsman bungalow that sat at the back of a large, treed lot. Though vintage, the place was well maintained. Brick posts supported a front porch, brown trim paint and matching gutters and downspouts looked new. A scrap of lawn edged a short sidewalk leading to the porch.

Sweeps of native grasses and wildflowers blanketed the rest of the property.

Parking behind a silver-colored Jeep Cherokee, he walked to the porch and glanced at his watch. Six-fifteen. Hearing Mackie yell, "It's open," he let himself in. Boycott met him on the run, ramming him in the crotch in his excitement.

"What the hell," he said, running his hand over the dog's croup. "You're *wet*."

"We both needed a bath." Rubbing damp hair with a towel, Mackie grinned at him. "It was a hard day at the office."

She stood on the landing of an oak stairway wearing faded jeans, a white western shirt with silver embroidery down the front, and short-topped western boots. "There's iced tea in the fridge," she said, pointing her chin toward the back of the house. "I'll just be a minute." On the way upstairs, she called out, "Why'd you change clothes?"

"Wanted to," he said.

More like *needed* to, he thought. The heat in the courtroom and intensity of the trial had heated both his body and blood. His trial clothes needed airing out and he needed to cool down. Shaded by trees, this house was a good beginning.

Chitto took in the place before heading for the kitchen. The front rooms had been remodeled into an open-concept living-dining area. The inside décor was as natural looking as the outside. Overstuffed furniture in earthy shades surrounded an entertainment center. Floor-to-ceiling bookshelves along one wall indicated Mackie had an eclectic worldview when it came to reading material. Scattered throughout the books were pieces of old pottery and figurines, looking to be authentic, and stacks of archaeology magazines: *Archaeolog-*

ical Diggings, World Geology, *Archaeology of Native North America.* He paused, noting the address labels on some of the magazines were addressed to a Dr. Frank Pederson.

"Frank," he murmured, vaguely remembering a reference to someone by that name. But right then, a cold drink was top of mind.

Walking through the dining room, he noticed a natural-fiber rug under hickory chairs and plank table in the dining area. Expensive, he thought.

The kitchen lived up to the rest of the house. Custom craftsman. The archaeologist not only had good taste, she had money. Maybe I chose the wrong field, he reflected. Neither cops nor field geologists made a salary that would have afforded this.

Hearing Mackie walk down the stairs, he called out, "Boycott behave himself today?"

"Perfect gentleman," she responded.

Opening a cupboard, he reached for a glass and noticed a half-empty bottle of Jack Daniels. Pushing it aside, he grabbed a tall glass and filled it with ice cubes from the freezer. Filling the glass with tea, he downed it in three gulps.

"Good grief." Mackie watched him from the doorway. "Must've been a tough day. I can hardly wait to hear the gritty details."

"I'd rather hear about yours," he said, using the back of his hand to wipe his mouth. He waved a hand toward the living area. "Nice place."

"Thanks. A young couple did most of the renovations." She shook her head, sighing. "Then the recession hit and they had to sell. I got it for a steal."

"Shit happens," he said.

"All too true." Nodding toward the front door, she said, "My insides are craving an onion burger big time. How 'bout we discuss *our* day on the way."

"Works for me." Rinsing his glass, he set it in the sink.

"*Huh*," she grunted, eyebrows arching. "Someone trained you right."

"Make that plural. Mother, grandmother, and . . ." He paused. "My wife. She died a few years back. Cancer."

As he said the words, Chitto paused, wondering if those words would ever become easier to say.

Her eyes darkened. "Sorry."

"Shit happens," he repeated. "Where do I put Boycott?"

She opened a sliding door that led to a shady screened porch. "His food and water are out here already." She smiled quickly. "He's a tired boy. Got plenty of exercise."

"He dig up anything?" Chitto watched Boycott turn circles on the blanket, then plop down, head resting on his front paws.

"Nothing we don't have plenty of." She handed him an irregularly shaped rock. "Thought you'd like to keep one of his finds as a memento."

"Hell, *yeah*." Examining the piece of chert she handed him, Chitto recognized minute fossilized shells embedded in the rock's face. The small stone told an eons-old story of when the area was sea, not land. "I'll add it to my collection of worry stones," he said, slipping it into his jacket pocket. "They help me think through a case."

"*Worry* stones," she said, walking toward the front door. "Well hopefully, this one doesn't get used anytime soon."

Chitto smiled as he fell into step with her. He was already fingering the stone in his pocket.

∞

Chitto rolled down the windows on the truck, opting for fresh air instead of the AC. The heat from earlier in the day dissipating quickly, the evening promised to be pleasant. On the way to the Four Corners Bar, Mackie filled Chitto in on the progress at the dig.

"The site's matching up nicely with what the geophysical survey showed. Dark oval shapes likely mark positions of roof posts. We're hoping the findings will get funding to develop more sites." She explained that less than fifteen percent of the total site had been tested.

"Good luck with that," he said. "Money for scientific research is hard to come by."

A minute passed. "All this is probably dull compared to your job," she said, glancing at him.

He laughed. "Actually, I'm jealous. My plans were to become a field geologist."

"*Field* geologist? How'd you end up in police work?"

In the fading light, her blue eyes were filled with the inquisitiveness of a scientist. They also brimmed with sincerity. After a long pause, he said, "My father was a cop. He and another tribal officer were murdered out there at Mayo dam."

When she didn't respond, he looked at her again. Her eyes expressed surprise. Her silence demanded more. Sighing, he gave her the bare bones of the incident.

"At Mayo," she said, shaking her head, "and I'm just now hearing about it. Lord help, I live in a vacuum." She faced him again, eyes wide. "You became a cop because you wanted to find out who did it."

"Still do. But it's been ten years now and . . ."

She stared at him a bit longer, then shook her head. "No, it isn't in your nature to give up, settle for less. That's the *real* reason you're up here, isn't it?"

"Let's just say I'm doing double duty." He exhaled slowly, deciding it was time to change the subject. "You mentioned that you'd been here four years. You must've started here right after you finished your doctorate." He glanced at her. "That was some kind of lucky break."

"Luck and a lot of hard work," she said, laughing softly. "My dad helped out with tuition, but I waitressed to work off other expenses." A pause followed. "I also did a couple of internships here, which moved me up the candidate roster. I like to think I paid my dues." She glanced his way. "Your turn. How'd the trial go?"

He took a minute, debating choices. Did he want to re-live the day? In a word: No. In two words: Hell, no. Did he have a choice?

Hurriedly, he briefed her on Susan Dayton's cross-examination of Buster Littlejohn and the bartender, Mick Weddle.

"*Aha*—that's why we're going to Four Corners, isn't it. To see if Mick might be wrong, if Buster could've slipped out unseen?" The broad smile made a showing.

She was already thinking Bobby would be set free, Chitto thought. He needed to set realistic expectations—and fast.

"A look at the place might settle that *particular* question," he said.

"*Particular* question," she repeated, blinking eyes indicating she was dissecting the implication. "Were they the only ones to testify?"

"Nope, they just kicked things off." He briefed her on Dewey Poindexter's testimony next.

"*Oh. My. God.*" Her eyes had become orbs. "I know Dewey—but then, everyone knows Dewey." She looked at Chitto quickly. "Littlejohn did it, didn't he? That rat bastard killed Muriel."

"Whoa now, slow down. Doesn't pay to rush to conclusions." Spotting the neon sign at the Four Corners Bar, he flipped on his turn signal and listened to gravel crunching beneath the tires. Halogen lights on telephone poles were only slightly dimmed by the thick shrouds of insects creating a mantle.

Shutting off the engine, he reached across and opened her door. "Let's have a look inside."

She looked around the lot as she undid her seatbelt. "It won't be as busy as a Saturday night, but they do karaoke later. The place will be jammed then." Noticing Chitto continuing to look at the place, she said, "What?"

"Just having a hard time envisioning cowboys and bikers doing karaoke." Opening his door, he stepped to the ground.

"Beats soap operas." She walked around the truck, joining him. "When boredom strikes out here in the boondocks, you get resourceful. C'mon, we'll find a quiet spot where you can finish telling me about the trial."

Mackie led Chitto to a table in the back corner. "We'll be out of the high traffic area here," she said. "And it has a good view of the entire place."

The "entire place" consisted of a room filled with square tables, minus a twelve-foot circle of bare floor reserved for dancing and karaoke. A low murmur in the room accompanied Merle Haggard pouring his heart out on a boom box. The *pop* of beer cans echoed from a long bar near the front entrance where barrel-chested Mick Weddle stood watch. The aroma in the room fit the atmosphere: cigarette smoke, beer, and loud perfume.

"Where's the back door?" Chitto asked, scanning the room.

"I never paid any mind." She craned her head, looking around. "Kitchen maybe?"

"There," he said, watching waiters coming and going through a door at the end of the bar. He also noted that Weddle would have a clear view of both the entrance and kitchen door. "Bathroom have windows?" he asked, looking toward two doors in the corner of the room.

"Umm . . ." She paused, blinking. "Women's doesn't. Can't speak for the men's."

"Be right back." Sliding from the booth they'd taken, Chitto located the men's room, where he washed his hands before returning.

"Window?" Mackie said as he sat down.

"Cinderblock. You'd need a masonry chisel to get out."

"What do you think?" Though the light in the place was low, expectancy made her eyes lustrous.

He drummed fingers on the table. "I think Mick would've had a bead on anyone coming or going."

"*Rats*, so Buster Littlejohn's innocent." The luster in her eyes faded. "Well, sounds as if you've learned everything you needed to. We don't have to stay for the karaoke, you don't want to."

"Not yet," he said, watching the activity at the bar. "Let's see how Mick does when it gets crowded."

"Oh, *right*." She looked toward the bartender. "Think he'll recognize you? He seems inordinately vigilant tonight."

"Not a chance. The courtroom was packed and I sat in the back." He watched the bartender a minute. "He's probably still smarting from the cross exam. It wasn't pretty."

A woman wearing scuffed red boots and a bandana neckerchief around her neck walked up. "Your usual?" she said, looking at Mackie.

"You bet. Oklahoma onion burger, well done, and a Bud Light."

"How 'bout you, doll face?" she asked Chitto. He skimmed the menu quickly, assessing his options.

"I can recommend the burger," Mackie said. "They do it right here."

"Then make it two," he said. "Medium rare and a glass of iced tea. Sweet."

"Only kind we serve, honeybun."

When alone again, Chitto looked at Mackie. "Your *usual?*"

She flushed slightly. "Don't get the wrong idea. Sometimes I accompany the archaeology dig team when they're in town—their dorm mother if you will. The students try karaoke occasionally but I'm not that brave. Or is the right word *young?*" She shrugged. "But like I said, out here, you look for things to break the boredom."

"Young?" He shook his head. "I figure you're crowding thirty. I've got a few more than that punched on my ticket." He studied her face in the dusky light. "What surprises me is that you're still single."

"No big mystery." She traced a square on the patterned oilcloth. "The man just hasn't shown his face that I want to wake up to day after day . . ." She tilted her chin, looking at him. "After day."

Chitto looked into eyes made hazy from cigarette smoke and dust off the parking lot, wondering what she was seeing. Was she thinking that one and one made two, that they might enter into a relationship? That thinking morphed to what type of relationship. Long-term or one-night stand?

Pete Brody's report that Mackie Green was known for frequenting bars rose to the surface, as did the all-night date that was her alibi the night of the murder. Instinct, plus his training and experience, also told him she was not the dorm-mother type. The bigger problem, however, dealt with him.

He was not the sex-to-relieve-the-boredom type. He was a commitment guy. Long-term relationships, not one-night stands. An innate wariness told him that she was talking about the other type.

The moment dissolved as a beer and iced tea showed up at the table, accompanied by a man and half-dozen young, sun-bronzed people. Chitto recognized them as the dig team he'd seen that morning. The students had been a blur but he remembered the man being the one who'd worn the floppy hat. The professor in charge of the dig. Now bareheaded, a receding hairline was evident. His face, however, was that of a younger man. Maybe Chitto's age, early to mid-thirties. He also wore a gold band on the left ring finger.

Chitto extended a hand. "Sam Chitto," he said.

Gripping his hand, the man said, "Pederson. Dr. Frank Pederson."

Frank, Chitto thought, recalling the magazine labels at Mackie's house.

A couple of the dig team members intercepted the waitress as she walked by. "Beer," they said in unison. "Buds for everyone . . . except the boss there." Attention moved to the professor. The waitress looked at Frank Pederson.

"Jack Daniels, neat," he said. "Make it a double."

And one and one makes two, chimed the voice in his head.

Chitto sat back, watching the proceedings. The dig team was an expressive lot, all laughter and chatter. It seemed his view of scientists being Spartan in nature was outdated. The professor, on the other hand, was subdued, studious looking. And right then, those studious eyes were glued to Mackie Green. It didn't take a genius to figure out there had been more than an interest in archaeology between the two.

"Well, don't just sit there, Mackie," a strawberry blond in jean shorts and ankle-high boots said. "Tell us all about this tall, dark, and hunky man you're with."

With a quick shrug, Mackie told them Chitto was an old friend from Oklahoma U. "He's in town on business," she explained, "and needed someone to watch his dog."

"*Oh*," the blonde said. "You're Boycott's human."

"He likes to chase sticks," a tall, gangly male student said. "Fetch them outta the creek."

Chitto nodded. "He's only a year old. Lot of play in him yet."

"Now you see why Boycott's so tired," Mackie said to Chitto.

He nodded again, then faced Pederson. "Join us? We can up pull up a table."

Pederson shot Mackie a quick look, then said, "Thanks, but I need to discuss scheduling with the team."

I bet, Chitto thought, noticing Mackie was practicing avoidance when it came to the professor.

"Scheduling, my foot," Strawberry Blonde snorted. "We need to talk about our act tonight."

"Their *karaoke* act," Mackie translated for Chitto's benefit. Turning to the others, she said, "Okay, scram guys. And don't get too rowdy or I'll have the bartender throw you out. Remember, you have to work tomorrow so count your drinks." As they departed, she smiled at Chitto. "What'd I tell you? Dorm mother."

He returned the look, minus the smile. "Frank the dorm father?"

She stared at him, a flush crawling up her neck. "He's a friend. We both went to school in Austin. Same field of study, same classes, same level of poverty. Neither of us wanted to carry too much loan after we graduated so we also worked at the same restaurant. He bussed tables and I waitressed. He's just . . ." She waved the hand again as if brushing away a pesky gnat. "A friend."

He nodded slowly, lips pursed. "His wife go to school with you?"

"No, she worked," she said, the flush deepening. She began tracing one of the patterns on the tablecloth again. "Computer industry's big down there. She had a good job till she got pregnant." She paused to move to a different pattern. "They have three kids now."

Chitto nodded, knowing when it was time to change the subject. "I didn't know there was a creek on the property."

She looked at him, blinking. "A man-made one. Why?"

He shrugged. "Just curious. I noticed an irrigation ditch when I walked around. That what you're talking about?"

She nodded. "It's the reason that particular spot was chosen for the first dig. Frank got permission to work on four sites where there could be potential structures, but there was concern flooding would erode the bank that runs near this one. So, in addition to research, the team's working with the Army Corp of Engineers to preserve it."

"Four sites . . ." He looked toward Frank Pederson. "Sounds like the digs will go on for quite a while."

She fell back in the booth, arms folded. "That's enough about archaeology. Now spill it, tell me about the rest of the trial."

Lowering his voice, Chitto told her about the redirect on Bernard Wasilewski.

"God, that sounds brutal," she mumbled, leaning elbows on the table. "And him a corpsman. Who would've thought he could do such a thing." She took a long drink of beer. "I don't even know what the man looks like, and he's lived here two years."

"Not surprising. He's pretty much a recluse. And after today, I don't figure he'll be sticking around. The other one either."

"What—?" She stiffened. "You think they're *both* innocent—Littlejohn *and* Wasilewski."

The waitress arrived, saving Chitto from answering. The burger lived up to Mackie's description: a mound of thinly sliced onions pressed into a beef patty on the griddle, a slice of American cheese, and a soft bun spread with mustard. Dill pickles lay to one side of the burger and French fries filled the other side of the plate.

"You weren't lying," Chitto said, tackling the burger. He looked up a few minutes later, noticing she had stopped eating. "What's up?"

"I can't stop thinking about Bobby." The smile had disappeared from her face, her eyes. "What do you think will happen now?"

Chitto pushed the plate aside, appetite gone. "I think he's going to skate," he said.

CHAPTER SIXTEEN

Karaoke kicked off at nine o'clock at the Four Corners Bar. Chitto ordered his and Mackie's drinks refreshed and they settled back in the booth. While others watched the entertainers, Chitto kept his eyes on Mick Weddle at the bar, unconsciously fingering the piece of chert.

A biker dressed head to toe in leather kicked it off with the George Strait oldie, "Amarillo by Morning." Not to be outdone, a bowlegged kid in pointed-toe boots and Stetson followed with "Friends in Low Places," a Garth Brooks' hit. The dig team took the spotlight next, the strawberry blonde doing the solo for "Wide Open Spaces" by the Dixie Chicks. The rest of the team sang harmony or pretended they were playing musical instruments. They brought the house down.

Chitto noticed that Frank Pederson did not participate. He could understand the decision. The professor's job came with responsibilities and responsibilities came with liabilities: long hours with no overtime and accountability for results. Accountability also led to public scrutiny. Public scrutiny required discretion.

"I'm regretting giving you that rock," Mackie said, indicating the stone in Chitto's hand. "You haven't taken your eyes off the bartender the entire evening. Something tells me you've made up your mind."

"Sorry," he said, pocketing the piece of chert. "But, yeah. I'm ready to leave if you are."

She nodded toward the woman's restroom. "Meet you out front."

Weddle gave Chitto the eagle eye as he paid out. "Where've I seen you before?" he asked, squinting.

Chitto shrugged. "Couldn't say, not from these parts." He had to give it to Weddle. The man had a sharp eye. Even though pressured by the cross exam, he recalled Chitto's face in the crowd.

Turning away, Chitto walked outside to wait for Mackie. He breathed deep, pulling fresh air into his lungs, and exhaled quickly to eliminate the remnants of the smoky bar. He wasn't looking forward to the drive back to Mackie's place. Weddle wasn't the only one with sharp eyes. She had kept one eye on the entertainment and the other one on him. He was in for a cross exam.

Mackie didn't disappoint. "Talk to me, Sam," she said as soon as Chitto turned onto the highway.

Chitto took time to watch clouds playing hide and seek with the moon, listen to the sound of the truck's tires slapping against patched asphalt, notice the smack of insects splashing against the windshield. "Burger was good," he said at long last.

The silence in the truck was thick enough to carve.

"Okay . . ." He cleared his throat. "I'm going to talk to you like a cop, Mackie."

"I don't care how you do it," she said, anger edging her words. "Just tell me what you're thinking."

Chitto drove in silence a bit longer, then nodded toward the glove box. "There's a pack of Doublemint in there. I could use a stick."

The light from the glove box illuminated the truck's cab. As she rummaged for the gum, Mackie found his pack of Marlboro Reds. Holding it under the light, she looked at him. "You smoke?"

"Not anymore."

Replacing the Marlboros, she said, "The cigs?"

"A test of willpower," he said, not divulging he'd given up smoking because his wife Mary had been concerned about the dangers of nicotine. The irony was she had died of cancer and Chitto had lived. But he had made her a promise, and he had not, would not, break it.

"And the gum?"

"A damn poor substitute," he said, peeling the paper off a stick. He chewed a minute and said, "I need you to take Bobby out of the equation for the moment."

"I'm listening." She closed the glove box, turning the cab dark again.

"You're right," he said. "I have doubts that either Buster Littlejohn or Bernard Wasilewski could be the killer. Which to a cop means the killer's still free. My biggest concern is that certain of the findings point to this guy either being a serial killer . . . or have the makings of one."

"I'm . . . listening," she repeated, more softly this time.

"In all likelihood, the psychiatrists will be addressing this tomorrow, and they'll use all the correct lingo, such as organized and disorganized killers, visionary killers, missionary and hedonistic killers. I'm going to skip that and talk about what this case is telling me as a cop."

Hearing Mackie exhale, Chitto continued. "A lot of serial killers take a memento, such as a body part." He relayed what the medical examiner had reported about the removal of Muriel Simpson's nipples. "If he was killing out of anger, the killer wouldn't have taken such care and . . ." He paused. "Whoever he is, I'd bet a dollar to a donut that he's stashed those mementos somewhere." He paused again, inhaling and exhaling. "Moreover, about now, he's planning how to add to his collection."

"She was also stabbed in the vaginal area," Mackie said, her voice raspy.

"Right, which could indicate the killer had unsatisfied sexual needs or believed he was ridding the world of someone he considered unworthy to live, like a prostitute or—"

"Good God, Sam. You're making Bobby out to be an avenging angel punishing mankind for their wicked deeds—"

"You're supposed to be listening," Chitto said sharply. "Many serial killers revisit the crime scene the next day—a need for confirmation—which is exactly what Bobby did."

"Okay," she sighed. "I admit the screech owl story sounded a bit farfetched to this non-native woman, but he had no reason to attack Muriel. She was a fun-loving girl, but not a prostitute. And Bobby *liked* her."

"I'm not saying she was hooker, but the landlord described her as a loose woman. It's a small town. Things like that get around." He lifted a hand when she started to protest again. "With these people, it doesn't have to be anything egregious or outlandish. Something small can trigger a need to get even . . ." He hesitated. "Like being slighted, humiliated."

She turned to look at him. "You're thinking about the girl who laughed at him" She shook her head. "But Muriel wasn't that girl. Good grief," she grunted. "If he were to get mad at anyone, it would've been me. I'm the one who talked him into calling that little bitch."

Chitto sat quiet, darkness hiding a deepening frown.

"Wait up," she said, turning toward him. "Are you keeping something from me? Did you see the other novels Bobby did, the ones the psychiatrists have? Is that why you're saying this?"

"Didn't see them but I was given a good description. And it sounded to me as if Bobby *did* look upon the protagonist as an avenging angel. This avenger character was doing away with people he considered monsters. Kids that, in appearance, looked like high-school teenagers. Boys in blue jeans, cheerleaders in ponytails. The kind who had bullied or ignored him over the years."

Mackie wagged her head side-to-side "All this is speculation, just speculation."

He glanced her way. "It's time to lay aside the dorm mother role, Mackie. Think like a scientist. There's speculation, and then there's hypothesis based on what the data shows."

She let out a long breath. "Well, one thing I know for sure. Charlie wouldn't lie."

"Could be," he said. "But there's a difference between telling the truth and *believing* you're telling the truth."

Considering this, she said, "But, how?" She stared into the darkness outside the window. "He swore in court that Bobby was home. He wouldn't have done that if he wasn't sure."

Minutes passed. "Tell me," he said. "Do you know when Bobby moved Shug's doghouse away from the house? It used to sit under his window. The ground still shows the marks of where it sat."

"No, Charlie's the one told me about the dog getting hit by a car. Bobby never mentioned it. But then, Shug was really Charlie's dog." She exhaled slowly. "Broke Charlie's heart—God he loved that dog. So did I, she was a sweetheart.

He saved a year to buy it. I figured it was a replacement for Bobby, you know, with him graduating soon and moving on."

An oncoming car's headlights showed her face in a frown. "What's the deal with the doghouse?"

"It's a long drop to the ground from his bedroom, but with something to stand on, Bobby could've gotten in and out without being seen."

She turned away, staring out the window again. Though he couldn't see her face clearly, Chitto knew she was blinking rapidly, resisting things she didn't want to believe.

"But, Muriel?" She raised a hand again, let it drop. "What reason would he have to kill her?"

"Exactly," Chitto said, pulling into Mackie's driveway. "That's the kicker." He cut the ignition. "Why Muriel Simpson?"

They sat a moment in the castoff light from the porch lamp, Mackie staring at her hands, Chitto staring at the silver Jeep parked in front of him. In the moonlight, the SUV appeared luminescent.

"So you're saying Bobby sneaked out." Mackie's voice was barely audible. "And the screech owl story was just an excuse to . . ." She let the last words hang.

"It makes the most sense. According to Walker, Bobby was in his bedroom working on his drawings. From his bedroom, Bobby would've heard a car drive into the Archaeology Center that night. There's no air conditioner in the trailer, so he would've had his window open to catch a breeze. With Shug gone and no other noises to interfere, he would've heard her pull in."

"I still don't believe it." Mackie rubbed the spot between her eyebrows. "Why Muriel?"

"Therein lies the rub." Chitto's eyes came to rest on the Jeep parked in the drive, at its silvery glow. Turning slowly, he looked at Mackie. "I never heard what kind of car she drove."

"Muriel?" Visible in the light from her porch, Mackie's face displayed concentration. "A Toyota, RAV4 I think. I remember because the locals gave her a hard time for buying a foreign-made car."

"Color?" Chitto asked.

"Silver . . ." Mackie swiveled her head, looking at her Jeep. "What are you thinking, Sam?"

"Nothing good," he murmured.

CHAPTER SEVENTEEN

Chitto woke before daybreak on Tuesday and immediately sensed the void in the cabin. At Mackie's request, he'd left Boycott with her the night before. "It would save a trip," she'd argued. He agreed to the arrangement, but for a different reason. After the implications about Bobby Taneyhill sunk in, Mackie was feeling vulnerable. He'd left her at the door, one hand gripping Boycott's collar, the other clutching the neck of her shirt.

His fault, he acknowledged now. Bobby was someone she'd known and trusted, and he had used an iron grip to crush that trust. Had he been presumptuous in his assessment? Was he guilty of making assumptions, as she'd said?

Fatigued from a night plagued with self-doubt, he rose and put on a pot of coffee. Changing into a T-shirt and sweatpants, he laced up his running shoes and gulped down a half cup. The trial resumed at half past nine. To brace himself for another long day closed up in a stuffy courtroom, he needed to fill his lungs with fresh air and expend pent-up energy.

He ran hard. At the place where he usually turned to start the return trip, he stopped to catch his breath. As his breathing slowed, he paused, listening to an unfamiliar sound. He concentrated, filtering sounds one from another. It was too early for most birds, but not for insects. Cicadas were called heatbugs for a reason. They droned endlessly on hot days and October had turned out hotter than usual. Katydids, on the other hand, took center stage at night. Right then, with one species finishing night duty and the other one just getting warmed up, it was relatively quiet.

The sound came again. A distant siren? The barking of dogs? A horse whinny . . .

He stiffened, recalling that Mackie had described a screech owl's call sounding like a whinny.

Slowly, quietly, Chitto made his way through the underbrush. He was about ten feet off the trail when he spotted the horned owl, sitting at eye level on a low branch. Only feet away, the owl returned his stare, unperturbed. Feathery tufts above its ears gave the appearance of horns. Streaks of dark feathers interweaved with muted grays the color of tree bark provided perfect camouflage for a small predator.

Ishkitini?

No, the scientist in him said. Just a little owl living the way predators were meant to live. Killing for survival. The fabled *Ishkitini* symbolized a monster that killed for no good reason.

Making a low *eh-eh-eh* sound in his throat, Chitto waited. A few beats later, he repeated the sound. The small owl's feathers vibrated as it warbled its reply. It repeated the sound again, and then again.

No way, Chitto thought. It would be damn near impossible for Bobby Taneyhill to hear the little owl from his bedroom *or* the woods behind the mobile home. Which meant the kid was either delusional or he'd lied.

In the next instant, Chitto was remembering how the bird was a sign someone was going to die. As far as Bobby Taneyhill was concerned, that could prove true if he were set free. Which, given the way the trial was going, was a good possibility.

And I helped pave the road for that possibility becoming a reality, he thought angrily.

Returning to the trail, he raced back to the cabin, his thoughts consumed with how to prevent a killer from going free. He was breathing hard when he walked inside. Wiping his face with a towel from the bathroom, he noticed a light on his cell phone. Hitting the Listen button, he heard Ramon Rodriguez's voice.

"Pick you up at the courthouse on the lunch hour," the message said. "Out front."

His heart rate elevating again, Chitto became a man divided. Concern about Bobby Taneyhill being set free comprised one half; seeing his father receive the justice he deserved, the other. He had no choice. He could not ignore either side. He'd told Mackie he was doing double duty, and he would.

Quickly finishing off the cup of cold coffee, he stripped and stepped into the shower.

∞

Skipping the cinnamon rolls at the lodge, Chitto left early to ensure he got a seat at the trial. Two nationally renowned psychiatrists would be the equivalent of the Mardi Gras coming to town. The only thing missing would be the beer and beads.

Parking in the courthouse lot, he hurried inside and found the same seat again. Scanning the room, he took a head count: Wasilewski, Littlejohn, Weddle, and the medical examiner were in the gallery. Two men in suits and ties caught his eye: the two psychiatrists. Key witnesses were accounted for.

Walker entered, made eye contact with Chitto, and took his seat near the defense table. As expected, the gallery filled quickly. Chitto idly watched the parade of people, then straightened as an attractive woman in a polo shirt and beige Dockers walked into the room. Mackie Green. In her hand, she held a tan portfolio with a garish picture drawn on the front.

What the hell?

Looking toward Walker, Chitto saw the older man lean forward in his chair, eyes glued to Mackie. The look on his face mirrored the same confusion he was feeling.

Mackie acknowledged neither of them. She walked with head down, shoulders hunched, her concentration on empty front-row seats. Finding one, she quickly claimed it. Now, she sat stiffly, her eyes trained on the other side of the bar.

Chitto stood, looking for an open seat next to her. Finding none, he sat down again. He wished he could see her face. Facial expressions spoke reams; the back of the head was mute. But body language was another story. Studying the set of her shoulders, he put his focus to what held her attention, on where her line of sight was directed.

The defense table? The jury? The witness chair?

The witness chair he decided, her reason for being there becoming clear. Mackie was a hard sell. She needed affirmation of Bobby's guilt, and the prosecution's psychiatrist would provide the proof she needed. She wouldn't have to wait long, he thought, watching the courtroom guard open the side door.

But, that wasn't all of it. Chitto rubbed the back of his neck, pondering something else that was needling him.

The portfolio. Why had she'd brought the portfolio?

All noise in the room ceased as Monty Powell led the way for the prosecution. Noticing Powell was back to his all-smiles-and sunshine-self, Chitto grew leery. The man had something up his sleeve.

Susan Dayton appeared next. Even in heels, she was a half-foot shorter than the teenage boy following behind. As in the past, Bobby Taneyhill seemed oblivious to things around him. *Inward*, Chitto thought, recalling Charlie Walker's description of his grandson. And he'd agreed that the boy's early years were enough to drive him inward. Scrutinizing Bobby Taneyhill's face now, however, he wondered whether he was witnessing a stratagem.

Time would tell, Chitto thought. Rabbit's best defense was to freeze in place, outwait his predator. If that fails, Rabbit runs.

Without warning, a woman in the front row stood, attracting the attention of those on both sides of the bar. Centered in front of her midsection, Mackie Green held the tan portfolio containing Bobby's last novel.

Damn, Chitto thought, recognizing Mackie's intent. She not only needed to hear what the psychiatrist had to say, she needed to see Bobby—face to face—and she wanted him to see her. She was calling him out, letting him know she was questioning his innocence.

As heads on both sides of the bar turned toward Mackie, Chitto put his attention on Bobby Taneyhill. Like the others, he was drawn to Mackie's abrupt movement. Seeing the portfolio, his eyes widened, his mouth drooped, his step faltered.

Turning quickly, Chitto looked toward Walker who was also staring at Bobby. Had he noticed the break in stride, the panic on his grandson's face?

"Sit down or you'll have to leave," a guard said to Mackie. She complied quickly. As the trial commenced, all eyes turned to the judge's bench. Except for Chitto's. His eyes were on Bobby Taneyhill.

"Run Rabbit, run," he murmured.

∞

Winston Barry was the forensic psychologist representing the prosecution. In appearance, he was unremarkable. Of average height and weight, he looked to be fortyish. His demeanor conveyed confidence. His clothes were professional but conservative. And he'd brought flip charts.

The quintessential expert witness, Chitto thought.

Monty Powell took time to set up an easel to hold the flip charts, then asked questions that would clarify Barry's expertise as a sexual homicide expert, which included a long list of other cases he had assisted with across the continental U.S.

"And . . ." Powell paused, radiating a smile at the jurors. "He's prepared charts to help clarify his testimony."

Chitto recognized Powell's strategy immediately: overwhelm the jury to sway the odds.

Completing the introduction, Powell moved to the Muriel Simpson murder. To ensure the jury grasped the full implications of the findings, he explained he would begin with general questions. Turning to the first chart, he asked, "Could you describe the offense characteristics of organized and disorganized sexual homicides, Mr. Barry?"

"Certainly," Barry said, indicating a chart with headings marked Planned and Spontaneous. "A planned or organized killing typically involves three different sites." He went into a lengthy discussion of abduction, assault/kill, and dumpsites associated with planned homicides, then moved to Spontaneous.

"Unplanned homicides are more disorganized," he said, explaining the body is typically left where it's killed and sexually assaulted. "But," he said, addressing Powell directly. "The two categories are not mutually exclusive. You should

208

think of them as a continuum with a predominance of one or the other."

"And in your expert opinion, was this case predominantly planned or spontaneous?" Powell asked.

"A combination of planned versus spontaneous actually. But in my opinion, it was predominantly disorganized."

"Clarify, please," Powell said.

"Random and sloppy initially, indicated by the blood on the ground where the assault happened. Then the murderer took control, dragging the body to a path some distance away."

"I see," Powell said. "Please proceed. You were explaining why you consider the murder to be *predominantly* disorganized."

"The violence appeared to happen suddenly," Barry said. "A blitz attack without use of restraints, and the body was left in view, not dumped where it wouldn't have been discovered right away. In addition, the sexual acts occurred after death."

Chitto exhaled slowly, thinking the description meshed with his assessment. Muriel Simpson was stabbed in the back. It was night, no light except for the headlights from the car, which were trained on the front door. Bobby could easily have mistaken the Simpson woman for Mackie. And once he was back in control of his wits, he would've tried to hide his tracks.

"What about the weapon used?" Powell asked. "Did that tell you anything?"

"Not the weapon itself," Barry said, "but the manner in which it was used does. The victim's vaginal area was brutally stabbed, yet her nipples were removed with methodical precision. Again, spontaneous then controlled."

Boy on the way to Serial Killer? No proof of that, Chitto reminded himself. Yet.

Powell flipped to a page marked *Modus operandi* on the flip chart. "Would you explain for the jury *modus operandi* versus the signature with sexual homicide?" Barry complied, explaining at length that *modus operandi* involved a method of operating, or necessary actions to complete an act.

"As I've just explained, in this case, there was a variable pattern. A blitz attack followed with deliberate actions." He paused, indicating Powell should turn the page on his flip chart to a page titled Signature. "You see, it isn't absolutely necessary to complete the kill in a sexual homicide. The attack is to gratify a psychosexual desire. In other words, it's the product of fantasy, where thinking and emotion tie into the act. Over time, a constant theme may evolve."

And according to what Mackie said, Chitto thought, Muriel Simpson radiated sexuality. Except Muriel wasn't the intended victim, he reflected, frowning. Mackie was . . .

"You mentioned fantasy," Powell said, looking toward the jury. "How does body mutilation tie into that?"

"Motivation. Mutilation speaks to anger or hostility toward women and the sexuality of women. In many instances, the person who does this is threatened by women or has a curiosity about female genitalia." Barry paused. "This can lead to disgust, a need to dominate and degrade a woman."

Chitto stared at the back of Mackie's head, wondering what her face was showing. He looked toward Bobby. His face was hidden too, but his gut told him it displayed the same as before. Nothing. Rabbit was back to hiding, frozen in place.

More charts came and went. Looking toward the jury box, Chitto noticed eyes glazing over. Even the judge was slumping in his chair. Powell's strategy might be backfiring.

Feeling muscles grow stiff from sitting too long, Chitto flexed his shoulders and glanced at a clock on the wall. The psychiatrist had been in the chair an hour. Wondering how many charts he'd prepared, Chitto willed the hands on the clock to move faster. Monty Powell, on the other hand, seemed determined to drag out the ordeal.

"Let's turn our attention to . . ." Powell flipped to another chart. "Rehearsal fantasy with planned sexual homicides." He looked toward the jury again. "And perhaps it would be good to start with a definition of just what fantasy is."

"It would," Barry said. "Fantasy is defined as conscious thought divorced from reality, frequently rooted in emotions and made sexual. Rehearsal fantasy takes place over an extended time, and there's usually evidence of rehearsal for the crime itself."

"Evidence," Powell repeated. "Are you saying that the killer produces something that shows the crime being committed?"

"That's right. But over time, that fantasy representation loses stimulation. That's when the perpetrator acts out the fantasy."

"Just to clarify," Powell said, facing the jury box. "What is the purpose of a rehearsal fantasy?"

"To express hostility to women in a private way," Barry said. "The fantasy serves as a compensating mechanism. If the world is painful, fantasy compensates, taking the place of real activity with real people."

A shuffling started up in the gallery. Chitto noticed people glancing sideways at their neighbors. Those looks said, now we're getting somewhere. He looked toward the jury next. Did they also see where this line of questioning was leading?

Without wasting time or showing sensitivity to feelings, Powell steamrolled ahead. Flipping to another chart, he said, "I believe there are different categories of mutilation."

Chitto eyed the chart and saw three categories listed. He rolled his head side to side to release the stiffness in his neck, then sat back to listen. The psychiatrist started with Defensive Mutilation, which involved disposal of the body to impede identification. Then he went to Aggressive Mutilation, which he dubbed "overkill," where more violence than was necessary suggested personal relationship or rage; in this category, the wounds were directed toward the face and upper body. Offensive Mutilation, the last in the category, satisfied sexually sadistic desires and usually involved strangers or casual acquaintances.

"In the last category," the psychiatrist said, "the mutilation is controlled."

"And which category does this case fit into?" Powell asked.

"Number three," Barry said. "Offensive Mutilation. To satisfy sexually sadistic desires."

More shuffling, murmuring. The jury was now sitting at attention.

"Let's talk about the people who create these fantasies," Powell said. "Who are they? And how long do these fantasies last?"

"They typically originate in the post-pubescent stage—"

"Teenage years?"

"Yes," Barry said. "But there's a period of incubation, months or years before it's acted out."

Powell took a position in front of the witness. "Doctor, would you confirm you've examined Bobby Taneyhill's graphic novels?" He paused, waiting for the psychiatrist's acknowledgment, then asked, "How far back did these *productions*, both the art and the narrative, extend?"

Barry shifted in his chair, looking thoughtful. "I would say the early ones date back to post-pubescence."

Powell turned, looking toward Bobby Taneyhill. "In boys, that would be since he was eleven or twelve, correct?

"Yes, about the time he entered the higher grades," Barry responded. "And if he was seventeen when the crime was committed—"

"Objection," Susan Dayton said, rising from her chair. "The witness is drawing a conclusion."

"Sustained," Alonzo Knapp said. Turning to the witness, he said, "This isn't your first rodeo, Mr. Barry. Your job's to provide expert testimony, not speculate."

"I'll rephrase the question," Powell said. "In your estimation, Dr. Barry, how long do you think Taneyhill has been creating his graphic novels?"

"Given the drawings and stories number over two thousand, I'd say four to six years."

The murmurings in the gallery became loud enough for the judge to call for order.

"Well, if I do the math right," Powell said once order was restored. "I believe that would put them beginning at post-pubescence." He shot Susan Dayton a smug look, then faced the witness again. "In your professional opinion, is it safe to say that, over that length of time, a blurring can occur between fantasy and reality?"

"Yes. Over time, it becomes harder to separate one's actual fantasy and the real world."

Powell commenced pacing again. "Are you familiar with the term Trigger Mechanism?"

"Of course," Barry replied. "It's also known as a precipitating event. There needs to be a point in time that compels an individual to go from thought to action."

"Such as?" Powell asked.

"Conflict with a job or at school, problems with parents, the death or loss of someone."

Chitto leaned forward, noticing Mackie's shoulders had stiffened. Of all those present, she had first-hand knowledge of what the precipitating event had been.

"Your Honor," Susan Dayton said, rising from her chair. "Must this continue? The jurors are intelligent people. Surely, they've heard enough—"

"The jurors must make an *informed* decision," Powell interjected. "There's not that many charts left."

Knapp paused, mulling over the two points of view. "I will allow the testimony to continue," he said. "Jurors can never have too much information."

As Dayton sank into her chair, Powell turned another page on the flip chart, on which was written Components of Rehearsal Fantasy. "Would you discuss the components of fantasy thought as you've outlined here, doctor?

"For the sake of brevity," Barry said, glancing at Susan Dayton, "I'll only provide what's necessary for understanding."

One by one, he went through the list on the flip chart. Components of a Situational Fantasy involved things such as a blitz attack and abduction through a ruse. Paraphilia, which Barry defined as sexually abnormal desire, involved states such as pedophilia or transvestitism. Demographic described physical characteristics of a preferred victim. Relational referred to a preferred relationship in a fantasy.

"For example," he said, "the perpetrator wants the victim to be a sex slave." He nodded at the last item on the list. "And Self Perceptual describes how the perpetrator sees himself during the act, which usually involves a component of dominance."

Chitto noticed the judge glance at the wall clock. Looking at his watch, he noted it was half-past eleven. The psychiatrist had his own definition of brief.

Powell had also noticed the judge's growing impatience. Standing before the witness with hands clasped behind his back, he said, "And now, Mr. Barry, summarize your findings regarding Bobby Taneyhill's productions."

Chitto noticed Mackie lean forward. Others in the gallery followed suit. The jurors' eyes were glued to the expert witness.

"I believe they were situational in that there were numerous examples of surprise attacks in the narrative. I also believe they displayed paraphilic components. In particular, piquerism, which involves penetrating the skin of another person, sometimes serious enough to cause death. The most frequently targeted areas of the body in piquerism are the breasts, buttocks, or groin. Cutting instruments were used representing acts of penetration, and . . ." He shifted his weight in the witness chair. "Several of Taneyhill's drawings involved knives, evisceration, dismemberment, and cutting certain parts of the body. There was also language associated with these drawings. For example, 'Die bitch' and 'I'll get even, you whore.'"

Chitto frowned, wondering why Bobby would look upon Mackie, the intended victim, in that way. He inhaled quickly, recalling Charlie Walker's comment that Bobby followed Mackie around like a puppy. Had he witnessed Mackie and Frank Pederson, a married man, being indiscreet?

215

Chitto wasn't the only ones assimilating that data. The murmurings in the gallery became full-blown conversations.

"Quiet in the court," Judge Knapp yelled. "Proceed, Mr. Barry."

"Yes, sir. In my estimation, the productions showed Demographic components in that they dealt with vulnerable female representations. In other words, chosen victims."

Looking quickly toward Mackie, Chitto noticed her shoulders slump.

"Let's turn to the main character in these graphic novels," Powell said. "Would you describe him, please?"

"An aggressor type, a warrior. A cold, unfeeling individual who killed others."

"And would you say Bobby Taneyhill perceived himself as this warrior?"

"Yes, I believe the writer identified with this main character. There were two graphic examples showing this aggressor character transforming from an ordinary person into this warrior. Not unlike like Clark Kent changing into Superman."

"I see." Powell faced the jury box. "Would you describe what this ordinary person looked like?"

"A dark-haired teenage boy with a slight build in jeans and tee shirt and wearing glasses, and . . ."

As the jurors turned to look at Bobby Taneyhill, Susan Dayton jumped to her feet. "*Objection.* That description could fit thousands of teenagers—"

"Allow the witness to finish speaking," Knapp replied.

"I was going to say . . ." The psychiatrist straightened in his chair. "In two instances, the words 'This is me' were written under a picture of this warrior hero."

Powell walked in front of the witness stand. "Taneyhill was seen leaving the scene of the crime the next day. What does that indicate?"

"Those living out a fantasy often return to the scene to relive the fantasy."

And if not stopped, Chitto thought, they do it again.

"Please tell the jury, Mr. Barry . . ." Walking to the jury box, Powell asked the rest of the question over his shoulder. "What is your overall opinion regarding Taneyhill's graphic novels."

Without hesitating, the psychiatrist said, "I believe they're sexual fantasies."

CHAPTER EIGHTEEN

Judge Alonzo Knapp withheld the cross exam of the state's expert witness until after lunch. A nervous chatter erupted in the gallery as he released the jury and left the courtroom. Chitto's efforts to reach to Mackie before she left proved futile. She was one of the first out the door and he was stuck behind a stampede of bodies on the stairs.

As he worked his way down, he glanced toward Susan Dayton's table. Chitto had predicted she would be busy attempting to bolster Charlie Walker's morale. But Walker wasn't conferring with Dayton this day; he sat in his chair staring at Bobby. Chitto turned quickly, looking at the teenager, but Bobby still wasn't showing his face. Even though the judge had left the room, he'd remained frozen in place, facing the empty bench.

Rabbit was back in his burrow.

Finally able to leave the building, Chitto jogged toward the parking lot. He saw Mackie's silver Jeep pull onto the street at the same time he heard a horn honk behind him. Looking over his shoulder, he saw Ramon Rodriguez's black SUV double-parked on the curb. Reversing directions, he climbed into the passenger seat next to the FBI agent.

"Didn't you pick up my message?" Rodriguez said, pulling away. He was back in his FBI uniform: dressy jacket over shirt and tie and Ray-ban sunglasses shielding his eyes.

"I was trying to catch up with someone. She left in a hurry."

"She?" Rodriguez glanced toward the parking lot. "That brunette running like the devil was chasing her?"

"One and the same," Chitto sighed.

"Doesn't have that much of a lead. Want me to catch up with her?"

A pause. "No, I'll see her later. She's taking care of my dog while I attend the trial." The comment brought another look from Rodriguez.

"Obviously, not today," Chitto said. "She's the archaeologist at Spiro Mounds. She must've left him with the dig team that's there excavating a site."

Rodriguez considered this. "Must've been something real interesting on the docket." He glanced at Chitto. "That hotshot psychiatrist? You need to catch me up on how that went." Stopping at the corner, he said, "Where to? You want more French-fried caterpillars or a change in diet?"

Sunshine reflecting off the SUV's black paint was glaringly bright. For the time of the day, it was a scorcher. Mid-eighties, at least.

"Someplace with air conditioning," Chitto said, looking at storefronts along Broadway Street. "Know where the Warehouse is? The guards recommend the burgers."

"Hell, yes," Rodriguez muttered, turning right onto Broadway. "I've eaten at every burger joint in the state." A block later, he made a left onto Dewey Avenue.

The Warehouse was a small corner building, red brick with green trim and a striped canopy over the windows. Low lighting, walls hung with memorabilia, and wood furnishings gave the place a cozy look. Most importantly, the AC was running non-stop.

Finding a corner booth, Rodriguez ordered iced tea with lemon and the Cuban sandwich. Chitto ordered a Coke with a cheeseburger.

"Pronto on the drinks," Rodriguez said to the server. "And toast the buns on both those sandwiches." As the server hustled off, he looked at Chitto. "They use soft bread here, gets soggy fast. Can't stand it when the bun falls apart in your hand. I like things neat."

Chitto just grinned.

The drinks were delivered promptly. "So, update me," Rodriguez said, squeezing a lemon wedge over his glass. "That shrink nail the lid shut on the kid's coffin?"

Chitto grunted softly, thinking Rodriguez didn't pull any punches. "Let's just say he gave the prosecution its money's worth. The defense's psychiatrist's due up this afternoon." He took a long drink of fizzy cola. "Surprised you didn't come. We don't see many sexual homicide experts up this way."

Rodriguez leaned back in the booth, sighing. "Wanted to but I needed to finish up here."

"Finish up," Chitto repeated. "You're done with your investigation?"

"Unless you can pull another rabbit out of your hat, I am." He shook his head slightly. "I'm not finding anyone in *any* branch of law enforcement that looks suspect and there's nothing else to go on." He paused. "Your father and Bert Gilly's weapons and cell phones weren't found. Like I said, they probably ended up in the river." Another pause and sip of tea. "Gilly's wife is dead and they didn't have any kids, so that's a dead end."

"Yeah, I went down that alley, too." Noticing Rodriguez staring into space, blinking slowly, he said, "But you did find something suspicious."

Rodriguez paused before responding, waiting for the server to set the food on the table. As she moved away, he looked at Chitto. "Not suspicious, just puzzling." He started on his sandwich.

"Puzzling . . ." Chitto took a bite of burger. "Can you be a little more concise, Raymond?"

"We agreed to Ray," Rodriguez said.

"Can you be a little more concise . . . Ray?"

Wiping his mouth with a paper napkin, Rodriguez frowned again. "You said Bert Gilly got a call from a friend up here."

"That's what he told my boss, Dan Blackfox." He paused, watching Rodriguez take another bite of his sandwich. "You found something I missed, didn't you? Like who that friend was."

"Nope, struck out there, too." He looked up at Chitto. "But if Gilly was coming up here to see a friend, tell me why he'd be wearing a Kevlar vest."

"A bullet-proof vest—" The words hung in the air. "And my dad?"

Rodriguez shook his head. "Had on his uniform and a windbreaker. Gilly was wearing a long-sleeve shirt over the vest and what appeared to be a ski jacket." He frowned slightly. "Strange combination."

The crow and the peacock, just as his mother had described.

Chitto leaned back in the booth. "My mom remembered that jacket. Not exactly dress code but lieutenants aren't required to wear uniforms."

"Well," Rodriguez said. "Maybe he was anticipating that land dispute would get ugly. If that was the case, it didn't work. The killers preferred . . ." He hesitated, glancing at Chitto. "A different part of the body."

Right, Chitto thought. The bullet behind the ear favored by professional hit men.

"And you're sure my dad wasn't wearing a vest." Chitto's voice was barely audible.

"Positive." Finishing off his sandwich, Rodriguez glanced at his watch. "Better finish that burger. If this afternoon's anything like this morning, the courthouse will be packed."

Chitto wolfed the rest of his burger and washed it down with Coke. They left money and tip on the table and walked into the midday sun. The black SUV had held the heat like a coal-stoker furnace but Rodriguez appeared unaffected. The dark sunglasses were back on, the jacket was free of any sweat stains, and every hair on his head was perfectly in place. Chitto was a different story. By the time Rodriguez left him on the curb in front of the courthouse, he was clammy head to toe. The sky overhead looked moist, dark and hazy. All the signs indicated another round of thunderstorm was building.

"Keep in touch," the FBI agent said. "Anything crops up, don't keep it to yourself."

"Got you programmed in my cell phone," Chitto said.

"That's what you keep telling me." Rodriguez gave a wave as he drove off.

Walking up the courthouse steps, Chitto stopped at the door, resisting the need to spend the afternoon in a stuffy courtroom listening to more psychobabble. But as people began to shoulder past him, he trudged inside and found his seat again. As he expected, Mackie was absent. She'd seen and heard all she needed to that morning.

Like a busy hive, a low buzzing filled the gallery, but Chitto heard none of it. He was staring into space, trying to bring into focus an image that surfaced again and again.

The crow and the peacock . . .

∞

Recalling Winston Barry to the witness stand, Susan Dayton launched into her cross exam. She started by stressing that there was no concrete evidence such as blood or hair, finger-prints or fibers linking Bobby Taneyhill to the Muriel Simpson's death, then moved to the graphic novels.

"There were several thousand pages of drawings and sto-ries seized from Bobby Taneyhill's home—his graphic novels." She stood before the witness. "In prior testimony, you stated that you examined these *fictional* pieces and found many depictions of stabbings, eviscerations, knife wounds, and so on. Would you confirm that you looked at each and every one of them?"

"I examined each of them thoroughly," Barry confirmed.

"So have I," Susan Dayton said, beginning to pace. "Many, many times." She stopped in front of the witness chair. "There is not a single narrative or a single picture of a woman being mutilated as Miss Simpson was, isn't that cor-rect?"

Barry hesitated slightly. "Uh, yes. There is not an exact duplicate."

Chitto rubbed his mouth, thinking about the drawings that had been hidden in Interpretation Center's storeroom. What would they have shown if Bobby had completed them?

Walking to the jury box, Dayton made eye contact with each juror, then turned to look at Barry. "Yet you've present-ed very *dramatic* data pointing to Bobby Taneyhill as the killer."

Chitto couldn't help but smile. The little lawyer was working the witness perfectly, pointing out his theatrical performance. The smile faded as he considered she might sway the jury to let BobbyTaneyhill go free.

"I presented data supporting this case was a fantasy killing," Barry responded.

"I see." Returning to the center of the court, Dayton faced the witness chair. "Just one last question." She looked toward the jury again, then back at Barry. "Doctor, have you ever been wrong?"

The courtroom took on a graveyard atmosphere. All eyes were trained on the witness, except for Chitto's. His were trained on Bobby Taneyhill.

"Yes," Barry responded faintly.

"A lot of times?" she asked.

"No," he said hurriedly. "Not a lot."

She looked at a paper she'd been holding. "But more than once or twice," she said, running her finger down the page.

"Three, maybe four," he said.

"No more questions," she said, spinning on her heel.

Did Bobby's shoulders just relax? Chitto wondered. He kept his eyes on the teenage boy at the defense table, wishing he could see his face.

The gallery erupted with chatter as Dayton sat down. Calling for silence, Judge Knapp asked Monty Powell if the prosecution needed to readdress the witness.

"No, your Honor," Powell responded.

Knapp looked at the clock on the wall, then at Susan Dayton. "I regret to say I have a prior appointment this afternoon that I could not reschedule. We have time for one more witness, Counselor."

"Please call Dr. Derrick Johnson," Dayton said. A middle-aged man with white hair and neatly trimmed beard took the stand.

Chitto leaned back, wondering how Dayton was going to play this rebuttal. Psychiatry was not a hard science. To ask Johnson to deny it had any validity would require he deny his own credibility. If she thought he was going to do that, she was whistling Dixie.

As Monty Powell had done with his expert witness, Dayton took time to establish Johnson's professional expertise. Off the bat, Johnson explained he did not label himself a sexual-homicide expert. He was a clinical psychiatrist, he said, with forty-plus years under his belt, and he had assisted on several criminal cases.

Dayton began to pace. Seconds passed, a minute. Frown lines creased Chitto's forehead. Did she not know how to proceed? Or was she sharpening her claws?

She finally came to a halt in front of the witness. "Doctor Johnson, many question clinical psychology as a science."

"That's true," he said.

"Given that," she continued, "do you question the accuracy of Mr. Barry's data?"

"Not at all. Matter of fact, I agree with it."

The gallery pulsed with low whisperings.

"Explain, please," Dayton said.

Johnson nodded toward the prosecution's expert witness. "Dr. Barry has outlined the five elements of a rehearsal fantasy, which are situational, sexually abnormal behavior, demographic, relational, and self-perceptional."

"I see," she said. "Do you also agree that these drawings and stories are in fact Bobby Taneyhill's fantasies?"

"I do," he said.

What the hell, Chitto thought, leaning forward.

In Dixie's Land, I'll take my stand, taunted the voice in his head.

As the whispers from the gallery cascaded into full-blown conversations, Judge Knapp gave his gavel a bang. After order was restored, Dayton turned to her witness again.

"Would you explain, sir."

"They may be fantasies," he said, "but they can't definitively tie the suspect to the murder."

Dayton followed quickly with, "Why is that?"

"You see . . ." The seasoned psychiatrist settled back in his chair. "While a number of people who've committed a sexual homicide have admitted to having violent fantasies, so do people who've never committed a crime. There's just not enough research to say fantasies are specific to perpetrators of sexual murders."

"In other words, the material presented is . . ."

"Questionable," he said, filling in the blank she'd left. "Studies like this are a good beginning." He gave a glance to Winston Barry. "But not enough to draw a firm conclusion. The state of knowledge at this point is premature. All we can say is that some people who commit these kinds of homicides engage in fantasies. But some do not."

Taking a position in front of the jury, she repeated, "But some do *not*."

Chitto's face reflected a new respect for the defense attorney. Susan Dayton was a law-school honor student for good reason. Her witness had been precise and convincing—and without the need for flip charts.

"No more questions," she said, facing the judge.

Alonzo Knapp looked toward the prosecution's table. "Mr. Powell?"

"No questions." Monty Powell didn't bother to rise from his chair to address the bench. He sat where he was, skillfully twirling a pencil between his fingers.

Chitto studied the prosecutor and the pencil doing its acrobatics, wondering what he was up to.

"In that case, court is dismissed," Knapp said. "We'll resume tomorrow at nine-thirty." He paused, looking between the defense and prosecution tables. "My other commitment requires my time again tomorrow afternoon. However, unless someone springs more surprise witnesses on the court tomorrow morning, you should be able to present your closing arguments." With that, he rose from the bench.

Chitto stood to get a better view of the actions on the other side of the bar. Monty Powell's research assistant entered the room and handed Powell a packet of papers. Susan Dayton and Charlie Walker went into a huddle. Bobby Taneyhill was back to being observant. As the guard that was to escort him to a holding cell entered the room, the teenager turned to leave. And the shadow smile made another show.

CHAPTER NINETEEN

Chitto wasted no time getting to his pickup after he left the courthouse. Keying the ignition, he glanced at the clock on the dash. Three-thirty A thirty, forty minute drive to Spiro, another ten or so to the Mounds Archaeological Center, where he'd pick up Boycott and confront Mackie about her court appearance. As he pulled out of the lot, he spotted Charlie Walker leaving the building. The old man walked slowly, eyes downcast, shoulders hunched, back bent.

The hangdog appearance puzzled Chitto. Susan Dayton was going toe-to-toe with Monty Powell and the trial was going well. Walker should be fired up, not looking like a man burdened. His grandson stood a good chance at being freed.

Moving into traffic, he turned onto Broadway and drove straight through Poteau, connecting with Highway 59 north. As traffic stalled at an intersection, he opened the glove box to retrieve his pack of gum. His eyes lighting on the Marlboros, he paused. Tribal elders looked upon smoke as a prayer; if he was to figure out how to proceed, he could use some divine intervention. Bobby Taneyhill might go free and he couldn't let that happen. Reluctantly, he removed the Doublemint rather than the cigarettes.

As he cleared the intersection, he thought about the other impasse that had surfaced. The curveball Rodriguez had thrown him over lunch. Why had Bert Gilly felt it necessary to wear a bulletproof vest on the trip to Spiro? That question ignited another, more burning one.

If Bert was *that* concerned, why had he let his dad go without one?

He chewed the gum hard as he drove, foot heavy on the pedal, thoughts roiling. Feeling his jaws start to ache, he lowered the window and spit the gum onto the right of way. As fresh air scoured the stale air from the cab, he eased off the pedal.

He glanced toward the Four Corners Bar as he reached the intersection of Highway 59 and 271, recalling the evening spent with Mackie Green. The night had ended with him having drawn a startling conclusion that she was the intended victim. Yet, though rattled, she had deliberately taken intimidating evidence to the trial. He admired her need to confront Bobby Taneyhill, but while he could understand her motivation, he doubted she realized the impact that choice could have.

If Bobby walked free, she would become a liability.

Turning onto Highway 271, he drove through Spiro and turned north on Lock and Dam Road. Swinging west where the road split, he pulled into the Spiro Mounds parking lot.

"What the hell," he mumbled, looking over the vehicles parked there. Mackie's Jeep was missing. Spotting the dig team in the distance, he jogged toward them. The strawberry blonde who'd led the karaoke song at the Four Corners greeted him.

"Well, if it isn't tall, dark, and dreamy," she said, grinning.

"Where's your boss," he said, looking around for Frank Pederson.

"Gone to fetch food," she said. "If you're looking for Mackie, she's gone home."

"Yeah," the lanky kid said. "Boycott went for another swim. This year, that ditch is more mud than water. She wanted to give him a bath before you picked him up."

"This year . . ." Chitto stared toward the manmade creek a short distance away. "Was it the same last year?"

Lanky Kid stared at the ditch, eyes contemplative. "Matter of fact, no. It was drier last year and the farmers downstream needed more water, so they opened the gates. Thing was a raging torrent."

"That's why we've been working our butts off," Strawberry Blonde said. "Banks were eroding too close to our site," She cocked her head, staring at him. "Why?"

"Just curious," he said. Silently, he was thinking a raging torrent would be a good place to dump bloodstained evidence.

"You need Mackie's address?" The blonde reached for a satchel lying on the ground.

"Got it," Chitto said, turning toward his truck. "Thanks for dog sitting this morning," he called over his shoulder.

"Anytime," Lanky Kid yelled.

"Don't be a stranger," the blonde called out. "We move a lot of dirt. No strong back refused."

∞

It was a quarter to five when Chitto pulled behind the silver jeep parked at the neat Craftsman. Boycott ran from the back of the house as he exited the truck, slinging water. Chitto gave his head a quick rub then looked up as a smiling Mackie Green appeared. A Hawaiian shirt was knotted around her middle, blue-jean shorts exposing tanned, muscular legs had replaced the Dockers, and she was barefoot.

"Come on back," she said. "I was just getting ready to towel him off."

"Nice shirt," he said, following her.

"Gift from my mom and dad. A few years ago, they made a trip to that big island senior citizens dream about. I'd worn it one time before today, just to please them." She laughed. "Definitely not my style, but today I felt like breaking it out."

"Let your wild side show?"

Grinning, she led him to the back porch where a bottle of shampoo sat next to a plastic storage container. A makeshift bathtub. The water hose was still running across a small grassy spot that served as rinse area. A stack of old towels was at the ready for the drying phase and a barbeque grill smelling of roasting chicken completed the picture.

"Hope that smell means I'm invited for supper," he said, drying Boycott's belly with a towel.

"Figured you'd be hungry after being cooped up in that courtroom all day. God, that place was a sauna." She turned off the spigot and wound the water hose around a reel attached to the wall. "How's Charlie doing?"

Chitto noticed she didn't ask about Bobby. "Hanging in there but the trial's taking a toll." He looked at her. "You ever tell him about that phone call Bobby made from your office?"

Her eyes widened in surprise. "I saw no reason to. Why?"

He shrugged. "You plan on attending the trial tomorrow?"

"No, I'm back on the job tomorrow, the rest of the week for that matter. But don't worry about Boycott, I'll keep an eye on him." She shrugged. "Besides, there's no reason to go again."

He paused, rubbing fingertips across his lips. "I have a better idea. A friend on the police force in Poteau has a fenced yard. I'll drop Boycott off on the way. You have your job to tend to."

"That might be best," she said after a short pause. "I hate to ask Frank and the kids to watch him again. They're working against a deadline."

Picking up a fresh towel, he asked, "Why would there be no reason to attend the trial again?"

She tilted her head, staring at him quizzically. "I got what I was after."

"Which was?"

She let out a snort. "To attract Bobby's attention, of' course. Make sure he saw me—and the portfolio."

"And that's why you were looking for just the right spot to sit?"

"Well sure. I didn't want to chance he wouldn't recognize me in the crowd."

Recognition . . .

Chitto looked away suddenly, mind racing backward ten years. It's wrong, he thought, pulling up a mental image of two men. The jacket Bert wore, it's all wrong. He wore it for a reason . . .

"Where'd you go?" Mackie said, waving a hand in front of his face. "You disappeared."

"Mind wandered," he mumbled. "You were saying?"

"I was saying, I wanted Bobby to see me." She slumped, sighing. "And the truth is, I wanted to see him—to see his face. He did it, Sam. Bobby killed Muriel." Her eyes deepened a shade. "All I could think about this afternoon was Charlie. How that boy's been the center of his life and won-

dering what he's going to do now. Which set me to thinking."

She sat down on a porch step and looked up at him. "As
I was washing Boycott, I started thinking about Shug. Charlie
really loved that dog. He even put up a grave marker when
she died."

Charlie put up the grave marker? Chitto frowned slightly. All this time, he thought Bobby had put it up.

"So I've decided to get him another Bluetick puppy,"
she said. "I checked the newspaper ads and *bingo*. There's a
breeder that raises Blueticks right outside Spiro. I thought
maybe you would help me pick out a good one."

Chitto drew a breath, let it out slowly. "What if Bobby
gets off?"

"Gets off—" She stared at him. "But he won't, not after
that psychiatrist's testimony. He proved Bobby was mentally
ill. I don't like to think about Bobby being in jail but he
needs to be someplace where he can get help."

Chitto picked up another fresh towel and began working
on Boycott's ears.

"Okay, spill it." She licked her lips. "What happened in
court this afternoon, Sam?"

He paused a beat. "The defense's psychiatrist was pretty
good. Not as flashy as the prosecutions, but convincing." He
looked at her. "Jurors are reeds in the wind, Mackie. They
blow one direction one minute, the opposite direction the
next. In short, it's a tossup. That means Bobby has a fifty-
fifty chance of walking."

Mackie covered her mouth with both hands. Seconds later, she let them drop. "Oh God, Sam," she breathed. "He
can't go free. He knows that I know—and he knows I have
that portfolio."

"That's the least of your problems. You're also the trigger mechanism, the reason he called that girl, caused him to be humiliated. Plus . . ." He looked at her directly. "I suspect he discovered you were having an affair with a married man. In short, he found out his hero has feet of clay."

She paled. "He thinks I'm a . . . a *Jezebel*?" Wrapping her arms around her knees, she whispered, "*Stupid stupid stupid.*" Seconds passed. A minute. Then, "You think you're helping someone and . . ."

Chitto thought about those who had influenced Bobby. Providing only neglect from birth, his parents had tossed him in the garbage can like a wad of trash. Socially inept, he'd become a pariah with his peers. To compensate, his grandfather had become overprotective, leading to Bobby living vicariously through fantasies. Then Mackie, his mentor and guide, had pushed him to come out of his shell. When it backfired, he'd chosen to retreat inside again, only to a deeper place.

Who to fault? Everyone and no one. Many had faced similar if not worse beginnings and come out stronger for it. When push came to shove, a person either stepped up or fell over the edge. Bobby had made a choice and the dark side that existed in all of us had survived.

Mackie looked up at him, eyes glistening. "What am I going to do?"

"This is what *we're* going to do." Giving the damp towel a toss, Chitto stood, walked to the grill, and opened the lid. "We're going to eat this chicken and then go look at Bluetick pups."

"Bluetick pups." She wiped her eyes with the back of her hand. "But that means you don't think Bobby will go free." Rising, she approached him. "But how? It's out of your jurisdiction. You can't get involved."

"Don't plan to get involved. At least not directly."

She hesitated, frowning. "Then, what *is* your plan?"

Forking chicken onto a platter, he said, "Apply a tried-and-true procedure."

"Which is?"

"Shake the tree and see what falls out."

∞

Boycott sat in the passenger seat, panting through open jowls. Reaching for the pack of Doublemint in the glove box, Chitto hesitated, eyes lingering not on the pack of Marlboros, but his service weapon. Resolutely, he slammed the box shut.

"This other plan will work," he mumbled. He looked at Boycott as if waiting for affirmation. The dog panted some more.

The clock on the dash read nine o'clock. He and Mackie had eaten a light supper at a picnic table in her backyard, surrounded by purple coneflowers and black-eyed Susans, then driven to the dog breeder outside Spiro. The kennel was clean. The breeder produced pedigrees, showing a strong lineage, and papers showing regular vetting. The Bluetick pups were well fed, healthy. Their coats, a black-and-white mottling that gave the impression of navy blue, was coarse and glossy.

Boycott had sat next to Chitto at the kennel, watching him examine the puppies. He alternated looking up at Chitto and down at the squirming mass of long ears and big feet.

"Don't worry, buddy," Chitto had told him. "They're not going home with us."

After studying the pups, he'd selected a female. Giving Boycott the Stay command, he set the pup beside him. Obediently, Boycott remained quiet as the pup cozied up to him. Blueticks were known for their good temperament and gentle

236

nature, the perfect friend for an honorable old man. This one lived up to the reputation. He'd picked up the pup and handed it to Mackie.

"That the one?" the breeder had asked. "I'll hold her for you, but need a deposit."

Mackie had hesitated. "I can't make a commitment just yet," she stammered.

"Make the commitment," Chitto told her.

She wrote out a check.

Now, Chitto let out a string of swear words. Boycott nosed his shoulder, looking at him with chocolate-brown eyes.

"Yeah, you're right," he said, scratching the dog's head. "It'll work out. It always has."

Ever heard of dumb luck, taunted the inner voice.

As he pulled down the lane to Cabin 4, he saw Bud and Birdie on their front porch. Slowing, he gave them a wave and pulled to a stop, window down.

"Where could I find a Laundromat?" he asked through the open window. "Looks like I'll be staying another day or two."

"Just drop your things off here in the mornin'," Birdie said. "I've got a washer and dryer."

"That's too much to ask," he said.

Birdie would brook no argument. They agreed that he would give her a couple bucks for soap, and he proceeded to the cabin.

Staking Boycott next to the porch, he walked inside where he flipped on a lamp. He'd forgotten to leave the windows open and the cabin was an oven. Remembering an oscillating floor fan in the closet, he pulled it out and turned it on high, causing curtains to flutter and dust motes to swim.

Tossing his revolver on the bed, he noticed a covered container on the kitchen table. Lifting the lid, he saw four large cinnamon rolls and a half stick of butter. Birdie was not only making sure he had clean clothes, she was ensuring he and Boycott didn't go without breakfast again. His landlords took care of undercover cops and their police dogs.

What else did they look out for? he wondered. Closing the lid on the cinnamon rolls, he checked the closet. The two long guns were still there. It seemed he had also earned his proprietors' trust.

Sighing, he punched numbers into his cell phone and waited for Molly Brody to pick up. She was prompt, though barely audible. Static was dancing along the transmission lines this night.

"Sam Chitto here, Molly," he said. "Pete still up?" He was.

"What's up, Sam?"

"Need a place to park a dog tomorrow. Shouldn't be all day. Judge is hoping to throw the case to the jury by noon."

"You can leave him here anytime you want. Drop him off on your way . . . Hold on a minute." A pause came on the line and conversation could be heard in the background.

"Molly has garden club in the morning," Brody said. "Just put him in the backyard. There's a spigot next to the door for water." Another pause, briefer. "How's the trial going?"

"Up for grabs."

Another pause, longer. "What about that other thing?"

That other thing. Brody wasn't comfortable discussing the murder of two cops in front of his wife.

"There *is* something I'd like to run by you," Chitto said. "You be in the office around lunchtime?"

"I will now. See you then."

Chitto stared at the phone after he cut the connection with Brody, then dialed another number. Four rings into the call, a voice growled, "It's my bedtime, Sam."

"Scouts work around the clock," he said.

"I demand a raise."

"Coffee's on me for a week when I get back."

"Two weeks," she countered.

"Deal," he said. Jasmine was a soft touch. He would've busted for a month. "Need you to dig into something—make that *someone*." He paused. "Bert Gilly."

"Bert Gilly—" The line went to static. "Someone slip a Mickey Finn into your Pepsi-cola?"

"I wish."

More static. "What am I looking for?"

"The face behind the face. You know, the one he didn't show the public."

A long pause. "You want me to dig up dirt on a cop who was killed in the line of duty."

Chitto rubbed a throbbing ache between his eyes. "That about covers it."

"Something tells me I wasted a lot of time looking into land transactions."

"Nope. You narrowed the field. Most of police work's elimination."

"Um-hmm. Am I to assume I should focus on dealings up there in LeFlore County? You know, petty things like drug running, prostitution, racketeering, illegal gambling."

He sighed. "Makes sense. Has to be a reason they ended up where they did. But don't' stop there. Look at anything and everything."

"Sounds like a ride on a merry-go-round to me," she said. "Lot of time's passed, trail's gone cold, old case file's in storage—or the hands of the FBI."

Chitto drew a breath. "Work your magic, see what you can conjure up. Gilly probably hadn't entered the digital age, so old email messages would be a waste of time. But there may be a paper trail. Did he have big debts, live over his budget, have any personal problems . . ." He left the list open-ended.

"All right," she said. "But I got a feeling all I'm gonna do is get dizzy."

He glanced at his watch. "It's late, Jasmine. Go to bed."

"Oh, *right*. I'm supposed to sleep now." *Click.*

CHAPTER TWENTY

Chitto dropped his laundry off with Birdie the next morning, then drove straight to the Brody place. He'd started the day early, not wanting to miss the closing arguments. The fate of more than Bobby Taneyhill hung on the outcome.

At the Brody's, he quickly put Boycott in the backyard and filled a water dish and food bowl. Hurrying to his truck, he drove hard. He wanted to intercept someone before the trial resumed. He was going to make a last-ditch effort, one he didn't relish, but he was out of options. Legal ones, at any rate.

The parking lot at the LeFlore County Courthouse was forgiving this day. Pulling into a close-in spot, he looked around for a black Ford pickup. There weren't any. Charlie Walker had not arrived. The day promising to be another scorcher, he lowered the windows an inch for air circulation. The lot was filling fast. If Walker didn't arrive soon, he would be forced to park on the street. Locking the truck, Chitto took a position with a clear view of both parking lot and street.

Charlie Walker entered the lot ten minutes later and parked near the back. The man's approach was unhurried, his head down.

"What do you figure Bobby's odds are?" Chitto asked, falling into step with him.

Walker's head popped up. Weariness had deepened the age lines in his face. His eyes appeared hollow.

Chitto didn't wait for a response. "I figure he has a 50/50 chance of being indicted," he said, "or walking free." He paused, making eye contact. "It's the walking free part that I find worrisome."

Coming to a halt, Walker stared at him. People pushed passed them, some curious, some irritated that the walkway was being blocked.

"A cop's job is to fit puzzle pieces together," Chitto said, his voice lowered. "It took me a while to make the connections."

"Connections?"

"Connections," Chitto repeated. Pointing his chin toward the front entrance, he resumed walking. Walker fell in beside him. "You know, between Shug's doghouse conveniently disappearing from under Bobby's window . . . the victim's body being dragged to a place closely resembling the one in the book in Mackie's storeroom . . . the close resemblance of Muriel Simpson's car to Mackie's."

"*What?*" Walker stopped again, eyes displaying confusion.

Chitto waved him through the entry doors. At the guard station, they emptied their pockets and Chitto dutifully turned off his cell phone. They caught up with each other in the hallway.

"They're not real stories," Walker said. "And just 'cause he makes up stories don't mean he did it. Our lawyer showed that."

"Yes, Susan Dayton's done a bang-up job doing that." Chitto paused outside the courtroom door. "But see, she didn't know about the phone call."

242

Walker frowned. "What phone call?"

"The one Bobby made from Mackie's office asking a girl out on a date. The one Mackie encouraged him to make, thinking she was doing a good thing—not setting the stage for what was supposed to be her own murder. How was she to know the girl would humiliate Bobby and that he would blame her for it." He leaned forward, talking in a low voice. "Think about it, Walker. What do you think Mackie's intent was yesterday when she brought that portfolio to the trial? She knows she was the intended victim and wanted Bobby to know he'd been found out."

"*Mack?*" Walker whispered the name softly.

"Look at the stories Bobby told. They were about this killer doing away with those he saw as evil, those he considered inhuman monsters." Chitto opened the courtroom door for Walker. "A wise man once cautioned monster fighters to be careful they didn't turn into monsters themselves . . ." He paused at the foot of the gallery steps. "For when you gaze into the abyss, the abyss also gazes into you." He stood quietly, looking into Walker's eyes.

"Thought you was on our side," Walker said, turning away.

"I am, Charlie," Chitto said to the man's back. "Bobby needs help."

Making his way to the top row of the gallery, he looked for the old man. Walker took a seat behind the defense table seconds before the defense and prosecution made their entrance. Bobby Taneyhill glanced quickly toward his grandfather, then sat down next to Susan Dayton.

Your job sucks said the voice in his head.

"You think I don't know that," Chitto snapped. The remark bringing looks from those around him, he sighed and put his attention on others in the courtroom.

243

All witnesses were present and accounted for. The gallery was unusually quiet but the tension showed in tight shoulders and straightforward gazes. The same applied to Susan Dayton, the darkness under her eyes a sign she'd spent another restless night. As was typical, Bobby sat staring straight ahead, frozen in place. Monty Powell, on the other hand, busied himself arranging neat stacks of papers on the table. Minutes later, the bailiff called for all to stand and Judge Alonzo Knapp took the bench.

As soon as court convened, Monty Powell jumped up like a jack-in-the-box. "Your Honor, I'd like to call Lavinia Tuttle. She has come forward with important evidence." Quickly, he walked a set of papers to the judge and Susan Dayton.

The judge looked over his glasses at the prosecutor. "I cautioned you yesterday about springing any more surprise witnesses on me, Counselor."

"Yes, sir, but the jury needs to hear what she has to say. Her testimony will affect their decision."

Alonzo Knapp pushed his glasses up his nose. "It involve flip charts?"

"No, sir. No flip charts."

"All right," Knapp sighed. "I'll allow."

The gallery went from impassive to animated as a woman in an olive-green slack suit took the witness stand. Recognizing her as the same woman he'd observed doing a tete-a-tete with the prosecutor earlier in the week, Chitto leaned forward.

Quickly establishing that the witness was Bernard Wasilewski's landlady, Powell said, "Do you remember the night Muriel Simpson met her tragic end, Mrs. Tuttle?" She did. "And you've heard Mr. Wasilewski testify that he encountered Muriel Simpson that night as he was taking out his trash." She confirmed she'd heard his testimony. "And that he went back upstairs to finish cleaning his apartment." She answered in the affirmative again.

Powell looked at Susan Dayton. "The defense has called into doubt that Mr. Wasilewski went back upstairs to complete that chore."

"Yeah, I heard that, too," she said. "But it ain't so. I know 'cause I heard Bernie running the sweeper at midnight."

Powell looked at the court recorder. "Let it be shown that Bernie refers to Bernard Wasilewski." He walked to the jury box as he addressed his next question to Lavinia Tuttle. "And how can you be so exact about the time?"

"The noise woke me up, that's how. I looked at the clock 'cause I was intending to call Bernie on the carpet the next morning, tell him not to do it again. That's one of the rules for living there. Keep it quiet after the evening news and weather is done with. That'd be ten thirty."

"In other words, there's no doubt that Bernard Wasilewski did *not* leave the premises that night," Powell reaffirmed.

Lavinia Tuttle stiffened her back. "Idn't that what I just said?"

"Yes, indeed," Powell said, smiling. "You have confirmed that Mr. Wasilewski didn't leave the apartment building once he went back upstairs." Turning to the judge, he said, "No more questions of the witness."

Seeking out Bernard Wasilewski in the audience, Chitto saw the ex-hospital corpsman's shoulders visibly straighten. Looking toward the defense table, he saw Susan Dayton's slump.

Score one for the cock of the walk.

"Bernie's the best renter I ever had," Lavinia Tuttle said abruptly. "It was that Muriel who was always disturbing the peace. Comin' and goin' all hours of the night. I was fixing to evict her once her lease was up—"

"Thank you, Mrs. Tuttle," Monty Powell said hurriedly. "No more questions."

The judge looked at Susan Dayton. "Counselor, any cross exam?"

"Yes, indeed." Briskly, Dayton approached the witness chair. "Mrs. Tuttle, you just mentioned you were planning to evict Muriel Simpson once her lease was up. Would you explain to the jury why you felt it necessary to do that?"

"Why, because of her loose ways."

Chitto watched Monty Powell's chin drop toward his chest.

"Would you please clarify what you mean by loose?" Dayton asked.

The witness stared at the petite attorney, blinking. "Well," she said, "it may not be considered a bad thing for you big-city types, but 'round here, a woman brings home a different man every time the wind changes directions, we call that loose—especially when those men don't leave till morning."

"Thank you," Dayton said. "Then am I correct in describing your feelings for Muriel Simpson as . . . extreme dislike?"

Monty Powell was on his feet in a flash. "Objection—leading the witness."

"Sustained," Knapp said. Looking over his glasses at Dayton, he said, "Continue, Counselor, but carefully."

Nodding, Susan Dayton faced the witness again. "Another question, Mrs. Tuttle. How many residents were there in your apartment building at the time of the murder?"

"Well, lemme see." Tuttle grew thoughtful. "A couple lives in one—a *married* couple so they're legit. The rest of us were single. Muriel's apartment's the only one I rented since it happened. There's a nice old lady lives there now. Eighty if she's a day."

Susan Dayton started to pace. "And which apartments did the other renters occupy?"

Lavinia Tuttle began to blink. "The married couple's upstairs, across the hall from Bernie. Their last name's Wallace. Bernie's apartment is above mine and Muriel lived across the hall."

Dayton made a *tsk-tsk* sound. "I'm troubled, Mrs. Tuttle," she said, stopping before the witness chair. "See, I live in a ground-floor apartment and I can't always tell if a noise is coming from inside the building or outside on the street."

She clasped her hands behind her back, still staring at the witness. "There are two apartments above you and a couple lives in one. Common sense tells me a couple would make more noise than a single person would. Common sense also tells me there would be traffic on the street on a Saturday night." She paused, eyes still on the witness. "Can you be certain, beyond-a-shadow-of-doubt certain, just what that noise you heard was . . ." She paused, leaning forward slightly. "*And* where it came from?"

"Well, I can tell you this much, girlie." Lavinia Tuttle puffed up like an adder. "Some of that noise I heard that night was the wheels on that sweeper squeaking. After I chewed Bernie out for waking me up, I loaned him my can of WD-40 so he could grease it up—and I haven't heard a squeak since."

247

A titter of laughter ran through the gallery. A look from Alonzo Knapp brought it to a quick end.

"I see," Dayton said, nodding slowly. "Might it be that you haven't heard it since because Bernie doesn't dare run the sweeper at night for fear you'll chew him out again?" The tittering turned to guffaws, requiring a bang of the judge's gavel. Chitto was one of those guilty.

Coolly, Dayton faced the witness again. "Tell me, Mrs. Tuttle, have you ever loaned your WD-40 to others there in the building?"

Lavinia Tuttle underwent a slow transformation: deflating by degrees, reddening from the neck up, tightening of the muscles around the mouth.

Susan Dayton leaned forward again. "Let me remind you, Mrs. Tuttle, you're under oath."

Olive-green Woman held the spotlight. Chitto heard footsteps *clip clipping* down the hallway, a siren wailing in the distance, and dead silence in the courtroom.

"Well, yes. Suppose I have," Tuttle said.

"Who, exactly?"

Tuttle sniffed loudly. "That couple upstairs," she mumbled.

Dayton leaned closer to the witness. "I'm sorry, did you say *that couple upstairs*?" Dayton got a nod in reply. "And what egregious act did they commit that required WD-40?"

"What kinda act?" The witness looked at the judge, a blank look on her face.

The judge looked at Susan Dayton. "Rephrase, Counselor," he sighed.

"Why did you give them the WD-40?" Dayton asked.

"Well, see . . ." Tuttle picked at a thread on her sleeve. "They have this exercise bike that sounds like two tomcats goin' to fist city when it gets dried out."

Turning to Alonzo Knapp, Dayton said, "No more questions."

Laughter rippled through the gallery again. Chitto knew one, however, who was not amused. Healing takes courage, Chitto thought, looking toward Bernard Wasilewski. The ex-corpsman shoulders had again hunched forward.

Exhaling loudly, Alonzo Knapp looked at Monty Powell. "What do I do with the witness, Mr. Powell?"

"Dismiss her." Powell waved a hand through the air, but as soon as Lavinia Tuttle was out of the witness chair, he was on his feet again. "However, I respectfully ask that this telephone record be added to the trial records." He handed the judge one printed set of papers, Susan Dayton another. Before either could comment, he added, "We just got this information so there wasn't time to distribute it in advance."

"What are we looking at?" Knapp said, flipping through the pages.

"A record from Buster Littlejohn's cell phone provider, tracking his phone usage the night of the murder. Cell carriers take note of incoming telephone numbers, the time, date and duration of the conversation, *and* because the call is sent through a network of cell towers, the location."

Knapp removed his glasses and stared at Powell. "That kind of record usually requires a court order. How'd you get this?"

Powell squirmed a bit. "You were out of the office, Judge. One of your constituents obtained it because it was relevant to an ongoing investigation." He produced a toothy smile. "And because you were sitting the bench on the trial, we thought it best not to involve you."

Lu Clifton

"How considerate," Knapp snapped. "Proceed."

Picking up a copy of the document from his table, Powell pointed out records on different pages. "You'll notice that these records indicate that Mr. Littlejohn was on his phone several times the night Muriel Simpson was murdered. He called two people multiple times. A Virgie Clark and a Velma Brownlee."

"And the significance of these calls?" Knapp asked, peering over his glasses at Powell.

Monty Powell looked at Knapp, then the jury. "The calls were made between the hours of eleven and one fifteen—from the Four Corners Bar. They prove conclusively that Mr. Littlejohn could *not* be Muriel Simpson's killer."

That's not all, Chitto thought. They also prove that the grieving boyfriend didn't waste much time replacing Muriel. Yon Cassius was, indeed, a devious fellow.

Powell glanced at Susan Dayton. "But if defense wishes, I can put Misses Clark and Brownlee on the stand."

"Your Honor," Dayton said, standing quickly. "In light of this new information, I request a delay. I need time to examine these documents before I proceed." She sat down as quickly as she'd stood.

Alonzo Knapp leaned back in his chair, fingertips tapping together. "Agreed," he sighed. "You've got till tomorrow morning." He looked at the bailiff. "In light of my commitment this afternoon, I hereby dismiss the court for today. We'll resume again tomorrow morning, nine thirty sharp."

The judge followed the jury out of the courtroom and a county officer escorted Bobby back to his holding cell. As both attorneys filed out, the gallery turned into a stampede. Chitto followed the herd, eyes on the only person who had not moved. Charlie Walker sat in his chair, staring at something visible only to him.

CHAPTER TWENTY-ONE

Chitto sat in his truck, engine running and air conditioner on, waiting for the traffic leaving the parking lot to ease up. The time did not go to waste. He pulled up a number on his cell phone, then hesitated, debating whether to call Jasmine while she was at work. The last thing he wanted was for Dan Blackfox to find out what he was up to. Giving his head a shake, he pushed the button.

"This must be important," she said, talking in a low voice.

"It is." The fact she was whispering confirmed his suspicions. Dan Blackfox was on the prowl. "How's it coming on that research you're doing?"

She made a grunting sound. "Mostly getting dizzy. The kind of thing you're after is buried in storage lockers or needs an official reason to release it. You know, like a subpoena?"

Chitto exhaled. "Well, it was worth a shot."

"Hold your horses," she snapped. "You think I'd give up that easy? When I struck out looking north, I started looking south."

"South? Only thing south of Durant's the Red River."

"You forget about Texas? I did some searching on that side. Did you know Bert Gilly almost bought a place on Lake Travis?"

Chitto sat up straighter. About fifteen miles northwest of Austin, Lake Travis was a large reservoir lake lined with resort communities and country clubs. "Damn," he mumbled. "How could he afford that on his salary? The smaller places don't come cheap and waterfront places cost *beaucoup* bucks."

"Upwards to a million these days," she said. "And we've been in a recession."

"Hold on," he said, pausing. "You said almost."

"Well, make a mark on the wall," she said, feigning shock. "You were actually listening."

"You said *almost*," Chitto pushed.

"Seems the deal was never closed."

"Why?"

"Don't know."

"What kind of place was it?"

"Didn't get that far. Wanted to run it past you, see if it was worth pursuing."

"Hell," he sighed. "At this point, anything's worth pursuing."

"Wonderful," she groused. "I'm back to land transactions."

He chuckled. "You find Gilly's cell phone number? I thought maybe someone there in the office still had it programmed into their phone."

"Cell phone number? Why you need that?"

Paraphrasing Monty Powell, Chitto said, "Cell carriers note incoming phone numbers, the time, date, and duration of the conversation—and the location."

"It's been ten years, Sam."

"They keep historical records a long time. It's a long shot, but possible."

"Unless he was using one of those prepaid cell phones."

"Yeah, didn't think of that." A pause punctuated with static. "I doubt he'd do that. Those things are unpredictable, run out of time fast. My money's on a cell phone carrier."

"Even so, there'd be no reason for anyone 'round here to keep Gilly's number after he died."

"Yeah," he said again. "You're probably right."

"Besides, like everything else, phone companies don't release that information unless there's a legal reason to. A court order or a warrant from a judge."

"I know," he said. "Something proving that a record is relevant and material to an ongoing investigation."

"Which isn't going to happen, is it?"

A deep sigh. "No, Dan wouldn't give me the go ahead."

"Of course," she said, "the FBI can skip all that rigma-role. Too bad you're on the outs with that Rodriguez."

Seconds passed.

A hoarse whisper. "Sam, you still there?"

"Just thinking. Thanks, Jasmine, keep digging on that other stuff. If you run across that cell number, let me know."

"Your fee just went to three weeks worth of coffee."

"Deal. Now, put me through to Dan."

"Dan?" She made a grumbling sound. "Call him direct. We're on the outs."

"I don't have time for that. Why are you on the outs?"

255

"He wants me to make coffee when I get here in the morning like Wanda used to."

"Cafeteria's right next door," he said. "We didn't even have a cafeteria when Wanda worked there."

"That's what I told him. Said, 'My job description didn't include making coffee.' Know what *he* said?"

Chitto rubbed an ache in his left temples. "I can only imagine."

"Said, 'I have meetings in my office sometimes.' So I said, 'Take them to the cafeteria, buy them a cup, and bring them back here—better yet, have the meeting there because the first refill's on the house.'"

"Where'd you leave it?" he asked.

"What do you think?" she snapped.

"You don't do coffee?" he said.

"I'll connect you now."

∞

Dan Blackfox wasn't long in taking the call. "What's up, Sam? Got a meeting in a few minutes so talk fast."

"Need a couple more days. Can you do without me?"

"We're keeping our heads above water. Why you need more time?"

Chitto took a few seconds, choosing his words carefully. "Things have taken a turn here I didn't expect."

"Like what?"

Chitto shook his head, wondering if he was too old to change his profession to field geology. Rock specimens weren't nearly as challenging as human specimens.

"I had a hard time getting a handle on this Taneyhill kid," he said. "As a result, I may have set something in motion I shouldn't have." He hesitated, licking his lips. "I need time to fix what I broke."

The line went quiet. "Sounds pretty serious."

"It could be."

"You sure it deals with this Taneyhill boy, not your dad and Bert?"

"Dead sure." Exhaling, he leaned back in his seat. "Besides, don't need to. Rodriguez is up here digging around. You were right. He's taking the case seriously."

"That's what I hear. Pete Brody filled me in."

"Sonofa—you were testing me?"

A chuckle came from the line. "Just keeping you honest. Take the rest of the week, come in on Monday."

"And one more thing," Chitto said. "My grandmother wants those drawings back—*muy pronto*."

"They're locked in my bottom drawer. Get 'em to you next week."

Chitto glanced at the dashboard clock after he hung up, then keyed the ignition. He had another appointment to keep. And he was hungry.

∞

Pete Brody was in his office, as planned. "'Bout gave up on you," he said when Chitto pushed through the door.

"Got time for a bite?" Chitto asked. "Had a couple sweet rolls for breakfast, compliments of the camp hostess, and one cup of coffee. Lunch is on me. You pick the place."

"There's a diner on Broadway. Parking's at a premium, but worth a walk."

"My preferred mode of transportation," On the way, Chitto told Pete he needed a dog sitter another day, which didn't present a problem.

The diner had a red tin roof and a sign out front that said, *Breakfast and Lunch*. The inside was small, big enough for a dozen or so rectangle tables with red Formica tops and a small salad bar. Flocked red wallpaper covered the walls and ceiling fans spun in lazy circles.

"Back here," Pete said, walking towards the rear corner. They ordered burgers and fries, iced tea with double the ice.

"First off," Brody said when the waitperson was gone. "Why's the trial been delayed? Rumor has it that skinny gal has done a whale of a job establishing reasonable doubt."

"She has, but the prosecutor shot a couple of spitballs at her this morning. She asked for a delay so she could reconnoiter and the judge gave her till tomorrow morning." He sipped iced tea through a straw. "But something tells me it's all over but the shouting. Attorneys will do their closing arguments tomorrow and the judge will throw it to the jury."

"What's your thinking?"

Chitto took another pull on the straw. "Jury's hard to read. Right now, I'd say it could go either way. Depends on how persuasive Greenhorn Girl can be against City Slicker."

Brody made a grunting sound. "What about our boys?"

They paused when the burgers and fries appeared, along with bottles of catsup and mustard. Noticing the glasses were almost empty, the waitress also brought a pitcher of fresh tea.

"I'll take the check," Chitto said, watching her tear it from her pad. He tucked it into his shirt pocket and began on his fries.

"Damn it, Sam, the skin on the back of my neck's crawlin'," Brody said, spreading mustard on his bun. "I'm not liking the silence coming from your side of the table." He handed the bottle to Chitto.

Chitto squirted mustard on his hamburger bun, then looked at Brody. "Bert Gilly was wearing a Kevlar vest when he came up here."

"*What?*" Brody did a double take, then took a long pull on his straw. "Why in hell would he be wearing a vest?"

Chitto chewed his burger, washed it down with tea, and looked across the table. "Thought you could help me figure that out." He paused, squirting catsup on his fries. "My dad wasn't wearing one."

Brody's eyes wandered a bit, then returned to Chitto. "You got that from a reliable source, I suppose."

"FBI."

"Hellfire." Brody chewed his burger slowly, blinking eyes showing a mind much more active. Looking at Chitto, he said, "Of course, you know what this is beginning to look like."

"A deal gone bad?"

Brody swallowed the bite he'd been chewing. "More like a double-cross gone bad."

Chitto rubbed a hand across his mouth. "I, uh, I've got someone looking into this for me, and she just learned that Bert was in the process of buying a place on Lake Travis, down in hill country. But my hands are tied. The case belongs to the FBI, but . . ." He shook his head. "The agent on the case is the one who told me about the bullet-proof vest, and he's reached a dead end."

Brody leaned back, staring at him. "I'm having a hard time wrapping my head around this thing."

"You're not alone." Chitto leaned forward, elbows on the table. "Tell me everything you know about Bert. Did he ever come up this way, maybe to work a connection with a case up here? Call you on anything—on his cell phone, maybe?" He leaned back in the booth, sighing. "Hell, I can't even find out what his cell number was."

Brody filled his tea glass from the pitcher, tossed the straw, and took a long drink. "Like I said before, Will and I chewed the fat now and then but I didn't really know Bert. He worked the other end of the Nation, kept to himself when we had joint meetings. Besides, so much time's gone by . . ." He looked away, letting his words trail.

"Something occur to you, Pete?"

Brody sat forward, arms folded on the table. "I'm a packrat, never threw one of my notebooks away. Got 'em stored in boxes in my basement."

"Like the one when you interviewed Wasilewski's landlady? That one was a year old."

"Hell, a year's nothing." Brody chuckled softly. "Molly's been on me to have a weenie roast, use them to fuel the fire." He sipped tea, looked across the table. "Let me take a look, focus on the timeframe before the murder happened. I've got the boxes indexed by year but could still take a bit."

"Appreciate it, Pete." Chitto glanced at his watch. "I've kept you longer than I should've. I need to fetch a dog and pick up your backyard." He grinned at Brody. "Don't want to leave a mess for you to clean up when you get home."

Brody grunted. "Believe me, a little dog poop's clean compared to what we've been discussing."

∞

Chitto spent a good two hours at Pete Brody's place but not because of Boycott. Molly Brody had walked out of garden club to a flat tire and hitched a ride home. Chitto drove her back to her car and swapped the spare for the flat. Worried the spare wouldn't hold air, Molly drove straight home and Chitto followed. He had taken the flat to a service station, waited for it to be repaired, then gone back and changed it out. His reward was half an apple pie in a plastic container, along with a wedge of cheddar cheese.

"Don't worry about returning the container," she said. "It's one from the grocery store I recycled."

He'd cleaned up the backyard before he left, then driven straight to Bud and Birdie's place. Cabin 4 was airless and stuffy again, but a stack of clean clothes lay on the kitchen table. He opened the windows and doors, aimed the three-speed oscillating fan at the bed, and turned it on high. To give the room time to cool down, he changed into his running clothes and took Boycott down the trail.

His mind roiled as he jogged, thoughts vacillating between Bell Gilly and his father, Bobby Taneyhill and Charlie Walker. Walker's was the face he couldn't get out of his mind. He'd dealt the honorable man a blow, removing the veil covering his eyes when it came to his grandson. But Walker wasn't the only one suffering undeserved consequences from the revelations this trial had produced. Bernard Wasilewski had suffered as well.

Could honorable men ever recover lost honor, he wondered.

Stopping at the turnaround on the trail, Chitto called Boycott to his side. He waited before starting the return trip, catching his breath and listening. The heatbugs had been in their heyday but even as they grew quiet, the katydids were starting their chorus. Though he strained his ears, Chitto did not hear the elusive little owl's warning cry again.

How many times you have to be told something? cautioned the voice in his head.

Dusk was settling when he returned to the cabin. Stripping down to his briefs, he walked toward the bathroom, then stopped, eyeing the light on his cell phone. Recognizing the number, he piled pillows up on the bed and sat down with them at his back. The oscillating fan did its job, blessing him with cool air as it made its revolutions around the room. Hitting the call back button, he waited for Jasmine to pick up.

"What you got, Scout," he asked.

"Don't get your bowels in an uproar," she said. "I didn't find a cell number but I did talk to a realtor down in Texas."

"Oh, yeah?" Chitto picked up a notepad and pen from the side table.

"The place Bert put a bid on *was* on the lake."

"Pricey?"

"Big time, but that's not the kicker. He was putting it in his name only."

Chitto's jaws went slack. "Why in hell would he do that?"

"Don't know, but sounds like it was a big place . . . and very la-di-da."

Chitto tapped the pencil on the pad. "Define la-di-da."

"Round bed in the master bedroom, wine cellar, hot tub, round bed in the master bedroom, three-car garage, private dock. Did I mention the round bed in the master bedroom?"

"Multiple times. What do you make of it?"

A weighty pause. "Midlife crisis leading to a major lifestyle change? Maybe a change of partners? One he felt a need to impress?"

"Damn." He ran a hand over his face. "So Wanda may not have known about it, which would account for it never being mentioned."

"Wife's the last one to know," she said. "He put down a deposit—a big one I might add—which he lost when he let the deadline fall through. That happens when you die unexpectedly." She paused. "I think maybe I missed the boat. Real estate's the job to have."

"Unless there's a recession," he said.

"Or a drought. Lakes in Texas have all but dried up in recent years."

"Might as well keep your job then. That it?"

"Told you not to get excited." *Click.*

Throwing his pen and notebook on the bed table, Chitto stripped out of his briefs and walked to the bathroom. Standing under the showerhead, he digested what the information meant.

Conclusion: Bert Gilly was not an honorable man.

Picking up a bar of soap, Chitto lathered all over, rinsed, then lathered again. Still, he did not feel clean.

CHAPTER TWENTY-TWO

Following his shower, Chitto had put on old jeans and gone without shirt and shoes. Dinner had been cold on the back porch: a meat and cheese sandwich on white bread with bottled water as a chaser. Dessert, the apple pie Molly sent with him, waited in the refrigerator. Boycott provided the entertainment. He had treed a squirrel and was standing guard. The squirrel chattered; Boycott growled at it menacingly.

Headlights coming from the front of the cabin pulled Chitto's attention away from the standoff. He listened to the sound of a car engine dying, a car door slamming. Abandoning the squirrel tree, Boycott walked as far as the tie-out cable allowed, tail wagging.

Translation? The visitor was friendly.

Rising, Chitto padded barefoot through the carpet of leaves surrounding the cabin. He stared at the silver Jeep parked next to his pickup, then turned his attention to the woman pounding on the cabin's door.

"Mackie?"

"*What the hell*—" She spun around, eyes glinting in the moonlight. "What are you doing out here in the dark?"

"I was on the back porch." He walked toward her, frowning. "Didn't mean to scare you. What's up?"

Wrapping her arms around her body, she said, "I was already scared." She looked at him. "I didn't know what else to do."

He took her arm. "Come inside. I'll fix some coffee."

Mackie surveyed the cabin as he filled the pot with water, the basket with coffee. Setting it on the burner, he motioned her to a chair and said, "Talk."

"It's Charlie. He waited until everyone left the center and I was alone. He wasn't scheduled to work because of the trial, so I wasn't expecting to see him." She looked away, eyes flitting. "He was standing behind me, not three feet away, just staring at me." She pushed her hair back from her face. "He was . . . different."

"How?"

She shrugged. "Darker, and I'm not talking about coloring. His eyes were penetrating. Probing." She looked at him, head shaking. "Scared the bejesus out of me."

"What'd he want?"

"The portfolio, he wanted to look at Bobby's novel again." She paused, eyes still skittering. "I didn't have a reason to refuse. I mean, it belongs to him. I was just holding it for him."

"So you gave it to him and . . ."

"He stood right there in the exhibit storeroom and looked at it, page by page—I mean, every inch of it. Then . . ." She paused, staring angrily at him. "You told him about that phone call Bobby made to that girl. It had to be you. I didn't tell anyone else."

"Guilty," he said, grimacing. "He asked you about it?"

"Wanted to know what happened, word for word." She leaned back, sighing. "So, I told him—about what I overheard, not what you and I decided it meant."

I saved you that trouble, he thought, deciding to keep that piece to himself.

Rising from his chair, he poured two cups of coffee and set them on the table. "You didn't get supper. I have sandwich fixings—"

"I couldn't eat," she said, taking a sip from the cup. Swallowing fast, she looked up at him. "But I'd take some milk to dilute this mud."

He fetched a carton of milk, the apple pie, and cheese. "No arguments," he said, setting two plates on the table. He split the pie and cheese, handed her a fork, and sat down again. He shoveled the pie. She picked at the cheddar wedge.

Minutes passed in silence. "He didn't intend to hurt you," Chitto said, noting the drained look on her face. "He just needed more than my word to connect the dots. I shook him up pretty good."

She laid her fork down. "*Charlie* was the tree you were planning to shake?" Her back stiffened. "You could have told me, Sam. I was caught flat-footed."

"I got busy . . ." He shrugged. "And I didn't know he'd react that way." He looked at her. "What happened after you told him about the call?"

"*Oh*, I had to repeat the story twice. He watched my face the entire time. I swear he was testing me, seeing if I would slip up."

"The truth can be a hard thing to swallow."

She rubbed the back of her neck. "I felt as if I was the one on trial." She shook her head, sighing. "And then he left, just turned on his heel and walked out." She looked across the table. "But he took the portfolio with him. The evidence is gone. If Bobby goes free, I'm hosed."

"I'll go see him," Chitto said, standing.

"He's not home. I checked as I drove away. His truck's not in the drive, and . . ." She shook her head. "His burn barrel is smoking."

"Damn." He sat down again, fingers tapping the table.

"Boycott wants in," she said, rising from her chair. Opening the door, she unclipped the tie-down snap on his collar and gave him a good rub.

"He's hungry," Chitto said, filling food and water bowls. As Boycott went to work on the food, he looked toward Mackie. She stood with arms wrapped around her body, shoulders sagging.

"I won't let anything happen to you," he said. "And just so you know, I'm known to be a man of my word."

She looked up at him. "All I know is, I don't want to go home." She looked toward the extra sleeping bag across the room "Mind if I bunk here? I've slept on the ground plenty of times."

"Take the bed," he said. "I'll take the floor."

∞

Neither could sleep, but neither talked. Night noises filled the void. Katydids, dog snores from the corner, and an oscillating fan created a nocturnal symphony.

Sam stared at shadows moving across the ceiling. He'd put on freshly laundered sweatpants and loaned Mackie an undershirt, then listened to her toss and turn, plump her pillow, and sigh for an hour. He knew she would never go to sleep if she couldn't stop thinking about Charlie Walker's visit.

"How'd you end up in archaeology," he said to divert her attention.

"What?"

"You need to think about something else or neither of us is going to get a wink of sleep. How'd you end up in archaeology?"

"Oh . . ." She paused a minute, then laughed softly. "I was given a sign."

"What kind of sign," he said, thinking of the horned owl in the woods.

"I was about twelve," she said. "You know, that time when kids start wondering about things."

"Like sex?"

She snorted. "That's what the boys do. Girls think about *important* things."

"*Ow*," he groaned. "That was cold. What kind of important things?"

"Nothing revolutionary, just questions waiting to be answered. Like, what did I want to do the rest of my life? I grew up on a ranch and loved it, but it seemed . . . I don't know, restrictive. Dull. A future fixing three meals a day for a dozen ranch hands and watching soap operas to break the boredom didn't appeal to me." She grunted softly. "Can you believe my mom still can't wait for *The Bold and the Beautiful* to come on? Holy hell—talk about living vicariously."

Chitto smiled into the darkness, thinking those few words spoke volumes about Mackie Green. "Where is your dad's place?"

"The Blanco area. It's a small spread, not like those in deep west Texas."

"Hill country," he said, thinking that explained the drawl. "Go on," he said. "I want to hear about this mysterious sign."

"Oh, right . . ." She faced the ceiling again, turning pensive. "See, I was walking across this patch of ground my dad

269

had let go because it wasn't fit for grazing or haying. Spring had been wet that year and the bluebonnets were beautiful." She paused. "It's pretty all the time, but that year was exceptional." She made a lazy wave through the air. "Anyway, this one spot is different, unnatural looking. The rocks almost look like they've been stacked up, arranged deliberately. Even as a little girl, I was drawn to it." She laughed. "The Texas version of a fairy ring, I suppose."

Studying shadows waltzing across the ceiling, he said, "How'd that lead to archaeology?"

She flipped onto her stomach, looking down at him. "That day I was telling you about when I was twelve, I walked up to this spot. As I was sitting on this outcropping, a gust of wind uncovered this stone right in front of me."

"What kind of stone?" He folded an arm behind his head, looking up at her.

"Nothing special, just a chunk of sandstone. But it had been worked into a tool. A groove on one side, the other side wore smooth from where a hand had held it. I showed it to my dad and he said it was probably used to smooth arrow shafts. You know, natural sandpaper."

"I've seen those," he said. "Still have it?"

"Sure do." She flipped onto her back, staring at the ceiling again. "Keep it on my bookshelf at home." She took a breath, released it. "It's what made me aware that I was not the first one to sit at that spot, that there were whole civilizations that had walked and lived and breathed there long before our kind was a twinkle in God's eye." She paused. "I wanted to get to know those people."

"A sign for sure," he said.

"Yeah." She looked over the edge of the bed again. "I know how you got into police work but how'd you get into geology."

270

He thought a bit. "I wasn't given a sign exactly," he said. "It was more a baptism."

"Baptism?" she snorted. "Oh, I've got to hear about this."

He paused briefly. "My dad was a fisherman and wanted me to share his passion. He took me bass fishing every chance he got, but I was more interested in rocks than baiting hooks. I alternated between cracking rocks open to see if there was a geode inside and searching for smooth ones flat enough to skip over the water."

He stretched out, fingers laced behind his head. "On this one trip, he was fishing from a long dock and I, of course, was skipping rocks across the water. He'd warned me several times about scaring the fish away till he finally got fed up." Chitto paused, chuckling softly. "I sliced a flat stone across the water and while I was busy counting skips, he walked up behind me. He picked me up, threw me over his shoulder, and walked to the end of the dock. Next thing I knew, I was in the lake—*way* out in the lake."

"You had to swim to shore?"

"No." He smiled into the darkness. "Dad fetched a tree limb and held it out so I could pull myself in. As I stood dripping on the dock, he looked at me and said, 'It's clear you prefer rock hunting to fishing, which is fine by me. We all have our passions. But here on out, the only thing I want to see you lob in that lake is a fishhook and bobber.'"

"Better than baptism by fire," she said, laughing again.

They laid a while without talking. Then Chitto heard her begin to toss again. "I'm a man of my word, Mackie," he whispered. "Sleep now."

Mackie turned on her side and soon enough, he heard the sound of steady breathing. As soon as he sensed her sleep was deep, he slid out of the sleeping bag and threw the deadbolts on both doors. Easing to the closet, he took the box of shotgun shells from the top shelf, loaded the Remington, and slid it underneath the bed. The Glock earned a place under his pillow.

He slipped back into the sleeping bag but did not close his eyes. Thoughts of Charlie Walker kept sleep from coming. He'd pushed the old man hard, forcing him to consider something repugnant. The visit he'd made to see Mackie was proof of that. By nature, Walker was an honorable man, but Chitto knew that the public face often concealed a hidden one. If Walker had destroyed the unfinished novel, what else was he prepared to do to save his grandson?

Something in Chitto's memory pulled at him, something from a college philosophy course he'd taken. A saying by the Greek philosopher, Epictetus. As he watched the shadow dance on the ceiling, the truism emerged. It went, "Circumstances don't make the man, they only reveal him to himself." Now that push had come to shove, would Walker discover he was not the honorable man he considered himself to be?

CHAPTER TWENTY-THREE

Chitto was dressed and had a fresh pot of coffee made by the time Mackie woke. He laced a cup with milk and handed it to her. "I'll follow you home so you can change, then head to Walker's place."

"What are you planning to do there?" she asked, slipping into her clothes.

"Talk to him, try to get an idea of where this is heading." He slipped his Glock from his waist holster and made sure it had a full clip. "I'll make sure he heads for Poteau. After that, I'll drop Boycott off and head for the courthouse myself."

She took a sip of coffee. "Call me if he's not there."

He paused, considering what-ifs. Mackie was still the trigger mechanism in this psychedelic drama. What if Walker turned around and came back to eliminate all remaining traces of Bobby's guilt?

"I'm planning to keep him in my sights, but just in case . . ." He handed the Glock to her. "I figure you know how to use one of these."

"I've shot a few rattlers in my day . . . but no." Pushing the gun away, she began to pace. "For starters, it's illegal to bring weapons onto the grounds. Second, I was rattled last night, not thinking straight."

He stared at her, eyes showing confusion.

She stopped in front of him. "Look, what you said last night made sense. Charlie wouldn't hurt me." She raised a hand, putting an end to any protest. "The case goes to the jury today. He'll be there for Bobby. I'm the least of his concerns."

"My faith in human nature's a bit more tarnished than yours. What if Bobby goes free?"

She paused, licking her lips. "My grandma was full of these old sayings, but more times than not they were dead on. One of her favorites was, 'Don't count your chickens before they've hatched.'" She shrugged. "If Bobby goes free, I'll deal with it then."

"I've got a grandmother like that," he said.

∞

Walker's pickup was not in his driveway. After following Mackie to her house, Chitto had driven straight to the trailer home. He sat in his truck, engine idling, and looked across the meadow at the Archaeology Center. No truck there either.

"Stay," he said to Boycott and opened his door.

He walked toward the steps to the mobile home, listening for sounds of activity. The birds were quiet, the insects, too. A look through the front window showed a dark house, no lights burning anywhere. His knock on the front door shattered the calm but went unanswered. He tested the door handle. Locked. He walked around the trailer to the back door. Also locked. As he made the return trip, he paused, looking at something that caught his eye. A fresh pile of dirt in the woods back of the mobile home.

Had Walker buried something there? Maybe a troublesome varmint causing problems?

Spotting the burn barrel, he quickly looked inside. It was filled with charred remains of day-to-day living: empty food cans, glass jars that had shattered from the heat, scraps of cardboard. He paused, frowning. Picking up a stick, he stirred the barrel, trying to get a better look at something that had caught his eye. He sighed as he identified the object: the button closure on the flap of a tan portfolio. Incriminating evidence was now ash.

Walking to his truck, he drove the short distance to the Spiro Mounds entrance and pulled into the parking lot. Leaving Boycott in the truck again, he pulled his service weapon and walked to the front door. Finding it locked, he walked behind both buildings, checking for signs of activity. Nothing.

Boycott nosed him as he put the truck in gear again. "I know," he mumbled, rubbing the dog's ears. "Something's not right."

Dialing Mackie's number, he got a quick, "That you, Sam?"

"Yeah. Walker's not home and I checked the Center. Doors are all locked, nothing looks out of place."

"Where could he be?"

"Left early for the courthouse, I expect. I'll call you from there."

He wasted no time getting to the Brody's or putting Boycott in their backyard. Quickly filling a food and water dish, he hurried back to his truck.

"*Sam*," Molly Brody called from the front porch. "Pete had to go out on an early call but he said to tell you to come by his office on the lunch hour."

He paused, facing her. "He find something?"

"He doesn't talk work," she said. "But he spent the night in the basement and left with a handful of stuff. What's that tell you?"

"If he checks in, tell him I'll be there."

He pushed the speed limit all the way to Poteau. Still, the courthouse parking lot was filled by the time he got there. Mardi Gras was in full swing and the revelers had turned out to enjoy the trial's finale.

"Beats soap operas," Chitto mumbled, recalling Mackie's comment about breaking the boredom.

He drove up and down each row in the lot, looking for a black pickup truck. Spotting it near the back of the lot, he relaxed. Forced to park on a side street, he jogged to the courthouse, cell phone to his ear.

"Walker's here," he said, relieved when Mackie picked up. "Can't talk now. Call later."

Hurrying through security, he pushed through the courtroom doors and looked toward the place behind the defense table. A suit coat with oversized shoulder pads lay on the chair that Walker usually occupied, but he was not in the courtroom. Walking up the gallery steps, Chitto found an open seat and took it.

The gallery was noisy this morning, excited whispers and mumbles skittering up and down rows. Except for the expert witnesses, who had been excused from further testimony, local witnesses were in place. All of them looked tense.

Chitto turned as Monty Powell entered the court. Exuding confidence, the prosecutor took his chair and opened a folder, preparing to make his closing argument. Seconds passed, then minutes. Still, Susan Dayton and Bobby Taneyhill did not appear. The chattering and mumbling grew louder, accompanied by restless shuffling, then quieted as a familiar figure entered from the hallway.

Charlie Walker walked with his eyes on the floor, back stooped, shirt collar open. Even from a distance, fatigue was evident on his face. Quietly, he removed the suit coat from the chair and sat down. A minute later, Susan Dayton entered, her suit looking as creased and rumpled as its wearer. Bobby Taneyhill trailed behind: face pale, shoulders drooping, eyes on the floor.

Gauging from Walker and Dayton's appearance, Chitto figured they'd been in conference well into the night, if not all night. He leaned forward, heart-rate escalating.

As the jury was seated, the bailiff called for those in attendance to stand. No sooner had Judge Alonzo Knapp assumed the bench than Susan Dayton was on her feet.

"If it pleases the court . . ." She paused, looking over her shoulder at Walker.

Glancing at the old man, Chitto noticed him give her a nod. The go-ahead sign? For what?

Shoulders sagging slightly, Dayton turned again to face the bench.

Before she could speak, Knapp said, "Are you preparing to spring another surprise on me, Counselor?" Removing his glasses, he stared at her.

"No—yes." She paused, sighing. "With the consent of the court, the defendant wishes to change his plea to guilty by reason of insanity."

It took Judge Knapp several minutes to end the pandemonium in the gallery.

Once order was restored, Dayton said, "The defendant did not know what he was doing at the time. He was living in another reality. Defense respectfully asks the court to consider the age of the defendant at the time of the event and also requests that he receive a psychiatric evaluation." She remained standing, waiting for a response.

"But Judge—" a shocked Monty Powell protested. "Evidence against the defendant is overwhelming. There's ample evidence showing he'd been planning this kind of thing for some time—"

"A verdict was not reached," Dayton insisted, eyes on the bench. "And it's not the prosecutor's job to determine that verdict."

Knapp looked between the two attorneys, then faced Powell. "The evidence as presented shows a lot of things, Counselor. Take your seat."

As Powell sunk into his chair, Chitto looked at Walker. The man sat stock-still, head bowed. Those in the gallery waited, stunned into silence.

Knapp's sigh from the bench was loud enough to be heard throughout the courtroom. He looked at Susan Dayton.

"Criminal trials are extremely expensive to the public, Miss Dayton. That plea might have garnered you something earlier, but now . . ." Removing a handkerchief from his pocket, he took time to clean his glasses before slipping them on again. "That said, I will take into account the guilty plea and consider the evidence that has been submitted before sentencing."

With that, he rose and said, "The jury is dismissed, court is adjourned."

∞

Chitto stood outside the front entrance to the courthouse, waiting for Walker to appear. As he waited, he placed a call to Mackie Green and quickly briefed her on the outcome.

"*Oh my god,*" she said. "Charlie had to be behind it."

"Without doubt," he murmured. No two ways about it, the honorable man had lived up to his reputation.

"How is he—how's he doing?" she said.

"I'm waiting to talk to him now, but he's worn down to a nub."

"You don't think he'll do anything foolish, do you? With Bobby gone, he doesn't have much to live for."

He took a minute. "Go get the puppy after you get off work, bring it to his place. I'll talk to him in the meantime and meet up with you there."

Chitto waited an hour, pacing between the courthouse entry and the parking lot to make sure Walker's black pickup hadn't moved. As it neared the time he was supposed to meet with Pete Brody, he went through security again and began looking through conference rooms. He found only one with a locked door. As he was debating next steps, Susan Dayton's research assistant walked up behind him, looking as tired and wrinkled as Susan Dayton had.

"I remember you." She was carrying a legal sized file. "What're you doing here?"

"Looking for Charlie Walker. I'm a friend."

"He and Susan are in conference . . . *again*," she said, sounding weary.

"About Bobby's future?"

"Something like that. They don't want to be disturbed."

"Understood," he said. "Just give this to Walker." Pulling a business card from his pocket, he wrote, *Mackie's waiting for you at your place. I'll catch up with you there.*

"Read it if you want," he said, handing it to her. She did.

"Guess I can do that," she said, pocketing the card. "Lord knows, that man's in need of some friends right now."

∞

"Let's talk back here," Pete Brody said, leading Chitto through the office to a back room that doubled as storeroom and kitchen. He had ordered in a pizza and made a fresh pot of coffee.

A card table had been set up and two stacking chairs brought in.

"Keep soft drinks in that little 'frigerator. Thought it'd be best to look these over in private." He laid several well-thumbed notebooks on the table.

"Coffee works for me. Didn't sleep much last night." Chitto helped himself to a slice of pizza and stared at the pile of notebooks. "Where do we begin?"

"I write beginning and ending dates on the front. Thought I'd lead you through what I found, which could be something or what the little boy shot at and missed. This business we're in is mostly guesswork."

The first two notebooks contained entries tracking the Messina family's illicit activities, which were far-ranging and noted an increase in drug use in local schools. They had finished off most of the pizza and were on their second cup of coffee when Brody opened the next notebook.

"Your dad was seeing the same drug problem in his district," Brody said. "See here." He held open a page for Chitto to read. "I wrote down that I'd had a call from Will Chitto saying he'd heard the problem was spreading further south, down toward the Red River."

"Red River? That would've been Bert Gilly's district." Chitto paused, blinking rapidly. "Why did Dad call you instead of him?"

Brody leaned back, sighing. "He figured the Messina family was at the core of it and I agreed. Hell, that bunch has no morals. Sad to say, but kids are easy targets. To the Messina bunch, business is business."

"Wonder how he knew they were trafficking down near the Red?"

"Will kept his ear to the ground, had plenty of informants, too. I figure someone called him with a hot tip. Sounded to me like he was on the trail of something."

Chitto read the entry again. "Or someone?"

"Exactly." Brody leaned forward, pulling up another notebook. "Remember I told you I didn't hear from Bert Gilly much?"

"Yeah, said your trails didn't cross."

"Right. Well, sir, he called me this one time and I made a note of it—though there was no earthly reason to do so. The call didn't deal with a jurisdictional issue, you see." He glanced sideways, blinking. "As I think about it now, I think I noted it because the call made no sense. Take a look."

Chitto read the line in the notebook aloud. "'Might see Gilly around the county, looking at pontoon boats for sale.'" He leaned back, looking at Brody.

"See what I mean?" Brody said. "Thing is, I didn't hear from that man once in a blue moon. Why on earth was it so important to let me know he'd be up here looking at a boat?"

"Pontoon boat, at that." Chitto looked away, frowning. "Maybe it was for that big move he was planning on making down to Lake Travis."

Brody grunted. "To my thinking, there'd be plenty of boats for sale down that way. Pontoons are lake boats for the most part, not river."

"I see your point." Chitto read the comment again. "You know if he called you from the office?"

"No, indeed." Brody smiled. "From his cell phone. I recognized the number wasn't one of ours so I made a note of it." He turned the page. "Wrote it down right here and made a note that it was Gilly's cell phone number."

"I'll be damned." Chitto laughed softly. "Don't ever let Molly talk you into using these things for roasting weenies."

Brody chuckled, then turned serious, "Now, back to that pontoon boat. Care to guess what I'm thinking?"

Chitto sucked the spit from between his teeth. "An inconspicuous way to transport illegal drugs?"

"Guesswork only, you understand. Wouldn't want to tarnish a man's reputation prematurely, but . . ." He shook his head, sighing. "If it walks like a duck, swims like a duck, and quacks like a duck . . ."

Chitto wrote down the phone number.

∞

The clock on the dash read one-fifteen. Chitto was on the way to pick up Boycott at the Brody place. Taking out his cell phone, he pulled up a number and punched it. A hushed whisper said, "I'm at work, Sam."

"I know, Jasmine. But something's eating at me."

"Give me a minute."

He listened to background conversation, a one-sided one. Jasmine had been talking on her office phone.

"Okay, I'm back. What's gnawing your insides so bad it couldn't wait?"

"Pontoon boats." Time passed. "Did I lose you?"

"No, I was just cleaning the wax out of my ear. For a second there, I thought you said pontoon boats."

"I did," he sighed. "You think it's possible to find out if pontoon boat sales took an upswing here in LeFlore County ten, eleven years ago?"

More time passed. He waited.

"Don't those things have to be licensed?" she asked. "You know, like a car?"

"They sure as hell do," he said, thanking his lucky stars Jasmine was on his side. "Work your magic, Scout. Give me a call."

"Hold your horses. I expected you back down this way by now. What's the holdup?"

"Trial took a couple of detours. Dan gave me the rest of the week off. I'll be back in the office on Monday. Appreci ate it if you look into this pontoon boat thing soon as you can."

"Four weeks of free coffee," she said and hung up.

Chitto clicked off his cell. Jasmine's negotiation skills were improving.

∞

Jasmine's call came through just before Chitto made it to the Brody's place. Pontoon boat sales had risen in the county ten to twelve years ago—sharply. Did he want to explain the importance of that fact?

"Not right now," he'd told her. "I need to do some more checking."

After he hung up, Chitto reflected on what his next steps might mean. If correct, he would know why his father died and perhaps confirm that Victor Messina was behind it. It would also prove his father's trusted friend had been untrustworthy. And while that truth could no longer hurt Wanda, it would affect his mother. How he wasn't sure, but there was no way it would be good.

Sure you're not jumping the gun? his internal voice asked.

"Right," he murmured. "Right now, it's just a hunch."

Pulling a slip of paper from his shirt pocket, Chitto stared at it. He'd spent ten years waiting to find his father's killer and all he had to show for it was a ten-digit number and a hunch. Retrieving his cell phone, he punched a number he'd programmed in some time back but never intended to use.

"Raymond," he said when the voice came on the line. "Write this down."

Rodriguez had just gotten back to his office and had not yet reported his findings, or lack thereof, to his boss. Chitto's call made his day.

"How long will it take to check it out that phone number?" Chitto asked.

"Soon as we hang up, I'm on it. There anything else I should be checking?"

A pause. "This will sound like I've been out in the sun too long," Chitto said, "but I think pontoon boats were involved in hauling drugs."

The line went silent.

"Raymond, you still there."

"The deal was you'd call me Ray."

"Habits are hard to break."

"I'll let it pass this time because you might've just filled in a blank we've been trying to fill for years."

Chitto hesitated. "About pontoon boats?"

"Right. We knew how drugs were being carried because we caught Victor Messina's son hauling them. Son of a bitch tried to shoot his way out."

Tried, Chitto repeated silently, noting the use of the past tense. "That how he died?"

"It is. But we couldn't figure out who was on the receiving end. Maybe we just got the break we needed. I'll trace the number and get back to you."

"Wait up, Ray." Chitto hesitated. "Why was my father targeted?"

A pause on the line. "Someone fed us the info but didn't identify himself. Calls came from all over the place, and always from a pay phone. Sounds like your old man might've been the secret informant. He would know where to find every pay phone in the Choctaw Nation."

Chitto swallowed. "And he paid the price for it."

"Would appear so."

"And Gilly? Why was he killed if he was in on it?"

A humorless laugh. "Would you trust someone who'd betray his own partner?"

"You make a good point. Let me know what you find."

CHAPTER TWENTY-FOUR

Chitto looped Boycott's leash over a fencepost and walked toward Charlie Walker's mobile home. Without hesitating, he retrieved the key from its hiding place under the eave and walked to the kitchen. Putting a pot of coffee on to perk, he went back outside. Advancing shadows told him it was edging toward late afternoon; a glance at his watch confirmed it was going on four. Dark bellies on the clouds signaled a storm was brewing.

He'd gotten held up at the Brody's place. He'd cleaned up the backyard, which involved filling in a hole Boycott had dug in pursuit of a rabbit, then had a glass of iced tea on the back patio with Molly. Still, he'd beaten the others to Walker's house.

Glancing toward the Spiro Mounds Archaeology Center now, he frowned. A few cars were in the lot but Mackie's was missing. Had she gone to pick up the Bluetick puppy from the kennel? He glanced at his watch again. And why wasn't Walker home?

Sitting down on the front steps to wait, he ran through what probably transpired behind the closed door of the conference room at the courthouse. The stakes had gotten higher since yesterday. Bobby's life was at stake. Susan Dayton would have gone over options with Walker. Was the death penalty one of those options?

Not likely, he reflected. The fantastical novels Bobby produced, the supposed belief in things like *Ishkitini*, was enough to result in a psychiatric evaluation. Would the doctors find his mental state treatable? The result of those evaluations was what troubled him the most. In many temporary insanity cases, the prisoner was released after a few years if the doctors determined he was fit to rejoin society.

The experts could bandy around terms like *fantasy killing* and *rage-induced murder* all they wanted, but he knew the act Bobby committed was nothing short of premeditated murder. He had seen through his scared rabbit act in the courtroom. The kid was guilty as sin and an expert at deception—hell, he'd immersed himself in make-believe worlds all his life. Would the psychiatrists see through the act?

He stood as Charlie Walker pulled into the drive. The black pickup pulled to a stop and the engine died out by degrees, the engine block ticking methodically. In time, the door opened and Walker stepped to the ground.

"Long day," Chitto commented, watching Walker trudge toward the stoop. "Made a pot of coffee, figured you could use a cup."

"I could at that." Walker carried his suit coat folded across one arm. Sweat stained the neck of his shirt, his underarms. The lines around his eyes had bitten deeper.

"Take a seat," Chitto said. "I'll fetch us one." Returning with two steaming mugs, he handed one to Walker, along with several packets of sugar. "My grandmother says drinking something hot will help you cool off. Runs contrary to common sense but seems to work."

He sat down next to Walker. Sensing the man needed time to wind down, he held his silence. They sipped coffee, watching shadows lengthen and the grass ripple in the meadow between them and Spiro Mounds. Birdcalls and insect droning dulled as each man contended with his own thoughts.

Finishing his cup, Walker sat it on the stoop between them. "I lied," he said, staring at the Archaeology Center in the distance. "I said Bobby never left here that night."

"You told the truth as you knew it. That's all any of us can do. We're men, not gods. Even honorable men like you aren't all-seeing."

"*Honorable.*" Walker rubbed his face with both hands. "I raised him up, made him what he is."

"Hold on." Chitto set his cup on the stoop. "Bobby was already turned inward when you got him hold of him. You told me that yourself." He looked Walker in the eye. "He just reached a point where he fell over the edge."

A pause. "The abyss?"

Chitto nodded.

Walker looked away. "I feel like I let him down when he needed me. I've lost him forever—" His voice broke.

Chitto looked away. "No doubt Bobby will feel that way, but we both know he doesn't see things like others do. And if you think he's through needing you, you're wrong. Whatever happens, he's going to need you more than ever."

Walker rubbed a gnarled hand across his eyes. "Miss Dayton said those doctors could fix Bobby, that he's likely to get out in a few years." He looked at Chitto, eyes sorrowful. "Thing is, I'll probably be dead and buried. What'll he do then? How'll he take care of himself?"

Chitto had no response. While Walker was concerned about Bobby's physical well being, his concerns dealt with his mental. If the boy was a serial killer in the making, would he resort to his old ways once released, escape again into fabricated worlds?

Walker turned toward the Archaeology Center again. "I scared Mackie, too. Saw it in her eyes last night when I went to get that envelope she hid for me. You said in your note that she would meet us here. I figure she's planning on firing me and she has every right to."

Chitto shook his head. "You might've scared her but that didn't shake her belief in you." He nodded toward a silver jeep pulling in the drive. "And she's about to prove it."

Mackie was smiling when she turned off the engine. She groped in the floorboard a minute, then opened the door. She stepped from the Jeep cradling a squirming puppy.

"God a' mighty—" Walker's face showed his astonishment when she held the puppy out to him. "It's the image of Shug."

"Sam helped me pick her out," Mackie said, beaming.

Walker stood the puppy on the porch, taking stock of its back and legs. "She's a beaut, a real winner."

"Best of the litter," Chitto said.

Mackie pulled a document from her hip pocket. "Here's her papers, made out in your name."

"I can't let you do this," Walker mumbled, fondling the puppy's ears. "Blueticks don't come cheap."

"Deal's done," she said. "She's all yours. What'll you name her?"

Walker's face went blank. "I'd have to give it some thought."

"I'm partial to Shug," Chitto said. "You said she was the spitting image of the first one." He cocked his head toward the storage shed. "Would save having to paint a new name on that doghouse back there."

Mackie laughed. "Seems to fit, doesn't it, Charlie?"

"It does for a fact." He turned as a pickup and a van pulled up the drive. "What's goin' on?"

"It's the dig team," Mackie said. "They decided to put up a dog run. You don't want this Shug to suffer the same fate as the last one."

"No, I don't." Walker glanced toward the woods back of the house. "She didn't deserve to die the way she did."

Chitto followed the man's gaze. Catching sight of the fresh dirt pile behind the house, he caught his breath. Walker had dug up Shug's grave. Whatever the reason, the result had led to a decisive moment, forcing Susan Dayton to change the plea.

It *had* to deal with the way Shug died, Chitto decided. Had the dog *not* been killed by a car but by Bobby? If so, Muriel Simpson was the not the first victim to die at his hand.

Connections, Chitto thought, wondering what he'd missed.

Slowly, the dominoes fell into place. Like Mackie, Shug had been another trigger mechanism. A puppy that had taken his place with his grandfather, caused him to be slighted. And then Mackie had delivered another blow. Slight and humiliation, a repeating theme in Bobby Taneyhill's life.

Turning around, he noticed Walker staring at him. They exchanged looks, each knowing nothing else needed to be said.

Turning his attention to the dog run, Chitto helped unload the pickup and van. Frank Pederson supervised the team, which had pooled money and bought a chain-link dog run. All they needed were the tools to put it together and someone to tell them where to put it.

"Set it here so it's within sight of the Archaeology Center," Mackie said, pointing to a spot. "Charlie can keep an eye on Shug, walk over to check things now and then."

"I'll show you where the tools are." Handing the puppy to Mackie, Walker led the team to the garage where he fitted them out with the necessary tools. Looking at Chitto, he said, "It'd be smart to set the doghouse inside the pen before we finish setting up the sides. Been sittin' a while, might check for snakes before you pick it up."

Chitto studied the situation. Grass had grown up around the doghouse, cobwebs hung off its sides, and trash had blown inside. Finding a rake, he pulled out the trash and carried it to the burn barrel.

Yelling to get Walker's attention, he said, "Matches?"

"Workbench," Walker called, pointing to the garage. "Coffee can on the shelf. Wheelbarrow in there, too. Thing's too heavy to carry."

Chitto found the matches and set the barrel burning, then wheeled the barrow to the doghouse. Flipping the house on its side, he used the back of the rake to clean the dirt from the bottom and sides. Moving to the inside, he snagged something stuck above the doorway and pulled it free. A Ziploc plastic bag. Instinctively, he knew that the bag had been deliberately hidden there. Refraining from picking up the bag, he turned it with a stick so he could examine the contents. Without warning, the hair on the back of his neck stood up. He'd seen similar items just the previous year. Skin dried to bits of leather.

Mementos.

He looked closer, frowning. From the shape and size, he figured two of the bits belonged to Muriel Simpson, but the others had fur sticking to them.

"Aw, hell," he mumbled, glancing toward the dirt pile behind the trailer home.

Boy had become Serial Killer.

"What's keeping you, Chitto?" Pederson yelled. "We're on the last side."

Chitto gave him a quick wave. "On my way." His mind raced. He held positive proof authorities could use to put a serial killer on death row or earn him a maximum sentence. Was either a more fitting punishment than a lifetime in a psychiatric unit? Either way, a young man's life was over.

And an old man's had just been restored, he thought, glancing toward the back porch.

He eyed Charlie Walker, wondering if the old man had known the plastic bag was there, if he had deliberately directed him to the doghouse so he would find it. No, he decided, watching Walker playing with the puppy. He had been unaware of his grandson's penchant for collecting mementos.

He turned as Pederson called to him again. Giving another wave, he picked up the doghouse and placed it in the wheelbarrow. As he pushed it toward the workers, he noticed the blazing burn barrel and pulled to a stop. He laid a hand on his pocket, feeling the bag, and glanced toward Walker again. Did the old man deserve more pain in his life?

Ishkitini . . .

Chitto looked around quickly, wondering if he'd heard wind rustling leaves on the trees or a whisper. Slowly, he took hold of the wheelbarrow. Allowing the slightest chance that Bobby Taneyhill would be released was out the question.

Continuing toward the house, Chitto caught sight of Walker embracing the new puppy. The old man may not have many years left but those years would be filled with the unconditional love he deserved. And with the new evidence,

Bobby would not be released upon humanity. A sad ending for a young man; a proper ending for an old one.

The righteous prosper and the wicked suffer.

CHAPTER TWENTY-FIVE

After the work at Charlie Walker's place was finished Chitto had driven to the sheriff's office in Poteau where he explained that he'd been helping erect a dog run at the Walker place when he had discovered the plastic bag. He suggested fingerprints on the bag be compared to Bobby Taneyhill's and the DNA on the items compared with Muriel Simpson's. The sheriff was more than willing to deliver the evidence to the proper authorities.

After he left the sheriff's office, he'd driven back to Walker's place where he explained his decision. He'd stayed a long time with the old man. Walker aged a decade before his eyes but in the end, he understood why Bobby should not be released. Chitto left him holding the new puppy and made the trip to Cabin 4 for the last time. He was certain that Mackie and the dig team would keep close tabs on Walker and was thankful for it. The coming days would be another trial to endure, but as an honorable man, Walker knew Justice had been served.

The deed is done, the doers undone, Chitto thought recalling a line from Macbeth. But that didn't mean the suffering had ended.

∞

295

It was late when the call came through. Chitto was packing, planning to turn in early and get a head start for home the next day.

"Ray?" he said, recognizing the voice. "You can't have traced that number already."

"The FBI doesn't mess around," Rodriguez said.

"Oh, yeah? How come it's taken us ten years to have this talk?"

A laugh. "It's what you thought it was. Calls were placed periodically from Gilly's cell number to someone up there."

"Who?"

"Old Messina's boy, the one who died in the shootout."

"Damn." Chitto's chest felt like a hollowed out gourd. Bert Gilly had been a crooked cop, the most contemptible kind. A cop who was willing to sacrifice a friend and partner for gain. Out of respect for Wanda's memory, he couldn't let the truth about Bert leak out.

"What next," he asked, knowing what the answer would be. You couldn't squeeze blood out of a turnip or information out of a dead man.

"No choice but to close the file," Rodriguez replied. "There's no way to trace who the actual shooters were, we've tried that for years. We've also tried linking Victor Messina, with no luck. There's no place left to go, man."

Chitto scratched a place behind his ear. "Old Victor knew about the setup, the ruse to get my Dad and Gilly up there."

"How you know that?"

"His grandson let it slip."

"Explain."

Chitto replayed the interview with the grandson. "The kid knew it was a professional hit."

"And you're just now telling me this?"

"Roads run both ways," Chitto said. "The question to ask now is how'd that kid know about it?"

A long pause. "Could've been from his father, who's now dead," Rodriguez said. "Old Victor might not've had a hand in it."

Chitto laughed without humor. "You really believe that, you're dumber than a post."

Rodriguez let out a long sigh. "Sam, as of now the case is closed so you can stop your meddling."

"Yeah, well," Chitto snorted. "Habits are hard to break."

"You stubborn *pendejo*."

There was no need for Chitto to ask for a translation. It wasn't the first time he'd been called a jackass in another language and wouldn't be the last.

"Tell you what," Rodriguez said following an extended silence. "I'll keep an eye on old Victor—and that grandson of his, too. Maybe we can get them on something else."

More uninterrupted static.

"Aw, hell," Rodriguez growled. "Try to keep it out of the dirt, Sam." *Click.*

∞

Chitto had lain awake well into the night, thinking of Ramon Rodriquez's call and his decision to close the case file. He fell into exhausted sleep in the wee hours and woke later than planned. It was around eight o'clock when he checked in with Bud and Birdie.

Laying his credit card and the key to Cabin 4 on the counter, he said, "Thanks for everything." As Bud ran the card, he pulled a twenty from his wallet and handed it to Birdie. "For doing my wash," he said. "You saved me a lot of time and trouble."

"It's was my pleasure," she said, pushing his hand away.

"Anytime you need a place to hole up, your cabin's ready," Bud said. "Fill your thermos before you leave?"

"Already did. I'm ready to go."

"Let me fix you something for the road." Birdie walked to the kitchen and returned with a warm pan of rolls and box of waxed paper. In quick time, two packages appeared on the counter. One for the undercover cop. One for his police dog.

It was raining by the time Chitto turned west on the county road that intersected the highway. The plan was to take a more direct route to Krebs, exiting 59 for OK-9, which ran through the towns of Stigler and Whitefield, then head due south US-69.

As he drove, he thought about loose ends on the Bobby Taneyhill case that needed tying up. June Biggers would have been on the phone to his mother by now letting her know the outcome of the trial, saving him the trouble. One loose end taken care of.

After hearing from June, his mother would figure out he'd be heading back today, so no need to call ahead. Another loose end fastened down.

He also needed to let Dan Blackfox know what had transpired, how he'd almost screwed up and how he'd fixed it without fixing it, but that loose end was better handled in person. Besides, he knew what Blackfox's reaction would be. He'd shake his head, wag a finger in his face, and swear he'd never let Chitto out of his district again.

He also owed Pete Brody an explanation on both the old murder case and the new one, but he could call him next week from the office. He wouldn't be happy to learn their suspicions about Bert Gilly were correct, but the information would go no further. Pete not only knew how to hold things close to his chest, he was also an honorable man.

Which only left one other loose end, and that one required more thought.

∞

By the time Chitto reached OK-9, the rain had turned torrential. Sheets of water had the wipers working overtime. Lightning bolts splintered the sky; thunder shattered the eardrums. He'd never experienced a battlefield but he imagined the conditions right then equivalent to an all-out assault. In this case, the weather gods were the enemy. He considered pulling off the road to wait it out but he was using the center stripe as a GPS. A damn poor one. Finding a clear, unobstructed piece of right of way was out of the question. So he drove.

The cinnamon buns were gone by the time he made it to Stigler. The coffee by the time he reached the town of Whitefield. The Doublemint by the time he made it to the fork that merged onto US-69 S. He'd been considering the Marlboros the last quarter hour. Boycott had retreated to the floorboard an hour before. Normally, the ninety-mile trip would've taken an hour and a half. He'd been on the road over two and still had a good thirty miles to go. Was it just a week ago he'd been counting his lucky stars that a similar storm had made for a quiet Friday to catch up on paperwork?

As Lake Eufaula became recognizable out the passenger side window, he sensed the worst of the storm had passed, giving him time to catch his breath and think about that remaining loose thread. Seeing a sign for the OK-113 exit toward Arrowhead State Park, he made a split-second decision.

Way back, Arrowhead State Park had been one of his father's favorite fishing holes. Largemouth bass, white bass, crappie, channel cat. Now, the park featured tent and RV sites, a marina, playgrounds, a horse stable and trails. But he remembered it before all that, what it was like when he was a boy. One spot in particular.

Driving to one of the more remote fishing spots, Chitto parked on a slight incline and pulled a windbreaker from a bag under the passenger seat. Snapping Boycott's collar to a leash, he opened the door and stepped onto wet asphalt. Leading the dog to the back of the Chevy, he dropped the tailgate so the bed would drain, then walked toward the shoreline. Seeing a picnic table near the shore that was somewhat sheltered, he slogged through wet grass and over water-clogged ground to reach it.

"Stay close, pup."

Letting Boycott off leash, he sat down on the table, feet on the bench, and put his attention on the surroundings. The air was cool, the sky beginning to lighten. He lost track of time as he studied the color of the water, turbid from being stirred up, and a shoreline studded with rocks. Some round. Some flat. Watching mist rise off the water, he felt the hair on the back of his neck stand up.

Pushing away thoughts about restless ghosts, Chitto turned his attention to Boycott who was following his nose through soggy grass and around dripping bushes and trees, trying to pick up a scent on the scoured ground. A futile undertaking. There would be no trail until new scent was laid down. Pulling a slip of paper from his shirt pocket, he stared at it. He'd spent ten years searching for his father's killer and all he had for it was a ten-digit number. Rising from the table, he walked to the water's edge.

"I decided your rule about not talking work at home was a good one, Dad," he said, dropping the slip into the water. The paper started to drift, floating toward the mist on the lake. "And I figured you'd agree that it was more important to let Mom hold onto that last good memory than find out the truth."

Searching through the medley of stones on the shoreline, Chitto selected a flat, smooth one. He rubbed the stone between his fingers a few seconds, then let it fly.

"But just so you know," he said, watching the stone skip across the water. "This thing's not over till *I* say it's over."

ABOUT THE AUTHOR

Lu Clifton writes mystery that mingles Choctaw culture, science, and murder. She became interested in cultural traditions while tracing her mother's Choctaw roots. She was born in and spent her early childhood in southeastern Oklahoma, then moved to the Texas Panhandle with her family. She completed an Associate Degree at Amarillo Junior College in Texas and a B.A. and M.A. in English at Colorado State University. She now resides in northwestern Illinois with a five-year-old brown tabby named Mary Jane that she rescued from a shelter.

The Horned Owl is the third book in the Sam Chitto Mystery Series. *Scalp Dance* released in 2016 and *The Bonepicker* in 2017. *Scalp Dance* was a finalist for the 2017 Oklahoma Book Award for Fiction.

In addition to adult fiction, Clifton also writes novels for children. At this printing, she has three in print. *Freaky Fast Frankie Joe* (2012) received a 2012 Friends of American Writers Award for Juvenile Fiction. *Seeking Cassandra* (2016) was awarded the 2017 Oklahoma Book Award for Young Adult Fiction. Clifton is a member of the Oklahoma Writers Federation, Mystery Writers of America, and the Society of Children's Book Writers and Illustrators.

THE HORNED OWL, A SAM CHITTO MYSTERY
DISCUSSION QUESTIONS

Use this guide to facilitate your library or book club's conversation about the book.

1. Clifton opens the book with this quote from Mark Twain: "Every man is a moon and has a side which he turns toward nobody; you have to slip around behind if you want to see it." List the characters in the book that have a side they have kept hidden. Chitto's job in this novel is to uncover these hidden sides. Were you surprised by any of the revelations? Which one surprised you the most?

2. Because of the lack of evidence that has surfaced regarding his father's decade–old murder, Chitto comes to suspect even his contemporaries in law enforcement: his superior, Daniel Blackfox; his peer, Pete Brody; and FBI agent Ramon Rodriguez. Discuss why he did not suspect Bert Gilly?

3. Clifton includes references in her books to the Choctaw belief in the *Shilup* and *Shilombish*, inner and outer shadows or ghosts. Over time, Chitto, a scientist by training, has come to look upon these beliefs as more than superstitions. Jasmine Birdsong, whom Sam refers to as Scout, also mentions "the fiery trivets," which refers to a person's prophetic abilities. Chitto admits to Jasmine Birdsong at one point that he felt he was being led by a restless ghost. Have you ever experienced a feeling that you were being guided by something otherworldly? Know someone who felt

they were? Experienced a premonition? Or are you a skeptic? If the latter, did your skepticism affect your feelings toward the book?

4. Some of the characters in the book suffer moments of indiscretion and/or bad judgment. Identify them and discuss their reasons for acting in the manner they did. In particular, contrast archaeologist Mackie Green and the "honorable man," Charlie Walker. How did you feel about the explanations given for their decisions? Did you find them understandable or a poor excuse?

5. In the beginning, Chitto worked to prove Bobby Taneyhill innocent. Discuss his role with the green-horn defense attorney, Susan Dayton, to see justice served and how it backfired. Also discuss the inn-keeper Bud's methodology for solving a problem, i.e., "shake the tree and see what falls out." This last-ditch effort on the part of Chitto was an appeal to the nature of an honorable man. What do you think Chitto would have done if this effort had failed?

6. Also discuss Chitto's judgment call with regard to the condemning evidence he found hidden in Shug's doghouse. Did you agree with the call? Why or why not?

7. A young person's growth and development is a topic in the book. Discuss the ways Bobby Taneyhill was affected by his early experiences. Do you think Charlie Walker's view that his grandson's early childhood led to his becoming "inward" was accurate, an excuse for overlooking the obvious, or a normal reaction to protect one he loved? What would you have done in a similar situation?

8. Clifton uses description of the Oklahoma landscape to enhance the reader's understanding of the physical

and cultural geography of the American Indian people living there. Discuss how this cultural background affected Bobby Taneyhill.

9. Have group members discuss the types of pictures they drew as children. Would those pictures be deemed unhealthy by today's new knowledge of mental health? What was your view of the teachers in the story making the determinations they did regarding the drawings of both Bobby Taneyhill and Sam Chitto as boys? Did the teachers overreach their bounds? Why or why not?

10. Sam Chitto is not only a law officer but also a geologist. Discuss how Clifton uses Sam's collection of worry stones and his introspection about the history of the Earth to enhance the story. Discuss various world cultures' use of stones and formations to denote the seasons of the year, as almanacs to guide transitions between seasons, or as a belief in a higher order. Ask if members of the group have visited some of these other sites. How were they affected?

11. Discuss how the role of the American Indian law officers differs from others, especially complications they face that their counterparts in city, county, state, and federal do not. What is more interesting to you as a reader: the case the detectives investigate or the life and culture of the American Indian detective?

12. Chitto has had ongoing disagreements with FBI Agent, Ramon Rodriguez. Discuss the causes for these disagreements and how their relationship seems to change in *The Horned Owl*, i.e., what shared experiences do the men share that led to a better understanding of the other? Do you tend to lean toward others with whom you share commonalities?

One Last Thing . . .

If you enjoyed this book or found it useful, I'd be very grateful if you'd post a short review on Amazon. Your support really does make a difference, and I read all the reviews personally so I can get your feedback and make my books even better.

Thanks again for your support!

Amazon Author page:

https://www.amazon.com/author/luclifton

Lu Clifton's website: http://www.lutricia-lois-clifton.com

CPSIA information can be obtained
at www.ICGtesting.com
Printed in the USA
LVOW10s0928300518
578847LV00008B/310/P